PATRIOTS

The Untold Story of Ireland's Pro-Life Movement

JONATHON VAN MAREN

Life Cycle Books

ISBN: 978-0-919225-60-2
ISBN: 978-0-919225-61-9 *eBook*

Published & distributed by Life Cycle Books
www.lifecyclebooks.com ▪ orders@lifecyclebooks.com

Printed in Canada

Cover design by Sharon Grisnich

Table of Contents

This book is dedicated to Ireland's thousands of pro-life warriors who worked tirelessly for decades to defend pre-born children.

Generations live because of your deeds.

I hope that I have done your story justice.

O wise men, riddle me this: what if the dream come true?

What if the dream come true? and if millions unborn shall dwell

In the house that I shaped in my heart,
the noble house of my thought?

Lord, I have staked my soul, I have staked the lives of my kin

On the truth of Thy dreadful word.
Do not remember my failures,

But remember this my faith

And so I speak.

Yea, ere my hot youth pass, I speak to my people and say:

Ye shall be foolish as I; ye shall scatter, not save;

Ye shall venture your all, lest ye lose what is more than all;

Ye shall call for a miracle, taking Christ at His word.

And for this I will answer, O people, answer here and hereafter,

O people that I have loved, shall we not answer together?

Patrick Pearse, 1915

Acknowledgments

Once again, I must first thank my wife, Charmaine, the fiercest of critics. She read and reread each word, working long hours because she believed this story needed to be told. She is an essential half of this writing team.

Niamh Uí Bhriain, one of my pro-life heroes, who spent hours factchecking the book and tolerated my constant messages, interviews, and questions.

Kate Bryan, who is as passionate about this story as I am and was constantly ready with advice, feedback, and background information on the Irish pro-life movement.

The many Irish pro-lifers who took the time to share their stories with me, including Úna Nic Mhathuna, Vicky Wall, John McGuirk, Tim Jackson, Riaghan and Enya O'Callaghan, Shauna Flynn, Mary Rose Short, Andy Heasman, and others. I am incredibly grateful for their raw honesty.

Paul Broughton, our incredible publisher, and the team at Life Cycle Books, who have given more to the pro-life movement than most people will ever know.

Sharon Grisnich, for her excellent cover design, and willingness to redesign until everyone was happy.

The many others who took the time to proofread the manuscript: Caroline Slingerland (who has fantastic feedback, and pulled at least one all-nighter), Amy Kreft, Cana Donovan. Andrew Krul, Nick Rosendal, and many of those previously mentioned.

To everyone who contributed in ways, big and small, thank you all.

Introduction

On Thursday I had a strange sense that the day had the tenor of a Holy Saturday—a day lifted out of history. Except that here, history seemed to have gone into reverse: the Resurrection behind, Calvary in front. On Friday, the Irish people climbed Calvary backwards, in the name of progress.

Irish journalist John Waters, May 28, 2018, three days after the abortion referendum

---

I touched down in Dublin two weeks before the Irish abortion referendum with my wife Charmaine, my daughter Charlotte, and two of my colleagues from the Canadian Centre for Bio-Ethical Reform, Nick and Maaike Rosendal. We had heard that Irish officials were turning back foreigners who had come to join the pro-life movement's final push before the deciding votes were cast on May 25 but my eight-month-old daughter's beaming face warded off any awkward questions. Who would take a baby on a political campaign, after all? We were waved through into a country in the throes of a culture war.

We left the city and headed out into the countryside, our surroundings exploding into a hundred hues of green. We wound our way down twisty roads lined with slumping stone walls once intended to fence in the sheep picking their way across the pastures and around the bunches of yellow flowers dotting the rolling hills. Ancient stone houses and outbuildings almost disappeared behind creeping ivy. And everywhere, the signs: *If abortion at six months horrifies you, vote NO.* Another featured a baby in the womb sucking her thumb: *A Licence to Kill? Vote NO to abortion on demand.* A similar sign simply cited facts: *I am 9 weeks old. I can yawn and kick. Don't repeal me.*

It is scarcely an exaggeration to say that there were signs affixed to every lamppost, traffic light, and road sign in the country. The signs urging voters to bring abortion to the country were more Orwellian, remaining conspicuously vague as to what they were actually advocating for: *Vote YES for Compassion, For Dignity, For Care*. And: *Vote YES: Care, Compassion, Trust*. The first victim of a war on children is always truth, and the Yes campaign seemed acutely aware that they were unlikely to score points in their battle for legal abortion by actually mentioning abortion. It was far wiser, they had decided, to appeal soothingly to vaguely positive human emotions.

Signs of resistance to the threat were everywhere. A clergyman was balanced precariously atop a stepladder in front of his grey stone church, affixing a "Vote No to Abortion on Demand!" sign to his flagpole, the Irish tricolor flapping in the wind above him. Further down the road, someone had used black spray paint to turn the back of a traffic sign into a message urging voters to protect life, an enormous "NO!" followed by a spray-painted X in a ballot box. When I stopped at a gas station and asked a white-haired man behind the counter what he thought of it all, he replied that he hoped Ireland could "keep the Eighth," but shook his head worriedly: "But the media, you know. They are so biased."

Coming from a nation where politicians consistently insist that the abortion debate is closed and local authorities often attempt to suppress pro-life activism, it was hard for a Canadian pro-life activist like myself not to be encouraged by the vibrancy and volume of the Irish abortion debate. Not only that, but there seemed to be something *different* about the Irish pro-life activists that we joined on the Vote No Roadshow caravanning across the country and the men and women we went canvassing with in Dublin and the passionate young people we campaigned with in front of the bullet-scarred General Post Office.

It took me days to figure out what it was: they had an innocence that North American pro-life activists lacked. Not naiveté, not at all—they certainly knew that they could lose the referendum. That is why they were pounding the streets, manning the phones, and working from door to door. It was the sort of innocence one has when they possess both the courage to fight evil and the faith that good can defeat it. More than that, it was the faith that good could defeat evil *again*. Abortion activists had been striving to destroy and undermine the Eighth Amendment for decades, but always the pro-life movement had fended them off. Time and again, the sweaty panic of the final countdown to the campaign's end had given way to an explosion of celebration.

This time, it *had* to be that way, too. The dragon had to die, the knight had to win, and the innocents had to be saved. In some ways, any other result was almost unfathomable. Those of us from America and Canada lacked this faith simply because we were accustomed to evil winning the day. Betrayal by politicians is the rule rather than a rarity. Working alongside the Irish pro-lifers of the Vote No Roadshow and feeling their beautiful optimism, I genuinely envied them their lack of cynicism. I said as much to Tim Jackson, the leader of the Vote No Road Show that had been criss-crossing Ireland for weeks. He smiled wryly. "Be careful," he said. "This country'll break your heart."

On May 25, 2018, Ireland became the first nation on earth to bring abortion to her shores by popular demand. Her citizens knew what they were voting for. They had been warned by the tireless men and women who worked themselves to the bone to plead for the lives of pre-born children and warn of the grotesque horrors that are spawned when an abortion regime takes root. They were tragically ignored by 66.4% of those who cast their votes. The grief that followed was raw and awful, and the depression was deep and dark. It felt, as one pro-life activist said shortly afterward, like a death in the family. In so many ways, that is precisely what it was.

Over the months that followed, I kept in touch with many of the pro-lifers I had been privileged to work with during my short time in Ireland. The triumphalism of the media was nauseating, and the emerging narrative in not only the Irish press but around the world was a simple one: legalised abortion is inevitable. Ireland's Eighth Amendment had merely been a hangover from a different time, and Ireland's pro-lifers were the last defenders of a nation that no longer existed. The tide of what is today perversely called progress is unstoppable, the media declared, and those few Western nations clinging to protections for pre-born children were put on notice that they would fall next. The eye of Sauron swung to Northern Ireland within hours.

The story that the media, the politicians, and the abortion activists want to tell about the abortion referendum of 2018 is the story of scrappy progressives and feminists who wanted to modernize their country, and succeeded after years of blood, sweat, and tears (and there will be much, *much* more of all that to come in the years ahead). Because the elites own the media, the entertainment industry, and every major political party, that is the only story being told. They must persuade us all that they are on the right side of history, and delude themselves into believing that a future can be built by shedding the blood of generations unborn. Their triumphant shouts and cheers of celebration at Dublin Castle on May 26 were perhaps just loud enough to drown out their own whispering consciences.

The inverse of that story, of course, is that the pro-lifers who fought so hard were simply the flagging vanguard of the patriarchy, those who wished to oppress women and drag Ireland back to a different time. The media ignored the fact that those on the frontlines were fighting for the children of *other people*—they had nothing to personally gain for their sacrifices. I met students who were skipping university courses to hit the streets from dawn 'til dusk, elderly men and women who had been stiffly walking from door to door each evening for years, a middle-aged man who had sold his business so he could live off the proceeds and campaign against abortion. Young parents were out pushing children in strollers with others strapped to their backs. The passion of these people was not rooted in the desire for a totalitarian society that is a figment of the feminist imagination. It was rooted in a genuine, palpable love for little children. But *that* the media could not report on, because that would draw attention to the fact that it was, in fact, little children who were at stake in the referendum.

"What about the *babies*?" one elderly woman asked a Yes voter sorrowfully as she walked door to door in the Dublin suburbs with our canvass team a week before the vote. A shrug, and the door closed. That was a question that only the pro-lifers seemed to want an answer to. Loving both the mother and the child, it appeared, was not something many abortion supporters thought possible or desirable.

This story is being ignored. It is being ignored because it is an inconvenient and far different narrative, and also because pro-life activists have become masters at telling the stories of the babies lost to abortion and the men and women left broken in their wake, but have never quite learned how to tell their own stories. We often look back to other social reform movements: the abolitionists, the civil rights activists, the Holocaust rescuers. But we seldom tell the stories of those ordinary men and women, those unlikely heroes, who fought in anonymity for years to save children not their own, persevering in the face of a hostile culture, a contemptuous media, and an entertainment industry selling death with glamour and a smile.

That story is the story of men and women who responded to the news of *Roe v. Wade* in the United States by fighting to insert protections for pre-born children into Ireland's constitution with the Eighth Amendment, saving hundreds of thousands of lives over the ensuing decades while nation after nation succumbed to the abortion juggernaut all around them. It is the story of the thousands of people who put boots on the ground to fight tooth and nail for the life of every pre-born baby—*while abortion was still illegal*. It is the story of the men and women who fought with their ancestors at their backs and their children in their hearts, fired by the rock-solid conviction that Ireland's babies were worth fighting for.

It is time to tell this story. In the wake of death's temporary victory, it is essential. Upcoming generations of not only Irish pro-life activists but pro-lifers around the world should know that for thirty-five years, babies in their untold tens of thousands ended up in bassinets instead of dumpsters because there were champions willing to speak for them. They should know that abortion activists right around the globe despised the pro-life Irish activists precisely *because* their defensive war on behalf of the pre-born proved that an abortion regime is *never* inevitable, and that a culture that loves both mothers and children is possible if we only love hard and fight harder. They should know that the true heirs of Ireland's ancestors are those who fought for her future, not the gloaters who believe her children can be sacrificed on the altar of casual sex and selfishness.

The loss of the Eighth Amendment was a crushing one, and the Irish pro-life movement will need encouragement in the years ahead. That encouragement can be found in the examples of the very men and women who made up her ranks in years past, and those who make up her ranks today. To see glimmers of light at the end of the tunnel, the patriots of today must climb onto the shoulders of the giants who went before. On many days, it may seem as if the pro-life cause is a lost cause. But there is perhaps nothing as Irish as a lost cause, and nothing as Irish as defying those odds.

It is, after all, what Irish patriots have always done.

Chapter 1
A Nation for the Family

In the Name of the Most Holy Trinity, from Whom is all authority and to Whom, as our final end, all actions both of men and States must be referred, We, the people of Éire, Humbly acknowledging all our obligations to our Divine Lord, Jesus Christ, Who sustained our fathers through centuries of trial,
Gratefully remembering their heroic and unremitting struggle to regain the rightful independence of our Nation,
And seeking to promote the common good, with due observance of Prudence, Justice and Charity, so that the dignity and freedom of the individual may be assured, true social order attained, the unity of our country restored, and concord established with other nations,
Do hereby adopt, enact, and give to ourselves this Constitution.

Preamble to the Irish Constitution, 1937

Through the first strike for freedom in the 1916 Easter Rising and throughout the infant years of the ensuing War of Independence, the founders of the Irish republic were determined to create a different nation. Centuries of struggle against the British Empire had forged a unique identity and elevated the status of the Catholic Church in Ireland, which would become further entrenched by the massive social role the Church would play in day-to-day life, an ecclesiastical welfare and civil system stretching into every corner of Irish society. Much like the Catholic Church in Poland had become a bastion of cultural significance for the Poles throughout the decades of Cold War Communist rule, the Catholic

Church became an essential part of the two-fold Irish identity: not British, and thus not Anglican.

It was not only Ireland's Catholic identity that would make the new nation distinct. It was also her explicit recognition and protection of the family. In the 1935 Act that banned contraception, for example, Eamon De Valera's government specifically stated that this ban was an assertion of independence from England. Articles 41.1.1 and 41.1.2 of the 1937 Irish Constitution recognised the family as essential to a stable and healthy society, declaring that "The State recognises the Family as the natural primary and fundamental unit group of society and as a moral institution possessing inalienable and imprescriptible rights, antecedent to all positive law," and adding that "In particular, the State recognises that by her life within the home, woman gives to the State a support without which the common good cannot be achieved."

In short, Ireland would be different. Ireland would not only welcome children, she would fiercely defend the family with all available legal and constitutional protections. Despite the characterization of Ireland's constitution as an imposition by Catholics on the rest of the population, Mary Kenny notes in her book *Goodbye to Catholic Ireland* that De Valera's constitution was "supported as much by Protestants and Jews as by Irish Catholics."[i] The protection of the family and the centrality of children to a nation's wellbeing was not particularly controversial for most people, regardless of their faith.

Large families were the norm in Ireland, and progressive historians consistently assert that Irish women were made miserable by their numerous children, citing the physical toll of pregnancy as evidence. But is this actually true? Were these children as unwelcome as feminist chroniclers would now have us believe? It is possible that some women felt that way, of course. It is certainly true in some instances. But the danger of looking back on big families in hindsight—especially for those progressive writers who cannot fathom desiring one—is that many modern people simply cannot understand them, and thus also cannot grasp why any woman would be happy with a large number of children. I vividly remember the words of my grandmother, who had nine children and lost two of them as infants, when I asked her what it was like to raise such a large family. "You don't get old from having children," she told me. "You get old from losing them."

The progressive sentiment on large families, on the other hand, can be summed up in the scornful words of French president Emmanuel Macron, who in 2018 decried the African birthrate in a sneering speech to the Gates Foundation's Goalkeepers Summit: "I always say: 'Present me the woman who decided, being perfectly educated, to have seven, eight, or nine children." Hundreds of such women promptly responded to him on social media to explain, and Nigerian pro-life activist and bio-medical scientist Obianuju Ekoecha pointed out that according to the available data, the average African woman wants more than six children—and many want up to ten.[ii] There are cultures that still see children as a blessing, and their existence highlights the danger of retroactive historical revisionism. An Irish feminist's view of children today would seem just as foreign to the mother of a large family fifty years ago as that mother's views would seem to many today.

The 1937 Irish Constitution did not explicitly ban abortion because the Irish leadership did not see a need to do so at the time. Like almost everywhere else in the world, abortion was illegal in Ireland, prohibited by the British Offences Against the Person Act of 1861, a law that remained in place after independence.[1] That pre-born children were protected by law went without saying. It was, initially, an American Supreme Court decision that alerted the Irish to the fact that explicit protections for pre-born children might be necessary. First, the U.S. Supreme Court discovered a right to privacy in the 1965 contraception case, *Griswold v. Connecticut*. That same right to privacy was utilised in their 1973 *Roe v. Wade* decision, which mandated the legalisation of abortion in all fifty American states in one fell swoop. With a liberal judiciary, it turned out, everything could change overnight.

Irish pro-lifers noted this development with alarm: the Supreme Court had essentially invented a heretofore non-existent right, irrespective of what the framers of the American constitution had intended (or *not* intended). What mattered, it seemed, was that a handful of justices could subvert everything and throw out both historical context and decades of jurisprudence by reading their own interpretations into a "living document" that had, they insisted, evolved with the times. And the times they were a-changin'—everybody knew that. While Ireland remained a socially conservative place, the sexual revolution sweeping the Western world brought with it new attitudes about abortion, often driven by a need to

---

1 The 1861 Offences Against the Person Act, Section 58, stated the following: "Every woman being with child who with intent to procure her own miscarriage shall unlawfully administer to herself any poison or noxious thing or shall unlawfully use any instrument or other means whatsoever with the like intent and whosoever with intent to procure the miscarriage of any woman whether or not she be with child shall unlawfully administer to her or cause to be taken by her any poison or other noxious thing shall unlawfully use any instrument or other means with the like intent, shall be guilty of felony…" Section 59 went on to say: "Whosoever shall unlawfully supply or procure any poison or other noxious thing or any instrument whatsoever knowing that the same is intended to be unlawfully used or employed with intent to procure the miscarriage of any woman, whether she be or not be with child, shall be guilty of a misdemeanour…"

deal with the unfortunate (and inevitable) offspring that occurred as a result of the casual coitus enjoyed by their liberated and usually unattached parents.

Their alarm increased when the Supreme Court of Ireland ruled in favor of Mary McGee on December 29, 1973. McGee, a 27-year-old mother, had ordered spermicides from England in defiance of the ban on the importation of contraception. The Court retained the ban on the sale and promotion of contraception, but struck the ban on importation. The primary concern, however, was the language used by the justices, who spoke about a "living constitution." A "living constitution" meant a malleable and essentially useless constitution that would be putty in the hands of whichever justices sat on the court, and pro-choice journalist Kitty Holland noted in her 2013 book *Savita* that the McGee case awoke Ireland's pro-life forces because "such sentiments were of concern to those against abortion, who saw contraception and abortion as part of the same continuum."[iii]

It was the "right to privacy" that had been used in the United States to impose legal abortion on the entire nation, and now that right had been created by Irish justices, too. It appeared obvious to many that the Republic of Ireland was on the same track as the United States. Additionally, the 1861 Offences Against the Person Act had been repealed in Britain in 1967, resulting immediately in the implementation of a liberal abortion regime there.[2] Some Irish women began travelling to England to procure abortions—578 in 1971—and the numbers continued to slowly rise, increasing the chances that the issue could soon arrive in Ireland, as well.

---

2 It is important to note that opposition to the abortion law was initially expressed by the British Medical Association and the Royal College of Obstetricians and Gynaecologists, medical bodies which did not embrace a permissive approach to abortion until several years later.

Finally, the 1973 McGee ruling came on the heels of Ireland joining the European Community. Ireland was the only member state where abortion was still illegal, and pro-lifers were very concerned that other European nations would attempt to impose abortion in the Irish republic. The 1979 Health Act, which allowed the sale of contraceptives with a prescription while making allowances for physicians who had conscientious objections to being involved in the process, was a final warning to pro-lifers: The die was cast. Despite the fact that the Act reaffirmed the anti-abortion portions of the Offences Against the Person Act, pro-lifers knew abortion would be next.

It was this foresight that distinguished the Irish pro-life movement from nearly every other similar movement in the Western world: They saw what was coming, and they moved to stop it. Most historians generally categorize anti-abortion activism as reactionary, a knee-jerk response to the legalisation of abortion. In Ireland's case, the opposite is true—as Michael Dougherty put it, when it became clear to Irish pro-lifers that their Republic was likely to follow in the footsteps of America and other nations, "they endeavored to run around their liberal judiciary" with a brilliant campaign that constituted an unprecedented political coup.[iv]

Dr. Mary Lucey of the Society for the Protection of Unborn Children (SPUC) described that growing realisation at a pro-life conference ten years later. "We had thought that Ireland would be different," she related. "We had the 1861 Anti-Abortion Act. The vast majority of people did not want abortion. It was anathema to the 95% of them who were Catholic and we thought our Constitution protected the unborn. We also thought that there were not any abortion referral groups in Dublin. The decision in the McGee case in 1973 and the simultaneous decision in the *Roe v. Wade* case in North America in the same year brought us to our senses. From that time on we who were interested in unborn life knew that we must do something."[v]

Likeminded men and women began to seek one another out, and the grassroots began to stir as pro-lifers moved to come up with a strategy to protect pre-born children from the abortion industry that was materializing around Europe and across the Atlantic. These men and women have often been forgotten or reduced to a historical footnote, but the work they would embark on set the stage for the first explicit constitutional protections for pre-born children in the Western world, and their achievements, buttressed by a defensive war fought by successive generations of pro-life activists, would result in hundreds of thousands of Irish lives saved.

As the pro-abortion journalist Rosanna Cooney put it: "The story of how the Eighth Amendment came to be placed in the constitution is part of Irish history, yet relatively little is known of the campaign or the people that put it there. Not since the Civil War in the 1920s has anything been as politically and socially divisive as the abortion campaign of 1983."[vi]

Chapter 2
A Brilliant Coup

The attack on abortion through the formation of the Pro-Life Amendment Campaign took the form of a pre-emptive strike. Pro-Life lobbies in other countries have been formed only after liberal abortion laws were already on the statue books. In Ireland, the attack began before abortion had been taken on board the mainstream political agenda. The issue had been raised within the women's movement in a low-key way, but widespread public debate was not in process.

Emily O'Reilly, *Masterminds of the Right*[vii]

Ironically, pro-abortion journalists and historians have spent the most time carefully studying what Ireland's anti-abortion activists pulled off in 1983 when the pro-life amendment was inserted into the Constitution. As Rosanna Cooney put it: "The Eighth Amendment was a remarkable feat by a small group of Catholic right-wing conservatives, but their story has largely been lost to the archives and cemeteries where many of Ireland's first pro-life campaigners now lie. To forget the sophistication and efficacy of the Pro-Life Amendment Campaign (PLAC), which orchestrated a constitutional ban on abortion in Ireland, is to forget one of the great political coups of the 20th century."[viii] The enemies of Ireland's pro-life movement were forced to recognise the brilliance of what the pro-lifers had accomplished.

Cooney, like other pro-choice journalists and historians who have written on the formation of the pro-life movement leading up to the Pro-Life Amendment Campaign, saw the men and women who championed the Eighth Amendment as a shadowy cabal of powerful Catholics, and their descriptions conjure up images of men in cassocks meeting in dimly lit rooms to plot Ireland's domination. She described the "formation of the pro-life movement in Ireland" as being made up of "years of planning, the network of spies and international allies, and the institutional support they possessed at every level of Irish society."[ix]

Journalist and historian Emily O'Reilly, who would go on to serve as Irish Ombudsman and Information Commissioner, painted a similar picture in her 1992 book *Masterminds of the Right*, in which she makes the bold claim that pro-life activist and political campaigner John O'Reilly (no relation) was the puppet-master who almost singlehandedly brought the abortion ban to Ireland.[3] The more research she did, O'Reilly wrote, the more she found that "all roads led to John O'Reilly."[x] O'Reilly's paranoia makes her historical analysis hard to take seriously at times, as she details the formation of the Irish Family League, founded by Mary Kennedy, Arthur McDermott, and others, in May 1973 (headed by Mary Kennedy and acting Chairman John O'Reilly) by noting that they were connected to the Knights of Columbus, which she describes as a secretive organisation with a murky agenda filled with agents of the Catholic Church hoping to implement its doctrine on a national scale (which does not seem to be a particularly *hidden* agenda, all things considered.) She even traces the Knights of Columbus to a variety of other groups, as if they were some papist version of the Free Masons.

John O'Reilly was, according to his associates, "a good family man, who has a warm and loving relationship

3 She also served as the editor of *Magill* magazine from 1998 to September of 1999, but resigned when the magazine's sister publication, *In Dublin*, got banned by the Censorship of Publications Appeal Board for advertising prostitutes and brothels.

with his children...a great sense of humor, a nice line in self-deprecation, and a passion for the promotion of his...beliefs."[xi] Emily O'Reilly described him as "a big man, slightly stooped, wears thick-lensed glasses which convey the impression of a squint. The unprepossessing appearance belies totally, and deliberately, the extent of the man's power and the range of his contacts."[xii] His memory was exceptional, augmented by a massive library of press clippings, pamphlets, legal documents, and books on abortion and related issues. In short, she wrote, O'Reilly was orchestrating everything—and there was, to her mind, nothing he couldn't do. Because John O'Reilly was a man of impressive vision and capability, Emily O'Reilly attempted to assert that the collective successes of a massive Irish movement were primarily the work of a single man.

The affiliations she detailed will not come as a surprise to anyone remotely familiar with the Catholic Church in any country, and there is more than a touch of kneejerk anti-religious prejudice in O'Reilly's analysis. As John O'Reilly told a journalist later: "The most the Knights ever did was say a prayer before polling day. We used the Knights headquarters as a place to have meetings and sometimes to drink."[xiii] But the fact that the Knights were a group of men (women would be admitted later) was also suspicious to O'Reilly, who felt that these "men at the heart of the right-wing drive" to keep abortion out of Ireland *must* be inherently misogynistic.[xiv] One bit of evidence for this was references to women in Knights of Columbus documents as "ladies," with, in O'Reilly's words, "that traditional patronising gallantry that marks covert hostility to the opposite sex."[xv] Again, it seems very difficult for feminist revisionists to understand that husbands and wives might define themselves in relation to the family and to each other rather than in accordance with their sex and the grievance politics that apparently must accompany it.

It must be noted here, as well, that the claim of feminist historians that the battle over protections for pre-born children was largely an attempt by men struggling to maintain the power of the patriarchy and assert control over women by controlling their reproduction is not based in reality. This narrative resolutely ignores the pro-life women who fought fiercely for the children of Ireland, and ignores their outsize role in denying the carnivorous feminists the so-called right to exert the power of life and death over the youngest and most vulnerable members of the human family. The women of the pro-life movement believed they were fighting for what was good, true, and beautiful, and conversely felt that the abortion activists fought for the crude joy of power, selfishness, and pleasure.

For that reason and others, most feminist historians have attempted to ignore some of the most significant female activists in the pro-life movement while emphasizing the role of men. O'Reilly goes as far as to cite pro-life organisations that were obviously female-run as "fronted by women to disguise the role" of the men running the show.[xvi] The feminist view, in short, is this: Women who supported abortion were obviously independent and intelligent. Women who opposed abortion must be the puppets of men using them for nefarious purposes—or worse, traitors to their sex.

The full story is much simpler, albeit far more impressive: A series of enormous grassroots networks of men and women who believed in rights for pre-born children were mobilised in just a few years to join a massive push to keep abortion out of Ireland.

The Irish Family League, founded just months after *Roe,* began their campaigns against abortion and contraception (which was viewed as the gateway to abortion, both socially and legally) with a mass distribution of literature to every senator and TD[4] in the country. Their argument against contraception, extensively sourced and footnoted with information drawn from the resources of the international pro-life movement, was that the widespread use of contraception inevitably resulted in a spike in promiscuity which in turn led to a higher demand for abortion. These booklets included the names and addresses of those running family planning organisations that were suspected of supporting abortion legislation.

The potential solution of a constitutional amendment protecting pre-born children as a way of preventing a liberal judiciary from inventing a right to abortion was considered very early on. In fact, the "idea of a constitutional amendment appears to have had its first public outing in 1973/1974 in a small leaflet published by John O'Reilly's Family League."[xvii] In one passage referring to the McGee case, the authors proposed a national referendum and stated in part that: "The law does not have to be changed to conform to the Constitution. A clause could be inserted defining a citizen as a citizen from the moment of conception."[xviii] This succinctly summarized the view of the pro-life movement worldwide: Human beings have human rights. Human rights begin when the human being begins. Science tells us when a new human life begins, and thus that human life is entitled to legal protections from its definable beginning.

By the mid-1970s, the battle was building and forces were mounting on both sides. John O'Reilly and the Irish Family League warned that the increased availability of contraception would mean an increased demand for abortion and the IFL highlighted the risks associated with

4 A Teachta Dála (TD) is a member of Dáil Éireann, the lower house of the Oireachtas, or Irish Parliament.

various contraceptive methods.[5] British health statistics revealed that between 1968 and 1975, 10,000 women had travelled to England for abortions, and the Irish Family Planning Association received several calls a week from women who wanted information on how to best procure an abortion abroad. These statistics were released in September of 1976, and that same month the Knights of Columbus planned three massive speaking tours right around the country, fronted by John O'Reilly's wife Treasa. These tours were designed to stir up the grassroots and confront them with the threats Ireland faced.

The speakers attacked the growing abortion threat from a number of avenues. Dr. Herbert Ratner, an associate professor of public health at the American Loyola University, detailed the dangers of the birth control pill. Dr. Kevin Hume was a general practitioner (GP) and and spoke as the vice president of the Responsible Parenthood Association of Sydney, Australia. Father Paul Marx, who had done a tour in 1971 highlighting the barbarism of abortion by showing an aborted fetus floating in a jar to school children, was a professor of sociology at St. John's University, Minnesota, the executive director of the Human Life Centre, and the author of several books on abortion. A tanned, balding, and passionate activist, one presentation given by Marx at Maynooth University in the early 1970s that featured an "instructional video on how to perform abortions" resulted in students screaming, four people fainting, and one nun racing from the room, trying not to vomit.[xix]

5 Interestingly, Emily O'Reilly notes that back in 1975, John O'Reilly was writing about the dangers of many contraceptive devices—and actually admits that, considering the later complications that were discovered, he turned out to be right. Despite the fact that he was correct, she dismisses the accuracy of the pro-life literature by stating that his motive was to inspire panic and gain support for his position. In other words, according to a pro-choice author, John O'Reilly was wrong even when he was right.

Another voice warning early on that the McGee case could bring abortion to Ireland was Dr. John Bonnar, who had arrived in the country in the mid-1970s from Oxford to head up Obstetrics and Gynaecology at the Rotunda maternity hospital at Trinity College. In 1977, Bonnar warned that a "right to privacy" could be used as a Trojan horse to bring in legal abortion, and in 1980 Bonnar became one of the founders of The Responsible Society, an organisation that would be a key part of the fight for a constitutional amendment in 1983. In the interim, he championed the establishment of ethics committees in hospitals with the specific goal of responding to the ethos sweeping other Western countries. Eventually, these committees would be consulted by the government on the pro-life amendment, and would wholeheartedly endorse it.

That same year, barrister[6] and law lecturer William Binchy, who had served from 1974 to 1976 as a special legal adviser with the Department of Justice on family law reform, also penned a warning to Irish pro-lifers in the same Jesuit publication, *Studies*. In an article titled "Marital Privacy and Family Law," Binchy explained why the Irish respect for life could not be counted on to keep abortion out:

> That attitudes regarding abortion are changing rapidly throughout most countries in the world is hardly a matter of controversy. In the United States it was only in the recent past that a small but clamorous band began to agitate for abortion on demand. The changes there have been described as 'breathtaking.' In Ireland there has so far been little openly-expressed support for abortion. It would, however, seem reasonable to expect that within the next few years attitudes will change somewhat on

6 Lawyer

> this subject, as they have done so remarkably on contraception where religious matters play a part.[xx]

In other words, it was important that pro-lifers be pro-active and move to insert protections for pre-born children into the Constitution while public opinion was still onside. That meant moving swiftly.

The 1979 Health Act was the final event in a series of catalysts that led to the massive push for a constitutional amendment. When Fianna Fáil[7] returned to power in July of 1977 with a twenty-seat majority, the new Taoiseach[8] Jack Lynch announced his plan to introduce a Family Planning Bill by 1978. The pro-family forces mobilised in response, with a number of organisations banding together under the name Council of Social Concern (COSC), located at 8 Ely Place, Dublin 2. The chairman was Niel Darragh, with John O'Reilly serving as vice-chairman. COSC combined the disparate membership rolls of Youth Alert, Concerned Doctors Group, Parent Concern, Nazareth Family Movement, the League of Decency, the Christian Political Action Movement, among others, as well as being associated with a number of Catholic medical guilds. While some groups eventually disaffiliated, the Council of Social Concern wielded impressive clout.

In contradiction to her earlier statements on Ireland's pro-life movement being a predominantly male project, even Emily O'Reilly had to admit that the Irish women who joined the fray were singularly impressive in both their creativity and their effectiveness:

> The Christian Political Action Movement was run by a Mrs Manifold and a Mrs Comer in Galway. The two women were first heard of at a public meeting in Galway in 1976 arguing against the

7 One of Ireland's primary political parties

8 Prime minister

> setting up of a family planning clinic in the city. In 1977 they published a leaflet naming Labour politician, Michael D Higgins, as being in favour of contraception and urging people not to vote for him. (Clearly not helped by the women's actions, Michael D Higgins failed for the third time in a row to get a seat at the 1977 general election.) During the November 1982 election, they published another leaflet, this time naming the so called 'Pro-Life' candidates and omitting Michael D Higgins. Mr Higgins lost his seat.[9][xxi]

The carefully co-ordinated campaigns were a major success, with even Health Minister Charles Haughey admitting that the 1979 Family Planning Bill was intended to restrict rather than increase the availability of contraception, and the criminality of abortion was roundly reaffirmed. Haughey's restraint might also have been the result of a clever tactic employed by the Irish Family League, which helpfully provided him with a poll of his own bailiwick indicating that a full 80% of his constituents were not in favour of contraception being freely available. As a faceoff over abortion approached, pro-life activists began to realise that with the right tactics, they could exercise tremendous influence. In early 1980, COSC again discussed the idea of a constitutional amendment, and this time sought legal advice regarding the idea.

While Irish pro-life activists were ahead of the game, feminist campaigners were beginning to share their view that a "right to privacy" could be used to legalise abortion. In February of 1980, an article in *Hibernia* by journalist Paddy Prendiville detailed the activities of a

---

9 On December 20, 2018, President Michael D. Higgins—one and the same—signed the legislation formally legalizing abortion in the Republic of Ireland. The abortion law would take effect on January 1, 2019.

relatively new group called Women's Right to Choose (their first meeting that month at Trinity College Dublin had attracted about thirty people, mostly students) under the headline "Feminists Plan Abortion Campaign." In his article, Prendiville speculated on the plans of Ireland's abortion activists—and his reporting warned the pro-lifers of what was coming and jolted them into action. "In theory," Prendiville noted, echoing what people like Bonnar and Binchy had already been saying, "the privacy concept could pave the way for abortion rights."[xxii]

Further to that, Prendiville wrote that abortion activists were finally getting their act together and attempting to catch up with their international counterparts: "Already a group of determined feminists in Dublin are planning a programme of demand and agitation under the heading of a Woman's Right to Choose. Their demands include the decriminalisation of abortion, open referral for abortions at hospitals and health centres, and the removal of all social and economic discrimination against single mothers...They also plan to form the Irish section of the International Contraception, Abortion, and Sterilisation Campaign." They were still a very small group of people. Abortion campaigners would later say that they were even smaller than pro-life activists thought at the time, but their presence signalled the definitive beginning of the Irish abortion wars.

Just two weeks after Prendiville's article was published, in March of 1980, Dr. John Bonnar delivered another warning to pro-lifers gathered at the Knights of Columbus headquarters at Ely House in a lecture titled "Abortions on Irish Women." International pressure groups and feminist groups were pushing hard for abortion, he said, and if pro-lifers hoped to head them off, a two-pronged response was imminently necessary: the protection of pre-born life by "effective social measures" and sweeping educational initiatives to shore up the support of the public and steel the Irish people from the onslaught of pro-choice propaganda that was sure to come.[xxiii] In August, the feminist group glowingly profiled by Prendiville formally launched as the Woman's Right to Choose Group in the Junior Common Room in Trinity College, with their primary goals being the decriminalization of abortion and full access to abortion clinics. When the pro-choice Irish Pregnancy Counselling Centre opened at 3 Belvedere Place in Dublin a month later, 250 women had already obtained advice on abortion.

In September, two significant pro-life conferences were held in Dublin, and these duel gatherings would trigger the genesis of the Pro-Life Amendment Campaign (PLAC). One was organised by Bonnar at Trinity College under the banner of the Dutch-based World Federation of Doctors Who Respect Human Life, an organisation committed to "the sanctity of the human person from conception to death." Around 200 physicians attended, including Dr. Julia Vaughan, a highly respected gynaecologist with a practice at Dublin's Mt. Carmel private hospital. She would later become the primary spokesperson for PLAC, proudly stating that Ireland without abortion would "become a beacon" that could "turn the tide in the western world."[xxiv] The conference focused on abortion, with the delegates discussing the increasing pressure from organisations such as the International Planned Parenthood Federation and its ability to influence abortion laws worldwide. Representatives of the Catholic Doctors Guild, some of whom had already considered and discussed the idea of a constitutional amendment, were also present. Several of these doctors, including Dr. Arthur Barry, the president of the guild, and Professor Eamon de Valera, son of the Irish statesman, would become essential to the amendment campaign.

The second conference was a supplementary meeting of pro-life activists held at the Carysfort Teacher Training College in Blackrock, County Dublin. It was a who's who of the emerging movement, including the recently-formed Responsible Society, the UK-based Society for the Protection of Unborn Children (SPUC), Father Paul Marx, and a number of the doctors who had been present at the Trinity College conference. Dr. Peggy Norris of the International Pro-Life Service delivered the keynote speech, adding her own wake-up call to the growing clamour of warnings: Ireland would end up with abortion on demand if something was not done. The abortion activists would never give up, and if pro-lifers did not push back hard, abortion clinics would soon be built on Irish soil. In fact, Norris noted, an international conference on abortion would be coming to Ireland the very next month.

After that meeting, remembered PLAC member Bernadette Bonar, several pro-lifers "met in a Dublin pub. We knew we had to do something to stop abortion from coming into the country. We had lost the fight against contraception, and one thing was certain: We couldn't afford to lose this one."[xxv]

Meanwhile, the Society for the Protection of Unborn Children, which had met in Dublin in July for a series of meetings, was already putting boots on the ground. As the conferences were getting underway, the first Irish affiliate of SPUC began holding public information meetings in Finglas and Dundrum titled "The Case Against Abortion." By December, SPUC was hosting demonstrations across the country, speaking in high schools, and showing photographs of aborted babies at every stop. Their activism, writes Rosanna Cooney, created "a network of willing campaigners in every parish," and their presentations were impactful and effective:

> SPUC's formula for their meetings was adapted

> from the UK. They would show a film entitled *An Everyday Miracle*, which showed the development of the child in the womb to the background of dramatic music. Audiences heard that "just eight weeks after conception this new life has assumed a recognisably human appearance. After 10 weeks, it was "looking more and more like a fully-formed baby". Following the showing of the film, SPUC presented a slideshow under the heading "Death before Life". These slides showed the different ways by which a foetus could be removed from its womb...The slides included the remains of a foetus after it had been suctioned from a woman's womb and a black plastic bag filled with foetuses. By 1982 SPUC had visited over 250 schools around Ireland, had recruited over 4000 members and on at least one occasion spoken from the church pulpit itself.[xxvi]

Throughout the autumn of 1980, things moved quickly. John O'Reilly had circulated a letter proposing the idea of an amendment back in July, and in September the Irish Doctor's Guild confirmed that they had been considering the same strategy. By Christmas of 1980, the team that would become PLAC—roughly a dozen people—was in place, and by January of 1981, O'Reilly had recruited twelve organisations and was fairly certain that five others would also join. On January 24, a founding conference was held at Mount Carmel Hospital, attended by more than a dozen organisations.[10][xxvii] COSC chairman

10 Organisations at this meeting included the Congress of Catholic Secondary School Parents' Association, the Irish Catholic Doctors' Guild, the Christian Brothers School Parents' Federation, the Council of Social Concern, the Guild of Catholic Nurses, the Guild of Catholic Pharmacists, the Catholic Young Men's Society, the St. Joseph's Young Priests' Society, the St. Thomas More Society, the Responsible Society, SPUC, the Irish Pro-Life Movement, and the charmingly named National Association of the Ovulation Method.

Nial Darragh asked the organisations present to support a pro-life amendment, and the following week a similar meeting was held where delegates were addressed by Professor Cornelius O'Leary of Queen's University on legal and political aspects of the amendment proposal. (The Irish affiliate of the British-based Lawyers for the Defence of the Unborn joined later.)[11]

The executive committee was selected in short order. Dr. Julia Vaughan was chosen to be PLAC's chairperson, Michael Shortall of the Catholic Young Men's Society was elected secretary, Denis Barror of the Responsible Society became treasurer, and Professor O'Leary was selected as vice-chairman. Michael Shortall's brother Brendan, a PR specialist, was asked to lend PLAC his expertise in that area. O'Reilly's initial campaign plans, which proposed a massive grassroots effort to collect signatures for a petition and pressure the government into holding a referendum, were rejected by Vaughan, who felt it would be wiser to target top politicians directly. The Irish pro-life movement thus formed two main wings as the referendum campaign approached: The foot soldiers of SPUC, who were comfortable with confrontational tactics and exposing the ugly reality of abortion, and PLAC, which became "one of the most powerful and effective lobbying groups in Irish history."[xxviii]

Less than a year after the first meeting of Women's Right to Choose, the Pro-Life Amendment Campaign formally launched with a press conference on April 27, 1981, with the initial press release citing the support of John Bonnar, Eamon de Valera, and a range of other prestigious obstetricians and gynaecologists. A draft

11 William Binchy would become John O'Reilly's legal advisor, and Senior Counsel Dermot Kinlen and Senior Counsel John Blayney would also play key roles.

amendment written up by Senior Counsel John Blayney (who later became a judge on the High Court) was unveiled at the press conference: "The State recognises the absolute right to life of every unborn child from conception and accordingly guarantees to respect and protect such right by law."[xxix]

Just three days after launching, PLAC moved with both speed and impeccable timing, setting up meetings with the then-Taoiseach, Charles Haughey, and Garret Fitzgerald, the leader of the opposition. PLAC realised that the current climate of political instability—there would be four general elections between 1979 and 1982—could work perfectly to their advantage, as Haughey's minority government was barely clinging to power and both Fianna Fáil and Fine Gael[12] desperately wanted to secure the pro-life vote. Both Haughey and Fitzgerald agreed to a referendum, with Fitzgerald being particularly eager to display his cooperation due to a furor over recent media comments made by the vice president of Fine Gael, Maria Stack, who had indicated her support for abortion in certain circumstances. In his 1991 memoir *All In A Life*, Fitzgerald would later write that the PLAC delegation had told him that steps should be taken to protect pre-born children to prevent a judicial ruling similar to *Roe v. Wade*.

The meetings, arranged primarily by Brendan Shortall, were brilliantly choreographed. The delegations were often led by Julia Vaughan, and delegates were selected based on who would have the greatest impact on the politician they were meeting. For example, Julia Vaughan met with Taoiseach Charles Haughey, while Eamon de Valera met with Fitzgerald, as it was surmised that Haughey might not care for being lobbied on the Constitution by the son of its author. Loretta

12 One of Ireland's primary political parties.

Brown of SPUC was also on the PLAC delegation along with lawyers Frank Ryan and Denis Barror, and Brendan Shortall attended every meeting to ensure that everything was running smoothly. The message was a simple and persuasive one: Ireland's top gynaecologists and obstetricians were worried about the threat of abortion based on what was happening in nations across the West, and thus they wanted to discuss it with party leaders. They also happened to represent an enormous bloc of voters who were *very* interested in what the party leaders had to say.

A month later, Fitzgerald included his commitment to supporting a constitutional amendment in the Fine Gael election program, and on May 14, Haughey wrote to PLAC that he was fully on board: "Further to our discussion on 13 May, 1981, I wish to convey to you, on behalf of the Government, a solemn assurance that an appropriate constitutional amendment to give effect to that position will be brought forward as soon as circumstances permit. We are at present examining the form such an amendment will take so as to ensure that it will be fully constitutionally and legally effective."[xxx] Less than a month after launching, PLAC had already secured commitments from the leaders of Ireland's two largest political parties to implement their agenda.

In June, PLAC's executive began to discuss strategy for the campaign that they were now assured would come. O'Reilly and Darragh were in favor of emulating the no-holds-barred approach of SPUC, the Irish movement's shock troops. Courting controversy, they felt, would allow them to highlight the barbarism of abortion and push back against the lies that the pro-choice crowd would be spreading—and they fully expected that they would be facing the full force of the international abortion lobby as soon as a date was set for a referendum.

In a letter to PLAC's leaders, most of whom seemed more inclined to a moderate approach, they laid out their rationale:

> It would appear that PLAC fails to realise that the international abortion movement will launch an intensive brainwashing campaign as soon as the Referendum is definite—if not before...If a date next April is named, we could expect the counter-campaign to mount before Christmas, less than six months from now...we have been given a respite of some months. Let us use it fully to get our strategy right, our funds in order and to build up our human resources. The international abortion movement is more powerful than even well-informed people realise, often working through international agencies held in great respect...The strategy, no doubt, would be to spread confusion by arguing for abortion in cases of rape, incest, alleged 'life and death' situations, and in the case of foetal abnormality. As usual, the pro-abortion campaign will be highly emotive and libertarian. To counter it, emotion will have to be made to serve the unborn and their sense of human rights and justice invoked.[xxxi]

Because so many nations had already fallen to the global abortion juggernaut, Irish pro-lifers had the sad benefit of seeing how pro-lifers in other countries had been outflanked and defeated, and also recognised how thoroughly the abortion activists had infiltrated international organisations that presented themselves as neutral. They understood that the abortion activists would soon utilise precisely the same strategies in Ireland, and that it would be essential to block them and blunt their influence. It was in part because of this careful research, strategizing, and foresight that the Irish pro-life movement would successfully achieve what no other Western country could lay claim to: explicit constitutional protections for pre-born children.

Although initially hesitant, the other PLAC members were eventually persuaded that a high-profile campaign was the way to go. O'Reilly immediately began working on a plan to respond to the inevitable anti-amendment campaign that was sure to surface, noting that, "We need money for literature, radio, and TV coverage, newspaper promotion as well as quantities of coloured literature on pre-birth life…All this will require sums of money, say a bare minimum of 100,000 pounds, doing it on a shoestring; up to a high of 600,000 pounds."[xxxii]

Then, politics intervened. In June, a general election produced another Fine Gael-Labour coalition, and the pro-life movement waited for the specific commitment to an anti-abortion referendum that they'd been promised. Fitzgerald, the Taoiseach, indicated that perhaps the abortion issue could be included as part of a review of the entire Constitution, which would fit nicely into his self-described crusade to create a non-sectarian Irish constitution. The coalition government was toppled over a budget vote in January 1982 without PLAC receiving a firm commitment, and the pro-lifers realised that they were going to have to force action if they wanted to see the referendum happen. In the February 1982 election, PLAC demanded that leaders explicitly explain whether or not they supported a referendum.

Fitzgerald dragged his feet, worried that committing to an acrimonious abortion referendum would interfere with his other political priorities. His opponent Haughey, on the other hand, promptly made things more difficult for him by writing to PLAC that: "I am glad to be able to confirm to your executive committee that when elected to office the new Fianna Fáil Government will arrange to have the necessary legislation for a proposed constitutional amendment to guarantee the right to life of the foetus initiated in the Dáil Éireann during the course of the year, 1982, without reference to any other aspect of constitutional change."[xxxiii] Haughey won re-election, and Fitzgerald worked hard to prove his pro-life credentials, aware that PLAC now had the ability to effectively kill his career. As Emily O'Reilly would put it: "PLAC was now calling the shots, with the power to make or break Fitzgerald or any politician who stood in their way."[xxxiv]

In November of 1982, Fianna Fáil published their wording for a proposed amendment: "The State acknowledges the right to life of the unborn and, with due regard to the equal right to life of the mother, guarantees in its laws to respect and, as far as practicable, by its laws to defend and vindicate that right."[xxxv] Fitzgerald promptly endorsed the wording, eager to prove to the pro-lifers that he had not gone wobbly and would deliver on his promises this time around. Fine Gael promised that if they were elected, they would hold a referendum on the wording by March of 1983, with Fitzgerald writing to PLAC personally to assure them that there would be no delays if he formed government.[13]

Haughey lost to Fitzgerald in December 1982, and this time, Fitzgerald buckled in the face of overwhelming pro-life pressure, terrified of being labeled "pro-abortion." Years later, Minister for Health Barry Desmond, who served from 1982 to 1987, recalled that

13 The Fianna Fáil government collapsed only two days after the wording of the amendment was agreed upon, after a man who had murdered a young nurse and a farmer was discovered to be a house guest of the Attorney General of Ireland, Patrick Connolly. The acronym GUBU was coined by Conor Cruise O'Brien as a paraphrase of Haughey's comments on the matter: "Grotesque, unbelievable, bizarre, and unprecedented."

the pro-life movement was "powerful in nearly every parish in the country"—and politicians feared butting heads with this well-oiled machine.[xxxvi] "The pro-life group decided—a very articulate group, very clever group—to put the fear of God into every politician about this issue of abortion," Desmond later told a pro-choice interviewer. "The Dáil deputies in government and in opposition, they knew perfectly well that their seats would be in complete jeopardy if they opposed the pro-life movement and the idea of a referendum."

In June of 1982, abortion activists launched the Anti-Amendment Campaign (AAC) to try and foil PLAC's efforts, and they were predictably livid at the wording of the proposed amendment, claiming that it could potentially threaten the availability of some contraception (an unintended admission that some so-called contraceptive measures actually function as abortifacients). Interestingly, there was also some political concern at the time that the abortion issue could be seen as a sectarian attempt to make the Irish state more fully Catholic, and that this could hurt Anglo-Irish policy if the Unionists and Protestant churches in the North were to view it that way. Three and a half decades later, it would often be the strict Protestants holding the line against the forces of the international abortion movement, with pro-life Irish republicans uniting with Unionists in their opposition to abortion.

But by February of 1983, some of the politicians began to wobble under pressure, with some Protestant denominations expressing opposition to the amendment (and even support for abortion in certain circumstances). The Methodist church even claimed that the pro-life cause was explicitly Catholic, and some Unionist politicians claimed that the unity of Ireland was off the agenda if an amendment passed. (Again, it is ironic to consider that it would be the Unionists fighting desperately to keep abortion out of Northern Ireland decades later.) Pro-life activists responded with fierce pressure, and the party was "forced to restate its commitment to an amendment with an anti-abortion stance."[xxxvii] Alternative wording was proposed that stated that no right to abortion could be found in the Constitution, and PLAC rejected it on the grounds that the new wording didn't explicitly state that a ban *could* be found in the Constitution. After a series of political scuffles, the original Fianna Fáil wording was reconfirmed on April 27 and the referendum date was set for September 7.

The pro-life campaigners hit the ground with force. "We traveled the country wide," Bernadette Bonar would later remember, "and my greatest memory of that was we never had to stay in a hotel or guest house. The people were open arms, receiving us."[xxxviii] Representatives of PLAC crisscrossed the country, hosting meetings and delivering presentations. Other groups that pitched in for the referendum campaign included Family Rights Council established by Úna Bean Mhic Mhathúna, Bridget Bermingham, and Máire Breathnach, the first woman to hold the position of Assistant Secretary of the Department of Finance. They produced voter guides and posters for the referendum particularly popular with activists on the ground. The public was extremely receptive—to many people, it was transparently obvious that something as barbaric as abortion should be banned. As Bonar recalled: "It was very easy to sell it to the people, because a lot of people didn't even know we had a constitution and they couldn't understand why anyone would want to legalise the killing of innocent babies, it was the easiest thing in the world to sell. The key supporters of a politician were important to get to. We would go to the local organisations, the county councillors, the chairman and secretary of branches, they were the people instrumental in getting a

TD elected. We had conveyers in every constituency that would put pressure on these people."[xxxix]

The Anti-Amendment Campaign, on the other hand, found it very difficult to get any traction. Businesses often refused to associate with them for fear of losing customers. Many venues refused to host their meetings or events. Door-knockers often faced a hostile reception: One AAC canvasser remembered that "even after a day spent canvassing people in the pub would call us murderers and baby-killers."[xl] Pro-lifers showed up to counter-protest some of their meetings too, most famously at the Black Sheep Pub in Coolock in Dublin's northside. The AAC had booked a meeting room in the pub, but it was cancelled after locals objected, and AAC decided to meet in the carpark instead, bringing a lorry and sound equipment. They were met with a vociferous protest, as pro-lifers and local kids drowned out the AAC with megaphones and chants of "let us vote" (the AAC were against holding a referendum) and shouts to "go home." Some of the pro-lifers had brought guitars and banjos. "Anything you can do, we can do better," crooned one into a megaphone, channelling Irving Berlin. One sign read that "The abortion mills of England grind Irish babies into blood that cries out to heaven for vengeance." The AAC eventually gave up and dispersed. Prominent activists, such as Úna Mhic Mhathúna and Míne Uí Chribín, a Santry woman whose work in educating those left behind by the system was legendary, made the papers. As far as they were concerned, they needed to use their voices for the voiceless pre-born children threatened by what the AAC was proposing.

The pro-life pushback was effective. Stumping for abortion was seen as a genuinely horrible thing to do, and although the visceral responses the AAC campaigners received can seem jarring to more sophisticated pro-life activists today, they emerged from a deep loathing of abortion and a genuine and justified anger that anyone could defend the killing of pre-born children. It was a different era, one in which many ordinary people could still be outraged at the very thought of their fellow citizens pushing for abortion. Abortion activists, one pro-life leader remembered decades later, were often nasty and vicious if they could get away with it—but during the 1983 referendum campaign, "the ordinary, decent, working-class men and women didn't let them get away with anything."

As Cooney put it, the pro-life movement had utterly outflanked the abortion campaigners: "They were entirely unprepared to tackle a well-funded, efficient, and sophisticated PLAC that had already been putting in years of groundwork in parishes around the country."[xli] Additionally, the AAC's message was vague because even they didn't dare to explicitly endorse abortion, choosing instead to quibble about the wording of the amendment and the financial cost of the referendum. As Cooney noted, PLAC's message was crystal clear: "Don't murder babies, abortion is murder, vote yes to the referendum."[xlii] The final leaflet issued by the AAC, on the other hand, was catchy but nearly inscrutable: "If you don't know, vote no."[xliii] The AAC campaigners did, however, use tactics that would be used in every abortion referendum to come: They trotted out extreme cases to insist that protections for pre-born children were dangerous to vulnerable women.

Ironically, after years of campaigning for the votes of the pro-life movement, Garrett Fitzgerald and Fine Gael actually campaigned against the amendment, joined by the Labour Party. Fitzgerald's attempts to change the Fianna Fáil wording had been foiled by PLAC (who had been tipped off about the proposed wording change and were immediately prepared to go to the media), and thus he decided in the end to declare his opposition to the movement he had courted. As the date of the referendum neared, however, AAC campaigners realised that victory was almost impossible. The final PLAC advertisement, issued on the eve of the referendum, issued a simple, powerful plea to the Irish people: "At the end of the day, this amendment is about preventing abortion—the direct and deliberate killing of individual, unique, human beings. If you want to make certain that this can never happen here without the consent of the Irish people, then vote Yes in tomorrow's referendum."[xliv]

The final evidence of what the Irish pro-life movement had accomplished was on display on referendum day, when AAC campaigners watched glumly as busloads of voters, carefully organised by the pro-lifers, rolled in a seemingly unending stream up to the polling stations. Hundreds of people had also volunteered their cars to pick up pro-life voters, and nearly every Catholic institution emptied out as the Irish flooded to the polls. On the seventh of September, 1983, 841,233 people voted to put protections for pre-born children into the Irish constitution—66.9% of the vote. On the other side, 416,136 people, 33.1%, had voted No, with a total voter turnout of 54.1%. The Eighth Amendment to the Constitution was passed by a two to one majority.

That day, the Irish pro-life movement achieved something that was virtually unprecedented: constitutional protections for pre-born children. They were, Fintan O'Toole later wrote bitterly in the *Irish Times*, the "most successful single issue movement in the history of the State."[xlv] The global abortion movement was enraged, and the international pro-life movement was inspired. Ireland became both a prominent target and a beacon of hope. It would remain that way for thirty-five years.

Chapter 3
Baby X

I would like to see evidence that our legislators and our Government are intent to implement the Eighth Amendment—to implement it to the full. We gave the right to life to the unborn—we pledged that in our laws and by our laws we would defend and vindicate that right. Have we done so? I suggest to you that our Dail, that is, our Parliament, has ignored that part of the amendment. If over 5,000 Irish babies are aborted in Britain every year, are we defending their right to life? In order to defend the right to life of the unborn, we must close these abortion referral agencies which are operating in Dublin quite openly and underneath the eyes of the law. These clinics must be closed and if the 1861 Act cannot close them, we must have a new Act that will. Is our Government sincere about the amendment or do they believe in the right to choose to abort Irish babies in Liverpool, Birmingham, or London?[xlvi]

SPUC President Dr. Mary Lucey to a pro-life conference in Rome in September 1983

Having achieved what no other Western nation could lay claim to—explicit constitutional protections for pre-born children in the womb—the pro-life movement pushed forward. Again, the Irish pro-lifers proved prescient. They were not simply satisfied with constitutional protections, but wanted to ensure that the abortion business did not slink in through a back door or attempt to ooze through a loophole, as had happened in so many other nations. John O'Reilly, in fact, wanted to maintain the PLAC infrastructure for the future campaigns that he was already anticipating, although that proved impossible due to internal disagreements. At a speech at a pro-life conference in Rome the same month as the referendum victory, O'Reilly explained to the crowd that there was still much work to be done:

> Another organisation will however have to be formed; perhaps using the structures and grass roots organisations already built up, if at all possible. We still have many problems. Abortion referral is rife and open. Despite the amendment, the anti-amendment lobby is united and vigorous and will not go away but will continue to press on their sensitive areas. There is room for more caring organisations for unmarried mothers…And, as the amendment vote shows, the attitudes of the media are totally out of tune with popular opinion; but if the media remain as they are, popular opinion will eventually take its lead from the media. There are many things which must be done. We know that if we retire from this fight, the advantage we have gained will be eroded and that whilst we choose the battleground we have the initiative.[xlvii]

O'Reilly's words proved prophetic. Thirty-five years later, the pro-life movement would conclude that the influence of the media played a key role in bringing abortion to Ireland. In the meantime, however, Irish pro-lifers shifted their focus from the amendment campaign to defending Ireland from the abortion activists. Following the defeat of the divorce referendum of June 26, 1986, which many of the key pro-life activists opposed, the movement achieved another goal they had been working towards: In December, "just seven months after the divorce referendum, John O'Reilly scored another stunning success when the President of the High Court ruled as illegal and unconstitutional the abortion counselling carried out by the Well Women centres and Open Line Counselling."[xlviii] [14]

The methods the pro-lifers utilised were both shrewd and clever. The two clinics they targeted had been referring Irish women for abortions in England, and several women agreed to go undercover to expose this fact. They went "on the abortion trail," which meant heading all the way to the operating table in a British abortion clinic before "opting out only at the last moment, pleading a change of mind."[xlix] The undercover investigators first went to Well Women, and then headed to Open Line, telling the staff that they were seeking abortions and needed assistance. The women were given counselling, and arrangements were made with British abortion clinics. Upon their return from England, the women promptly authored affidavits on behalf of the Society for the Protection of Unborn Children detailing their experiences, and SPUC initiated legal action to have the abortion referral centres banned from arranging abortions for Irish women in other countries.

The direct result of this undercover investigation spearheaded by female Irish pro-lifers was the closure of Open Line Counselling, the cessation of abortion counselling at Well Women Centre, and the abrupt decision by several British magazine publishers to cancel abortion ads in the Irish editions of their publications such as *Cosmopolitan* for fear of being shut down. An appeal by both centres failed, with the judges again affirming that their actions violated the pre-born child's right to life as laid out in the Eighth Amendment. Because killing a pre-born child was a human rights violation under Irish law, assisting women in procuring

14 The pro-family forces won the anti-divorce referendum with 63.1% voting against legalisation. Emily O'Reilly again claimed that it was John O'Reilly and a handful of activists who pulled this off, reemphasising her thesis that a tiny cabal of key actors held off modernity in Ireland for decades.

such a "service" was obviously illegal. As Emily O'Reilly put it in *Masterminds of the Right*: "All abortion counselling and information was now banned in the state. PLAC's tentacles had now spread wider and would spread wider than they ever dared admit."[1] The Eighth Amendment had now been tested and proven solid: The Court ruled that providing information and counselling about abortion was contrary to Article 40.3.3.

A similar campaign was launched when SPUC discovered that student unions were seeking to fill the void by providing information about British abortion clinics in their student manuals at both the University College of Dublin (UCD) and Trinity College. The stereotypically left-wing student unions went so far as to provide both the addresses and phone numbers for abortion clinics in England in order to make abortion arrangements for their members as simple as possible. SPUC promptly took the case to court in September of 1988, seeking an injunction to prevent the UCD handbook from being published the following academic year, as it would presumably again contain information on how to obtain abortions. The case went to the High Court, the Supreme Court, the European Court of Justice, back to the Supreme Court, and then to the European Community and the European Council.

Pro-lifers won the case at the Supreme Court and then, shockingly, at the European Court of Justice in 1991, where the student unions were represented by the future president of Ireland, Mary Robinson:

> [I]n October 1991, the full European Council Court of Justice followed the advice of the Advocate General and upheld the information ban. The court ruled that while medical termination of pregnancy was indeed an EC accepted service: 'It is not contrary to Community law for a member state in which medical termination of

> pregnancy is forbidden to prohibit Students' associations from distributing information about the identity and location of clinics in another member state where voluntary termination of pregnancy is lawfully carried out and the means of communicating with those clinics, where the clinics in question have no involvement in the distribution of the said information.'[li]

The victory was short-lived. Irish pro-lifers had always been concerned that Europe might attempt to interfere with their country's protections for pre-born children, and from a strictly strategic perspective, the zealousness with which the movement attempted to restrict information on procuring abortions abroad may have been a well-intentioned overreach, as it exposed them to attacks on issues like freedom of speech. The European Community pushed back, declaring in October of 1992 that the Irish court injunctions prohibiting the provision of information about abortion services outside the country were a violation of the European Convention of Human Rights Article 10, which protects freedom of expression. The European Court of Justice also took aim at the injunctions against the abortion referral clinics, claiming that they were a disproportionate measure that posed a health risk to Irish women who might be seeking abortions abroad.

But the most significant event of 1992 was the case of Baby X, which jolted forces on both sides of the abortion wars like a sudden thunderclap.

The story broke on Wednesday, February 12, when the *Irish Times* ran a small news item on their front page by Niall Kiely titled "State attempts to stop girl's abortion." In the article, Kiely reported that the State had taken legal action to prevent a 14-year-old girl, who had been impregnated by rape, from leaving the country to get an abortion in the UK. The girl was from a middle-class family in South County Dublin, and the abuse she had suffered at the hands of a friend's father had come to the attention of authorities when her parents asked the Gardai[15] if DNA from the aborted baby could be used as evidence to prosecute the rapist. The Gardai sought answers from the Director of Public Prosecutions, who spoke with Attorney General Harry Whelehan, who moved to secure an injunction.

Political chaos ensued immediately. Abortion activists knew that they had a sympathetic case to present to the public and moved swiftly to frame the tragic situation as evidence that Ireland's pro-life laws were cruel and unjust. Four members of the 1983 Anti-Amendment Campaign released a statement saying that they had warned that the Eighth Amendment would restrict the right to travel, and that "the so-called 'pro-life' amendment was nothing more than an exercise in national hypocrisy."[lii] Both abortion activists and their allies in the national press announced with feigned shock that pro-lifers were opposed to abortion in *all* cases, even in cases where the child was conceived through sexual assault. Despite the fact that this was not news, the pro-life movement's response—that attempting to address one act of violence with a second act of violence was not a humane solution—was presented as horrifying and callous. Pro-lifers attempted to respond but, as one leader remembered years later, were "shouted down."

Sensing an opportunity, the abortion activists mobilised and took to the streets. After Mr. Justice Declan Costello of the High Court upheld Whelehan's application on February 17, they protested outside Government buildings, with speakers such as Maxine Brady of the Union of Students in Ireland calling on the crowds to condemn the Eighth Amendment. Inside the Dail, some

15 Police.

politicians predictably began to buckle. Former Fine Gael leader Alan Dukes and spokesman Justice Alan Shatter said the Eighth Amendment needed to be revised, and Fine Gael TD Nuala Fennell said that it should be either amended or scrapped entirely. On February 19, abortion supporters held a candlelight vigil outside Leinster House. The same day, the Catholic hierarchy caved and presented shocking legal advice that stated their view that the constitutional protection of the right to life of the pre-born should not necessarily restrict the girl from travelling. The Government agreed to accept an appeal by the family, with Taoiseach Albert Reynolds insisting that the case was about the right to travel, *not* about abortion. Supporters of the original Anti-Amendment Campaign, however, thought otherwise, and began planning for a campaign to repeal the Eighth Amendment.

On February 26, the Supreme Court overturned the High Court's ruling, and the Taoiseach averred that he was "delighted" that "the family [was] now free to take whatever action they wished."[liii] Many politicians, and even many pro-lifers, hoped that this would resolve the case, with Dr. Mary Lucey of SPUC and Des McDonnel of Family Solidarity echoing the Taoiseach in stating that the ruling was not about abortion, but rather about the right to travel. Abortion groups, predictably, had other ideas, and almost without exception called for an end to the Eighth Amendment. But a week later, relief that the case might be over without the issue of abortion becoming front and centre vanished when the texts of the rulings by the five Supreme Court justices were released. By a 4 to 1 majority, it turned out, the justices had not merely overturned the High Court's ruling regarding the right to travel, but had instead stated that the threat to the pregnant girl's life by suicide was "real and substantial" and that she should be legally entitled to abortion.[liv]

This changed everything, as it transformed the case of Baby X from one about the right to travel into a case about abortion itself, essentially legalizing abortion when suicidal ideation was claimed by the mother. Justice C.J. Finlay said that permitting abortion in such circumstances was acceptable because the pregnancy could at that point be defined as a threat to the mother's equal right to life, while Justice Niall McCarthy posited that if pregnancy caused mental and emotional distress, this could result in suicidal ideation, meaning it consequently also posed a threat to the mother's life. McCarthy's ruling also eviscerated lawmakers for failing to pass laws that explicitly laid out the rules surrounding abortion. Pro-lifers pointed out that the judgement was fundamentally flawed because the evidence of mental distress provided to the Court was from a non-medical psychologist rather than a psychiatrist, but this was largely ignored. In the end, Baby X's mother suffered a miscarriage, and the right to travel, for her at least, became moot.[16]

In response to the case of Baby X, three referendums were presented to the Irish people on November 25, 1992. The so-called 12th Amendment, which would have declared suicidal ideation an insufficient threat to justify abortion, was rejected by a margin of 65% to 35%. The 13th Amendment proposal that an abortion ban could not limit travel to countries where abortion was available was approved by a margin of 62% to 38%. And the 14th Amendment, which proposed that Irish citizens could learn about abortion services in other countries, was approved by a margin of 60% to 40%. These three referendums, it seemed, definitively confirmed the right to travel abroad for the purpose of procuring an

16 The girl's assailant, named in 2003 as one Seán O'Brien, was sentenced to 14 years in prison, which was reduced after an appeal to 4 years. He served a mere 3 years, but was sent back to prison in 2002 for another three and a half years for the sexual assault of another teen girl in 1999.

abortion. Abortion activists, however, were still unhappy: It seemed that the case of Baby X would not result in the desired repeal or revision of the Eighth Amendment. The referenda might have been a victory for freedom of expression, but they wanted abortion on demand.

For the duration of the uproar surrounding the case of Baby X, the media maintained a de facto pro-abortion position. It was simply taken for granted that the pre-born child at the centre of the maelstrom was disposable, and the humanity of the child was intentionally ignored along with the inconvenient facts that pro-life spokespeople attempted to put forward. There are those who claim that the media was unbiased due to the fact that they also solicited statements from pro-lifers, but this ignores the reality that the media largely failed to take into account the core scientific facts at the heart of the pro-life position: Baby X was a real human being with real human rights, irrespective of the circumstances of his or her conception. Even the crime of rape was only addressed primarily as an emotionally powerful argument for legal abortion, which the media desperately wanted to push. As one spokesperson for SPUC commented: "It is remarkable how much of this attention has focused on abortion and how little on the crime of rape and the right to life of the unborn."[lv]

To cite one typical example, on February 20, the *Irish Times* published an editorial condemning the Eighth Amendment, claiming bitterly that those who had voted for it were dupes who had been "used," and that the case of Baby X had roiled the Irish public with a "seething anger" that "safe, benign, family-loving Ireland…has visited such cruelty on one of its own children."[lvi] Again, it was simply taken for granted that Baby X was not *also* an Irish child, and that the only humane response to the horrible circumstances of the child's conception would be to procure and facilitate an abortion. It was also taken for granted that an abortion was in the best interests of all involved, including the mother. The "seething anger" referred to by the *Irish Times* was intentionally stoked by the media for the purpose of demonising the pro-life movement, reducing support for the Eighth Amendment, and launching Ireland on the path to legalising abortion.

But something else was also happening throughout that chaotic year of 1992, and it was not only the abortion activists who were mobilising for war. The smears of the press and the aggressive campaigning of the abortion activists had not gone unnoticed by a twenty-year-old woman named Niamh Nic Mhathúna, who watched the media and the mob call for the ending of the life of helpless Baby X with growing concern. Abortion was a subject close to Niamh's heart for several reasons: Her family was heavily involved in the pro-life movement, and her mother Úna had played a significant part in the grassroots campaign during the 1983 referendum campaign. In 1987, American pro-life leader Joe Scheidler, founder of Chicago's Pro-Life Action League, had visited the family home on a trip to Ireland. Despite growing up staunchly pro-life, Niamh remembered later, abortion wasn't something she thought about a lot.[17]

Scheidler's visit changed all that. "He was a big, tall man," Niamh recalled, "to me as a child he seemed almost like a giant. But he was also funny and kind and interesting. Even as a child you knew this was someone who was making a difference in the world." He left her mother several photographs of aborted babies for

17 Scheidler's 2016 memoir *Racketeer for Life: Fighting the Culture of Death from the Sidewalk to the Supreme Court* details his long career as one of the global pro-life movement's seminal figures, and also details several of his experiences in Ireland.

her to use while speaking with people about the issue, and decades later, Niamh could still vividly remember seeing these photographs for the first time. She stared at the photos in shock, utterly horrified that somebody could do something so cruel to *anybody*—but *especially* to a baby. Abortion was something fundamentally foreign, something profoundly antithetical to how she had been raised. "We were taught to see children as a gift—that their vulnerability entitled them to our protection," Niamh remembered. "That photograph probably made me realise for the first time that abortion was more than a word, it was more than a 'bad thing,' which was how we thought about it in childish terms. It was something that actually caused a child to die in a horribly cruel way. It was a revelation. It was something that remained with me as I grew up. I've never lost that sense of it. At the heart of all of this is the inescapable fact that abortion in itself is a terrible thing. The cruelty of it—towards mother and child—is a terrible thing."

American pro-life activist Dr. Monica Miller once described her first glimpse of abortion victim photography this way: "The sight makes us tremble and weep, and the shock solidifies within us a great, absolute, 'No' as we refuse to be part of this terrible darkness. Our being is filled with a resolve to stand against it. Nothing in this glimpse of Hell can be right, and the evil of it all is incarnated in broken bodies that cry to you for justice. Once you see the bodies with the right mind, you can never go back. They have taken you into their world."[lvii] Joe Scheidler, too, quit his job to work fulltime in the pro-life movement after seeing a photograph of a garbage bag filled with aborted babies—one of them looked just like his son. So did renowned pro-life apologist Scott Klusendorf, who once said that nobody joins the pro-life movement—they are "summoned into it." In many cases, they are summoned into the movement by the aborted babies themselves, their mangled little bodies frozen in horrific photographs that have the power to change the lives of those who see them.[18]

And so, as Ireland was convulsed with the shockwaves of the X case, not everyone was buying the lies pumped out by the media. Some, like Niamh, had seen what abortion really was, and were thus inoculated from the media reports designed to disguise abortion as a compassionate solution. Just weeks after the story broke, she and a group of five friends (all between the ages of seventeen and twenty) decided to start fighting back. Somebody, they felt, had to defend the heart and soul of Ireland from those who wished to utterly transform and destroy what their ancestors had built and what their children were owed. Everywhere they looked, the media was claiming that the young people were clamouring for legal abortion. Journalists were tracking down young people who agreed with this assertion, and amplifying their voices as best they could. Entire classes of high school students were showing up at protests demanding that the Eighth Amendment be repealed.

The establishment pro-life groups were doing their best, but it seemed to Niamh and her friends that nobody was standing up to rebut one of the media's core assertions: the young people of Ireland wanted abortion. Nobody was standing up and saying: *I'm a young person, and I'm pro-life*. The pro-life movement needed young voices, too. "We saw a well-orchestrated campaign screaming for the blood of Irish children," she said in 1992, and it was time "to put an end to the madness."[lviii]

The movement they launched would shape Irish politics for years to come.

---

18 In my 2017 book *Seeing is Believing: Why Our Culture Must Face the Victims of Abortion*, I detail the stories of pro-life leaders who joined the movement after seeing abortion victim photography.

Chapter 4
A Generation Rises

We are too young to realise that certain things are impossible... So we will do them anyway.

William Wilberforce

We didn't have the inhibitions of an older, cautious person, who is worried what the neighbors think of him. Does anybody get anything by being called "respectable"? Because usually that's the opposite of respectable. Usually it is a lack of self-belief in the opinion you have, because you think it's not important enough to get angry about. It's not important enough to get upset about. It's not important enough to lose something over. It's just: If I say something in a meek voice, maybe they'll eventually see that I'm right. No. That's not how the world works. They hated us, but we were relevant.

Úna Nic Mhathúna

The sight of the funeral procession was enough to stop passersby dead in their tracks. Young men and women dressed in mourning black made their way somberly down the street in silence. Many of the men wore tuxedos, and the women wore long black dresses, their faces obscured by mourning veils. They carried the white coffin of a child on their shoulders as they marched to the place where the baby they mourned had been sentenced to death: the Irish Supreme Court.

The crowd of marching young people had come to commemorate the ruling of the Supreme Court in the X case, and to stand against the clamour of demands from abortion activists that Baby X be killed. One extraordinary image from this procession stands out starkly. It is a photograph of a beautiful young woman, a black cape knotted at her throat, her pale face and red lips and black hair covered with a black veil. She is clutching a white cross and a fistful of blood-red roses. It is a picture of the battles to come: The flower of Ireland's youth in bloom mourning the cruel trampling of one who had scarcely had the chance to bud. Baby X could not be saved, but she could be wept for.

The 1993 first Annual Commemoration of the Death of Baby X was led by Youth Defence, an emerging force made up of driven young men and women who would go on to be described as "the shock troops" of Ireland's pro-life movement. Annual funeral processions for Baby X were one example of their resolute refusal to allow anyone to ignore the fact that they believed abortion to be the human rights issue of their generation. The slick strategists and pro-life politicians may have wanted to forget Baby X and the accompanying controversies as swiftly as possible, but Youth Defence relentlessly and repeatedly dragged the public gaze back to the core issue: the babies, dead and alive, who were owed their nation's remembrance and protection.

The commemorations of the X case ruling would become an annual event, with leaders summoning the creative power of youth and the symbolism of traditional Ireland to draw powerful comparisons that the press felt predictably helpless to ignore. One stark procession was led by mock judges carrying signs that confessed "We sentenced Baby X to death." Black flags flapped in the wind over their heads, the breezes ruffling the mourning veils of the women wielding crosses with knots of yellow daffodils hanging from them. When they arrived at the Marie Stopes clinic[19],

19 Marie Stopes International is a global organisation peddling abortion and contraception, founded by the renowned eugenicist who gave the organisation her name.

the flag-bearers formed an honour guard flanking each side of the walkway, and the pallbearers processed past. At the head of the coffin, a tall white tombstone: *RIP Baby X*. Mourners walked one by one to the coffin and laid flowers on the lid.

These funeral processions were a perfect microcosm of Youth Defence's modus operandi: a refusal to allow the abortion debate to devolve into a discussion that distracted people from the reality that abortion killed babies in the womb. They were fully willing to utilise bold tactics and shocking street theatre to draw attention to this reality, and their strategies were designed to ensure that the media would be forced to cover their demonstrations. They didn't mind making people uncomfortable, and they didn't care if people were offended. The young men and women of Youth Defence were foot soldiers, and that meant taking to the streets and forcing the discussion. Those pushing to bring abortion to their island would talk soothingly about anything but the act itself: *Reproductive healthcare, the right to choose, bodily autonomy*. Time and again, Youth Defence would snap the public gaze back to the reality hidden behind the rhetoric.

Just as *Roe v. Wade* had spurred the forces of PLAC and SPUC into action to obtain the Eighth Amendment, the case of Baby X also triggered a new groundswell of pro-life activists. Twenty-year-old Niamh Nic Mhathúna, a student in accounting, listened to the relentless calls for legal abortion throughout the chaotic month of February 1992 with growing frustration, and she and a handful of her friends realised that if something was not done, those calls might very well be heeded by increasingly skittish politicians. As a young woman she felt that "a 14-year-old girl's pregnancy as a result of rape was being ruthlessly exploited." She phoned into Fr. Michael

Cleary's popular radio show on Dublin's 98 FM that month, decrying the exploitation of the case and urging that Ireland's abortion laws be tightened so that they could not be undermined by legislation, and, within days of that programme, had begun to form Youth Defence and organise the group's first public event. The first members of the group were all friends and family. By the end of 1992 they would be an army.

They wasted no time mobilising to respond to those calling for an end to the Eighth Amendment. On Tuesday, March 2, 1992, six members of Youth Defence were invited onto Fr. Cleary's radio show, where they explained why they had founded the new organisation and discussed the X case. A rally outside the Dáil was announced, and hundreds of people showed up on short notice and in the freezing cold. Youth Defence reported that the rally was attended by "1,197 people, a dog, two bicycles, and a man with an umbrella and a fake beard," highlighting another of their defining characteristics: Abortion was the *only* thing they took seriously.[lix] That first rally, and those that followed that year, would not be the visually coordinated festivals of colour that the Irish pro-life movement would become famous for in the years to come. They were simple crowds marching down the street with huge, home-made banners and slogans written on pieces of paper and cardboard. Sophistication would come later. The compulsion to respond came first.

This was before the days of social media, and so Youth Defence built their movement the old-fashioned way. To get people to come to the rally, they began by phoning everyone they knew, asking them to call everyone *they* knew. "We were doing everything on the mega-cheap," Niamh recalled. "We were going around, probably illegally when I look back at it, pasting up posters, advertisers, all around the city centre (probably over electrical boxes that said things like 'Post No Bills.') We didn't have experience organising anything. We were just hoping people would hear and respond." The message was simple: *If you don't like what you're hearing from the Irish Times and the media establishment, if you're pro-life, if you want to keep the Eighth Amendment—come, and be heard!* The boost from Fr. Cleary's radio show helped, too, and when people began showing up at the first rally, nearly everyone who came was a stranger to them. But not for long: these people were pro-life, and they had cared enough to show up. The handful of Youth Defence members took down their names and contact information so they could stay in touch.

A month later on April 4, the first Information Street Session, which would become a staple of Youth Defence's activism in the decades that followed, was held in Dublin. The pro-life activists gave a soap-box style populist presentation, speaking to people as they passed by or addressing the small crowds that gathered to listen. Photographs from 1992 show the power of this simple tactic: Attractive young women with their jaws set firmly wielded signs with slogans such as "Abortion Kills Children" and "Abortion Kills Women," as well as signs depicting babies killed by abortion to buttress their point. To complete the picture, some young mothers took their children with them, sleeping babies snuggled peacefully in strollers that sent a message all their own. They answered questions, passed out leaflets, and handed out the famous pro-life "Precious Feet" pins the shape of the tiny footprints of a ten-week-old baby in the womb. Only weeks after formation, Youth Defence had boots on the ground.

Just over a month after their first demonstration, Youth Defence organised the first Rally for Life on April 25, 1992. Over 10,000 people showed up, marching from the Garden of Remembrance to the Dáil in a powerful counterpoint to the never-ending media calls for abortion on demand. As the first major counterpoint to the calls for change since the X case, the size of the rally gave the politicians pause. The forces marshalled by Youth Defence were attracting attention now, and requests for speaking engagements began to come in. Youth Defence activists gave their first pro-life presentations at schools in Tralee, Dublin, and Roscommon scarcely four months after launching. This would become the beginning of an entire school program. Another rally on June 6 included a demand for a pro-life referendum to insert even more explicit protections for pre-born children into the Constitution, and film actor Michael Ahern addressed the crowd, declaring to loud cheers that he was pro-life. There was, Niamh said, "tremendous energy, great commitment from people, a real sense that this was a pivotal moment."

After the rallies, Niamh recalled, "the organisation just took off. We set up a committee, we started having meetings, we got a little office, and it grew from there. From the beginning, we had this desire to talk to our peers, to go to the streets. It was a different approach because until then, campaigns (outside of referendums) had been run through the media [and] media debates." The media, predictably, did not react well to the fresh upstarts: "Abortion campaigners attacked us, [and] then their allies in the media began a sustained and relentless campaign to shut us out and silence our message. It had real consequences for people." The media was used to serving as the gatekeepers of the abortion debate, but the X case had clearly revealed just how biased they were. The media was not simply reporting on public opinion, they were attempting to *shape* public opinion. They had an agenda, and abortion legalisation was on it.

To Youth Defence, this was obvious. Many Irish pro-lifers were seeing the coverage of the X case and hearing, over and over again, that "the country is demanding change." As this went on, pro-life leaders recalled later, doubt began to creep in for many people: *Is* the country demanding change? People with pro-life convictions would begin to fall silent, and thus the media narrative of a shrinking pro-life consensus would become a self-fulfilling prophecy. By taking to the streets, Youth Defence circumvented the media's monopoly on the abortion discussion, and when they began to show abortion victim photography, "confronting the other side with the reality of what they were supporting, the media found it horrifying," Niamh remembered. "They just wanted this nice, calm debate where the pro-lifers rolled over and gave in, and where they could get on with telling everyone what to think." Youth Defence stepped onto the scene just in time to fill a void. People wanted to fight back and they wanted to do something, but they didn't know how or what. Youth Defence provided the answers they were looking for. The new movement promptly exploded. As C.S. Lewis once said, "Friendship is born at that moment when one person says to another: 'What! You too? I thought I was the only one.'"

Niamh recalled those first heady days as a time when everything seemed to be going at warp speed. Many of the first meetings took place in hotel rooms or the backrooms of social clubs, and "they were packed—it was such a great feeling. You're more radical when you're young, because you're less afraid." Youth Defence, like other movements powered by young people, presented that curious paradox: Although lacking in experience and some of the wisdom that derives from it, passionate young people also often have a sense of certainty and justice that frees them from the burden of over-concern for the opinions of others and makes them more willing to take the risks necessary to launch a movement in the first place. At times, the young pro-lifers were being driven more by truth than by the tactical considerations of more political groups, and at times, that is precisely what the moment called for. Mistakes, of course, were made. But a movement was also created in a matter of months.

"It was definitely one of those things that change your life, that sets you on a course that you might not have otherwise embarked on," Niamh reflected decades later. "There was no intention to set up a pro-life group [initially] because there was no need to. I think if the X case hadn't happened, something else would have happened. The push for abortion never ends. The first group of people who came to the meetings directly after we founded were brilliant people. A lot of them stayed involved throughout and are still involved now. We were very lucky in that regard. Almost immediately, we met people from different parts of the city, different parts of the country, who we'd never met before. They were just people who felt the same—[they] had this deep, very passionate belief that everyone has a right to life and that this was something that they needed to do. And we were very lucky because between us we had a very useful mix of skillsets. Some people had design skills, others had organisational abilities, some of them were really charismatic, and that combination really helped with growth and shaping the organisation nationally."

Youth Defence was fortunate in other ways, as well. The young men and women who joined, Niamh noted later, were mostly principled people who weren't motivated by any desire to be seen as leaders or to seek personal political capital. "We were all young, mostly good-humoured, doing this for the right reasons: people didn't have notions and if you did, you wouldn't have them long before being taken to task—in a nice way," she reflected. "We were friends who would hang out and go for drinks together. People weren't afraid to tell each other if something had gone wrong, or if we'd made a mistake. We didn't always see eye to eye and of course there were disagreements and everything like that, but I do think we were really blessed in the people we had when we were just starting off."

Úna Nic Mhathúna, who remembered her mother going door-to-door during the 1983 referendum, recalls sorting through "all the bits of paper" they'd used to hurriedly scrawl down people's information so they could begin creating a database. Úna ended up doing much of the administration, but back then, she says, "it wasn't like anyone had roles." Everyone just did what they needed to do to get things started. "I used to go to work, and then go to the office afterwards. Or I'd take time off, or do it on my holidays," she remembered. "It was actually such good fun, as well. Somebody would say something on the radio and we would say *let's go protest!* At the start, we could pull together a picket at the drop of a hat." Often, the pro-lifers became as close as family.

There were no big donors, either—just lots of people giving small amounts. "When you don't have people pumping in hundreds of thousands, it makes you leaner, it makes you hungrier," Úna noted. "It makes you more strategic, and it makes you make less mistakes because you can't afford to make mistakes." The activists who joined became unpaid professionals, and there was a lot of work that had to be done to get things formalised: Infrastructure, a database, an office, a name, a bank account—"doing all that stuff that's so boring, but it has to be done."

In those first days, planning was simple. "We'd sit down and have a brainstorm and come up with loads of whacky ideas, and then we'd do one of them or three of them," Niamh recalled. Short-term plans were created and implemented, and then they headed back to the drawing-board. But they quickly struck on projects that would become the hallmarks of Youth Defence, such as roadshows, campus talks, and school tours. To assist with these projects, they created pro-life literature, which helped enormously with both recruitment and infrastructure because Youth Defence had several good writers and designers and the material packed a punch. People liked the literature, found it effective, and wanted to use it. To set up sustainable country-wide infrastructure, Youth Defence organised much like many other Irish institutions, centralising in a head office with largely autonomous branches set up throughout the country wherever willing volunteers could be found. Each group would adopt similar projects that were agreed upon by the grassroots.

This proved to be one of the most effective ways of keeping people engaged in their own regions for sustained periods of time. The inevitable downside, of course, was that when particularly passionate volunteers with important leadership qualities would leave for one reason or another—moving for work, or college, or to get married—the health of individual branches would suffer. Whether or not regional pro-life branches thrived was thus largely dependent on whether or not natural leaders existed within them, and branches were often petering out and sputtering back to life again. The annual roadshows proved to be an essential part of keeping the movement vitalised, activating more people, starting up new branches, and giving a big boost to existing leaders and activists that could energize them and keep them going for months. Youth Defence's networks thus spread quickly.

Youth Defence also joined forces with other pro-life

organisations to campaign against the Maastricht Treaty, which proposed the Eleventh Amendment to the Constitution. This would permit Ireland to ratify changes to the founding treaties of the European Union (which was still then known as the European Community). Many pro-lifers feared that being drawn further into the European Community would result in the legalisation of abortion, and John O'Reilly, Des Hanafin, and others directed a newly-founded organisation called the Pro-Life Campaign from headquarters off Parnell Square, Dublin, while PLAC veterans William Binchy and Bernadette Bonar toured the country rousing the public with warnings that a vote for the Maastricht Treaty could mean a vote for abortion. At every stop, they showed Dr. Bernard Nathanson's searing abortion film *The Silent Scream* to remind voters of the stakes.[20]

The Pro-Life Campaign organised a huge pressure campaign to target politicians in an attempt to replicate the success of PLAC in 1983, and politicians were sent petitions, pro-life literature, and some pro-lifers even mailed glossy photographs of aborted babies. Youth Defence's contribution was the first sign that they would become a potent political force, canvassing 20,000 homes and distributing 200,000 leaflets, an incredible feat considering that the organisation was not yet six months old. Despite the fact that the June 18 referendum to approve the Eleventh Amendment was successful (69.1% voted in favour with a turnout of 57.3%), Youth Defence was just getting started, launching pickets on

20 Dr. Bernard Nathanson was a founding member of the abortion lobby group NARAL Pro-Choice America and a New York abortionist before defecting to the pro-life side after his studies in fetology convinced him that abortion killed a human being. *The Silent Scream*, a film he released in 1984, is a 29-minute documentary that showed an abortion unfolding via ultrasound. The title comes from a particularly horrific moment in the film when the baby in the womb appears to emit a soundless scream of pain.

Easons Store on Dublin's O'Connell Street to protest the distribution of *The Guardian*. The British newspaper had been featuring full-page advertisements for the Marie Stopes abortion clinics, and Youth Defence demanded that the ads be pulled.

In August, Youth Defence launched their maiden roadshow. Dubbed the first National Youth Defence Information Roadshow, they drove around the country and visited twenty towns and cities over two weeks, hosting Street Sessions by day and organising grassroots meetings and powerful pro-life film screenings by night. It was all done on a shoe-string budget, and made possible by the kindness of activists such as Mary White, Deirdre Manifold, Br. Kevin Treacy, Maureen Normoyle, and the Hogan, O'Connor, Brauder, Caulfield, and Buckley families, and others who turned their homes upside down to house and feed carloads of young pro-lifers. It was an effective way of both capturing attention and drumming up support—hundreds of people joined their ranks, and another roadshow was launched in early September after rural towns and villages insisted that they receive a visit from Youth Defence, as well. The tactics of direct action, a hallmark of Youth Defence, were partially inspired by America's "Godfather of Pro-Life Action" Joe Scheidler and his use of street theatre, powerful imagery, and clever baiting of the media.

That November, Youth Defence threw itself into campaigning on all three issues proposed in the trio of referendums presented to the public. They hosted a press conference announcing their opposition to the referendum on traveling and referral for abortions, and proposed instead that a referendum be held on the issue of abortion itself. By the end of 1992, eleven months after formation, the membership of Youth Defence had swelled to 5,000, with almost non-stop national and international media coverage taking note of the youth movement that seemed to have come out of nowhere. Youth Defence had given 63 TV interviews, dozens of radio interviews, and were endlessly analyzed in print.

Youth Defence would become the target of endless media smear jobs in the years ahead, with seemingly unlimited journalistic energy expended in relentless searches for any potentially unsavory associations or former members who might have uttered distasteful things, often accompanied by outright slander. Too often, other pro-life leaders would be quick to condemn youthful fervor or aggressive tactics and thus play into the hands of pro-abortion media commentators—left-wing journalists are always delighted to be able to use one pro-life organisation to club another. This often proved easy to do because the pro-life movement in most countries is generally divided into two primary wings: the street activists capturing the attention of the public and shifting the Overton Window, and the more respectable spokespeople who usually work the political arena and utilise strategies more suitable to political ends.[21]

This tension often comes from a failure of leaders in one wing to recognise the role of another. The political arm of the pro-life movement needs respectability in order to act as effective lobbyists, and thus it is important that they appear reasonable, even to the media. The activist wing of the pro-life movement (often referred to as the "prophetic arm") has a different role, working to draw public attention to the horrors of abortion and attempting to shore up and reshape public opinion.

---

21 This is true for most social reform movements, and the tension between the more radical, prophetic wing and the respectable, political wing is common. It is important to note, however, that both of these factions are necessary in any successful movement.

The political wing is, by definition, working to see the existing consensus reflected in law. The activist wing, on the other hand, works on the cutting edge of public opinion, thus by definition pushing the boundaries of respectability. Both wings are necessary for success, but it is common for their respective leaders to misunderstand each other.

To many, the young men and women of Youth Defence seemed to be punks with a traditional twist, irreverent revolutionaries advocating a return to the values of their ancestors rather than demanding that they be trashed in the vein of left-wingers the world over. They accused the stuffy politicians of being pathetic in comparison with the great Irish patriots of the past, and scornfully refused to accord them the respect they craved. Niamh, the chairwoman of Youth Defence, was known to give fiery speeches, while the organisation defied attempts by the media and their fellow pro-life campaigners to control Youth Defence's strategy and message.[lx] This was Ireland's youth rising in defence of their inheritance and defending their future from the bumbling bureaucrats attempting to implement the rules demanded by Brussels.

They were a movement made up of young people from every walk of life. Some were students, and others were musicians, engineers, bar staff, or accountants. Some were unemployed. "Everyone was on the dole then," Niamh remembered. "This is the early 1990s in Ireland and we were just coming out of a savage recession—you take any group of six people and one of them was going to be on the dole." Even the skeptical and slanderous media had to occasionally accord them begrudging respect, with the *Irish Times* noting that they were the "most visible of the anti-abortion groups. Fearless...commitment beyond doubt." The *Evening*

Herald observed that they were "educated, articulate people, the vibrant voice of Ireland's future" and "on the offensive, but not off the wall." And Brenda Power at the *Sunday Press* described them as "bright-eyed, well-spoken, good-humoured, driven by that fierce, inspiring, transient youthful determination."[lxi]

That determination, as it would turn out, was not as transient as the press hoped. In 1993, Youth Defence escalated their Street Sessions to a weekly event, with tens of thousands of pamphlets and pro-life badges being distributed and thousands of conversations about abortion being held. Many passersby changed their minds about abortion as a result. "If you want to see Ireland's diversity in all its glory, try joining in a street session," Youth Defence announced, only slightly tongue in cheek. "You will meet the sane, the old, the young, the bold, the cold, the mad, the bad, the downright sad, the sleek, the slick, the couldn't care less, the life's in a mess, or doing their best, the big, the small, the tall, the bald, and a man called Thatch who has two cars where his chickens and pigs live. Yes, it's interesting who you meet when you stop to talk to people."[lxii] One of the key highlights of the roadshow each year became meeting mothers with young babies who had decided not to have abortions as a result of meeting Youth Defence the year before.

The same year, Youth Defence launched a magazine, *Solas,* which they published five times annually and mailed out across the country to a growing list of members, supporters, and donors to keep people updated on the abortion situation in Ireland and up to speed with Youth Defence's activities. The 1993 roadshow covered eighteen "assorted largish settlements," with Youth Defence announcing in their characteristically playful fashion that a "regular pattern becomes established, and lots of excellent stuff is done."[lxiii] For many Irish pro-lifers, participation in a roadshow became a defining event in their development as activists.

They also ramped up the political pressure: Brendan Howlin, the Minister for Health responsible for the Labour party's programme of legalizing abortion, became a prime target for Youth Defence's picketing activities. In response, Howlin angrily went on Wexford Radio to condemn the pro-life activists, which spectacularly backfired and had the unintended result of notifying his constituents of his role in the "pending nasty business" and becoming the subject of *their* ire, as well. As Youth Defence put it: "Legalising abortion was quietly dropped—as one wag wrote, 'who wants to deal with it when it means a crowd of Youth Defencers are permanently on your tail?'"[lxiv]

The following year, the politicians struck back. In what many believe was a direct response to Youth Defence's street activism, Marie Geoghegan-Quinn, then the Minister for Justice of the Fianna Fáil/Labour Coalition, introduced the Public Order Act, which effectively banned many forms of public protest and specified the display of "offensive photographs." Both abortion-supporting politicians and the media preferred to discuss abortion in an environment where their rhetoric could effectively cover up the gory brutality of what was being discussed, and although abortion activists insisted that abortion victim photos were ineffective and counter-productive for pro-life activists, the fervor of these claims was matched only by their attempts to get abortion victim photos banned from public places—a rather odd thing to do if it was in fact the case that the display of these images was backfiring.[22] Youth

22 My 2017 book *Seeing is Believing: Why Our Culture Must Face the Victims of Abortion* details precisely why abortion victim photography is such a powerful tool and includes polling data and studies indicating their effectiveness in changing minds on the issue.

Defence members were promptly arrested in Galway for showing such offensive photographs, "starting off a pattern that continued for years."[lxv]

The second round of arrests took place on the fourth National Information Roadshow, which traveled to more than twenty towns and cities and faced the "threat of arrest several times," but "the Roadshow pushed ahead despite some brief incarcerations."[lxvi] In October of 1994, nine pro-lifers were arrested in Wexford under the Public Order Act after another picket of Brendan Howlin. The protest began at 1 PM, but before the hour was up the Gardai had actually attacked the protestors, knocking several to the ground and, in the words of Youth Defence, "assaulting" some people.[lxvii] One 18-year-old girl was even hospitalized for four days after the police roughed her up, but of course it was the pro-lifers who were forced to appear in Wexford District Court on charges of public order offences. Two years later, in 1996, Youth Defence won its Circuit Court of Appeal case with video evidence showing that the police had not been honest in their characterization of events.

That said, the activists certainly didn't take the arrests lying down—unless they felt a prone position might make the arrests more difficult. Footage of the Gardai's unwelcome arrivals at Youth Defence protests throughout this period shows feisty young Irish women informing the police precisely what they thought of their censorship and cowardice, chanting at them as stiffly-uniformed cops collared pro-life activists and attempted to wrest them free of their "offensive" signs. The grimaces on the faces of the Gardai as the girls chanted "No to police state! No to police state!" indicate that some of the verbal darts struck flesh. At one point even the left-wing poet and HIV activist Pat Tierney intervened in a confrontation between pro-lifers and police, defending the right of the Youth Defence activists to their freedom of speech regardless of what one thought of their point of view, his eyes flashing above his black mustache, his face gaunt from the HIV he suffered from.[23]

The arrests did have a chilling effect on recruitment for a time. The new law meant that every time the activists went out, they could be arrested. At first, defiance, anger, and an aggrieved sense of justice were the order of the day. But slowly, the gears of judicial bureaucracy ground away at the will to fight, and some young people eventually weighed the costs and reluctantly decided to take their leave. After the third or fourth or ninth arrest, the days away from work to go to court would pile up, and the stress of hiding the reason for work absence from employers would mount. The arrests were also very effective at stigmatizing pro-life work, with the media gleefully reporting them as "scuffles" and casting the pro-lifers as lawless ruffians. Peer pressure from those who disapproved of the charges of obstruction and disorderly conduct were also a deterrent to activism.

Police crackdowns on pro-life activism continued until 1998, when two weeks prior to the annual summer roadshow, Youth Defence supporters received a copy of a letter from [Police] Superintendent Waldron of Cork. The letter confirmed the existence of a memo from June 23, 1997 that had been sent out by the Garda Commissioner on the instruction of the Office of the Director of Public Prosecutions, stating explicitly that "posters of aborted foetuses does not breach the law."[lxviii] This memo had gone out a year previously, but the police, who presumably had full knowledge of the memo and its contents, continued to arrest and harass members of Youth Defence in the meantime.

23 Tierney would later hang himself on his 39th birthday in 1996.

In the letter, Waldron stated that "I accept that certain individual Gardai have acted unwisely in dealing with protests." Youth Defence, of course, was very pleased to receive this information, and it lent credibility to their claim that the police simply didn't want to allow them to express their point of view.

Youth Defence's activism continued to grow in both scale and sophistication. In 1994, they threw their first National Conference in Cashel County, Tipperary, reporting that it was "great craic[24] for everyone except Evan who broke his arm climbing over a gate, lost his wallet and burnt his lips on a pizza. Apart from that, though, it was a resounding success with training workshops and information debates taking place."[lxix] They also hosted a media training weekend, drawing much of their material from Dale Carnegie's famous *How to Win Friends and Influence People* to prep their activists for sparring matches in the media ring. In January of 1995, Niamh and other members of Youth Defence attended the American March for Life in Washington, D.C., and after the Second National Conference in Dublin later that year, Niamh and John Heaney were invited to attend Pope John Paul II's private mass in Castelgandalfo, Rome. The pope then praised Youth Defence's work in a private audience, and urged them to carry on and "be courageous."[lxx] It was quite a vote of confidence, especially in the face of criticism from Church officials and other pro-life groups who thought Youth Defence was too radical.

In 1995, Health Minister Brendan Howlin, who had by then been dogged across the country and back by persistent pro-life activists, resigned from office and stated that public pressure had prevented him from legalising abortion. Media commentators and abortion

---

24 Entertainment, good conversation

activists angrily pinpointed Youth Defence as the cause of this public pressure, and the pro-lifers accepted this tacit evidence of their effectiveness with great cheerfulness. Michael Noonan, the new Health Minister, promised to at least legalise abortion referral, and managed to pass the Abortion Information Act, though not without strong resistance from Youth Defence, who promptly arrived in Noonan's hometown of Limerick to picket. Some even chained themselves to the doors of the Department of Health with handcuffs. The "gardai remove[d] the protestors in the time-honoured way of pleading, losing their patience, [and] resorting to cutting instruments" wrote Youth Defence, noting that the protestors' jumpers had been stretched past their knees in the process.[lxxi] While they did so, other pro-lifers wielded signs with the slogan "Freedom of Choice???" and a horrifying photo of the top half of an aborted baby's head, held gruesomely aloft by means of metal tweezers.

It would not be Youth Defence's last dust-up with government forces. In 1996, they launched Ireland's first pro-life advertising campaign, a two-week lineup of billboards designed and produced by Youth Defence. The media, which preferred to play the role of referee in regard to what information reached the public, promptly went nuts, "causing journalist Des Rushe to remark that Youth Defence received much more publicity than their budget could have bought for them." Publicity continued to grow when a thirty-second radio advert describing the development of a child in the womb was banned by the IRTC, the government body regulating independent radio stations. A number of radio stations had already accepted the ad and were furious at the state's heavy-handedness, causing another uproar. Again, the same government that was constitutionally obligated to protect the rights of the pre-born child in the womb was, at the urging of the media, censoring the pro-life perspective.

The non-stop activism of the new youth movement bore fruit. With their offices becoming cramped due to the growing team, Youth Defence had to decamp to a new office off Mountjoy Square in Dublin. In five short but action-packed years, they had gone from a handful of street activists pushing back against media lies and political spinelessness to the primary engine of Ireland's pro-life movement, almost single-handedly shaping and driving the national debate.

Chapter 5
Youth Defence

Such is the strength and professionalism of the Irish pro-life movement that activists from other countries are traveling here to see how it's done. "Our approach is multifaceted," says a spokesperson from Youth Defence. "It's focused on public engagement and strives for excellence in messaging. We've had teams of young pro-life activists come to Ireland from the US and right across the world to learn the Irish model."

John Hearne, *The Irish Examiner*

"Our next guest," TV host Pat Kenny of *Kenny Live* on RTÉ told the camera on January 29, 1997, "is lucky not to be in jail tonight. She's had almost 4,000 pounds in fines, she's had a total of more than two years worth of prison sentences suspended, but a further offence may well put her behind bars. When you see her, you'll wonder—how could all of this befall a beautiful young woman whose face was her fortune, modeling in Paris for the top fashion houses? Quite simply, the reason is that she's one of France's leading anti-abortion activists. She's sometimes dubbed 'the Lipstick Commando.'"

With that introduction, Noelia Garcia walked confidently onto the set in a black dress, smiling serenely as Kenny gave her an awkward peck on the cheek. Blonde with hazel eyes and the feline look of a French resistance fighter, Garcia was dressed to kill but pro-life to her core. Kenny's confusion at Garcia's anti-abortion activism was understandable: The twenty-two-year-old Garcia had risen to fame as one of France's top models, lending her face to big name clients such as L'Oréal and Air

France. Her experience in the modeling world, however, had repulsed her—she found that models were often pressured by agencies to have abortions so that their bodies would not be marked by motherhood.

"Modeling uses women as objects," Noelia noted. "I was surrounded by other models having abortions and became disgusted by it."[lxxii] She joined the French pro-life group Le Treve de Dieu (God's Reprieve), and began engaging in a controversial form of pro-life activism. "I have used my body and my face to sell products," she explained. "Now I am using them to protect unborn children against the consumer society that chucks away babies it does not want."[lxxiii] She rapidly became known as one of France's most militant activists, staging "rescues" at four abortion clinics and chaining herself to operating tables to prevent abortion procedures, getting arrested and fined by the French police. As the *Independent* put it, she had exchanged a life on the runway for becoming the "young blonde pasionaria" of the pro-life movement—and now she had arrived in Ireland at the invitation of an appreciative Youth Defence.[lxxiv]

Garcia had faced the media before. Two years prior to her arrival in Ireland, on October 26, 1995, she had participated in a nearly three-hour live televised debate on France's largest network, TF1. The media and the abortion lobby threw everything they had at her, but as one pro-life group later summarized it, her "determination, her conviction, and her charm totally reversed the effect sought and the general public discovered that the resistance to legalised abortion is today being led by young people of which the majority are under thirty years of age...the program was designed to kill off, in media terms, Noelia and her combat. However, it ended up making [her] even more popular."[lxxv]

Moreover, she made sure to emphasise that she was not pro-life simply on religious grounds, but because she "just loves human beings."[lxxvi] She made that fact crystal clear, telling the *Washington Times* on April 15, 1996 that her stance "has nothing to do with religion. Nor am I political. I am a true feminist fighting for women's rights. I don't want every boy I meet to regard me as a potential aborter, a piece of meat. How can a man respect a girl if he thinks she will abort a baby?"

Having a glamorous young model—who had given it all up to defend pre-born children from abortion—come to Ireland was a very effective media strategy. According to the *Irish Times*, two days before her appearance on Pat Kenny's show she urged attendees at a pro-life meeting to prove that "you would give your life" to prevent abortion from coming to Ireland.[lxxvii] To the nervousness of the press present to cover the meeting, Garcia told the audience that pro-lifers needed to show the media that they would "do anything non-violent" to stop abortion, and that if pro-lifers showed that they "would do anything, I'm sure they'll take you into account."[lxxviii] She was joined by Niamh Nic Mhathúna of Youth Defence who urged attendees to join the movement. "You are the only defence the unborn child has," she told them. "You are the last line of defence."[lxxix] A day before that, on January 25, 1997, Garcia gave a speech to pro-lifers in Limerick, telling a rally that "Ireland is the only country where there is no legalised abortion and I really admire your country." Garcia then joined a hundred Irish pro-lifers in marching on the residence of the Minister for Health, Michael Noonan, where a dozen police officers lined the entrance of his home.

Later that year, Youth Defence returned the favour by heading to Paris for World Youth Day and joining the Lipstick Commando and other French pro-lifers in protesting at several abortion clinics. One stark, memorable detail from the Parisian protests stood out for the pro-life activists: One clinic was "situated in a hospital and shared a hospital building with another clinic providing gynaecological and pre-natal care. On entering a common doorway, mothers turned left to prepare for their baby's birth or right to have their baby killed."[lxxx] *Left you live, right you die.* It was a simple, horrifying picture of the arbitrary power women held over the lives of babies in the womb—and why those voiceless children desperately needed pro-lifers to speak for them.

Trying to shut down clinic operations had become one of Youth Defence's Irish activities, as well. When the Marie Stopes Clinic in Merrion Square was accused of performing abortions by a woman who claimed that she had been hurt by one, Youth Defence called for the doctor to be charged with murder and began picketing the clinic daily right through 1997, when the fed-up landlord finally tossed Marie Stopes out, concluding that they were more trouble than they were worth. Precious Life, Youth Defence's sister organisation, started up with a "lively bunch" from Ballymena, working on opposing the extension of the 1967 Abortion Act in Northern Ireland, going "right for the jugular with a strategy of direct action…attract[ing] media attention and lots of local support."[lxxxi] The annual roadshow hit 22 towns and activists handed out 80,000 pieces of literature. A handful of American pro-lifers who joined them on the road were very impressed by the Irish hardiness to inclement weather.

And another political storm was coming. In August of 1997, a thirteen-year-old girl who would become known to the Irish public as Miss C was raped by her babysitter and became pregnant. Because of this assault, the Eastern

Health Board took her into state care, removing her from the caravan where she lived with her large Irish Traveller family.[25] According to pro-choice journalist Kitty Holland in her 2013 book *Savita,* the girl requested an abortion, but the EHB was told they could not facilitate one, which would require travelling to the United Kingdom. Abortion activists saw their chance, and moved to employ the same strategy they had used in the case of Baby X: make the victimization of a young girl primarily about abortion. In order for Miss C to have her pregnancy terminated, she would have to be transferred back to the care of her parents—but her father announced that he had changed his mind about consenting to an abortion. The *Irish Times* noted suspiciously that his "change of mind coincided with the appearance at court of prominent anti-abortion campaigners."[lxxxii]

On November 21, after an eight-hour hearing in Children's Court, the judge ruled that the girl was likely to kill herself if she didn't get an abortion, and as such she was entitled to travel to the United Kingdom to procure one. Thus, Miss C would not be returned to her parents, but would stay in the care of the Eastern Health Board. The High Court responded by staying the ruling in order to give Miss C's parents time to appeal. Some politicians responded by announcing that the case of Miss C once again proved the need for abortion legislation, with Taoiseach Bertie Ahern weighing in on the case from Luxembourg that night, stating that "I believe we have an obligation to prepare legislation for abortion."[lxxxiii] On November 27, Justice Hugh Geoghegen of the High Court upheld the ruling of the Children's Court.

---

25 The Irish Travellers are a traditionally nomadic ethnic group who maintain a set of unique traditions. They have long pushed for specific ethnic status from the Irish government, and finally succeeded in 2017.

Youth Defence's account of the events surrounding Miss C's case are radically different than the narrative pushed by journalists such as Kitty Holland. According to them, Miss C's parents had been "willfully deceived with regard to the abortion and what [was] best for their daughter," and when they decided to oppose the abortion arranged by the EHB and asked for assistance from Youth Defence, the parents became the target of vicious media hatred, as they were spoiling what abortion activists saw as a perfect opportunity to gain political ground.[lxxxiv] Social workers prevented the parents from seeing their daughter, they were offered no support, and the pro-life movement was savaged in the media for responding to the parents' requests for help. Miss C was then placed in foster care with a family duly described by the media as a "loving and caring" one, with the obvious insinuation that the parents who did not want their daughter to get an abortion were something quite different.

The Star went so far as to gain access to the girl by making a "small token" of their regard to Miss C's foster family, and then promptly ran an interview with the underage girl with "an easily distinguishable photograph of the rape victim" accompanying it.[lxxxv] In December, Miss C was taken to London, and she remembered later that she spent the plane ride gripped with nausea. On her CD player, the girl listened to a song that she later came to believe symbolized the rest of her life: *I'm leaving on a jet plane. Don't know when I'll be back again.*

"I'll never forget those lines," she said later. "Part of me never did come back again after that. I didn't know that the next day my life was about to change forever."[lxxxvi] Her memory of that day is one of trauma: "The next day, I was taken to a building. All I remember next was being wheeled on a trolley and screaming with the pain. They gave me an injection, and when I woke up, the pain was gone. Eventually they told me the baby was dead."[lxxxvii]

Once the girl's baby had been aborted in London, the EHB promptly lost interest in Miss C's family. Interestingly, "a member of the Eastern Health Board, [Councillor] Tommy Cullen, later [told] a YD conference that members of the Health Board with a pro-abortion agenda [were] trawling the cases under their control looking to use young pregnant girls to further their cause."[lxxxviii] Like vultures, the abortion campaigners were on the lookout for what they needed: a corpse, a girl in distress—something that would pique the public's appetite for abortion legalisation.[26] For her part, Miss C remained in care until she turned eighteen years old.

So what is Miss C's account of the storm she found herself at the centre of? It would be years before we would discover just how horribly she and her family had been lied to—and how radically her account differs from those of pro-choice journalists like Kitty Holland. Since leaving State care, Miss C, in the course of several interviews, revealed what really happened. Although a psychiatrist for the EHB had insisted she would kill herself if she was not given an abortion, Miss C said that, "All they explained to me at the time was that I was going to get the baby out. That's all I was told, I was going to get the baby out. At thirteen I didn't know anything about pregnancy. So I said okay. But when I woke up after the procedure, I asked the people that

---

26 This is one of the abortion movement's favourite tactics, and one they consistently use in nearly every nation where they are pushing for abortion on demand. In the United States, for example, feminist lawyers litigated the *Roe v. Wade* case by claiming that Jane Roe, a woman later revealed to be Norma McCorvey, was a victim of rape. In her biography, McCorvey said that she had been told to claim that she had been impregnated by rape because that would make for a more sympathetic case. It was a brazen lie.

brought me over to London to have the abortion, I asked them: 'Where's the baby?' And they said to me, 'There is no baby.' And I was like: 'But you told me I was going to get the baby out, so how is there no baby?' And after that, like, no one would speak to me, no one would answer me, no one would tell me…the truth of what happened."[lxxxix]

In other words, the girl who became the center of Ireland's abortion debate for nearly two decades because she was a rape victim who was denied an abortion says she did not even know what abortion *was*—and that even government employees referred to abortion as "getting the baby out," a blunt statement of fact that reveals the barbarism inherent to the procedure. Years later, Miss C would come forward as a mother of three children to excoriate the abortion activists who were using her case to push for legal abortion. "It still makes me angry because people don't know me," she told RTÉ, Ireland's primary TV broadcaster, "they don't know *anything* about me. Why keep bringing me up all the time? Stop bringing me up for abortion when I never wanted an abortion."[xc] In fact, Miss C said the abortion sent her into a spiral of depression—and, in a cruel irony, she became suicidal—the very reason cited for getting her an abortion in the first place.

"I have three other beautiful children now, and I'd be thinking: *They'd have an older brother or sister right now,*" she told RTÉ. "I'd *never* have had that abortion if I'd have known what it was going to do to me, to hurt me for the rest of my life. That lives with me. I'm in so much pain every day thinking about it."[xci] Despite the fact that pro-lifers were accused of cruelty for opposing Miss C's abortion, her view of what happened mirrors Youth Defence's account at the time: "The government made me go to England for an abortion…They killed my baby.

I was punished for what a rapist did to me. My baby was punished for what a rapist did to me. The government don't care about women like me. They just want to bring in abortion for any reason. They're using us. They don't know it hurts, and they don't care. If you're raped and get pregnant, you need love and support. Not to have an abortion, but you need the love and support of people," she said, urging a No vote in the 2018 abortion referendum. [xcii]

In fact, Miss C now says that the abortion was "harder to deal with than the rape."[xciii] She thinks about the baby she lost to abortion every day. "I still have dreams about a little girl with blonde hair running around a field and asking me to play with her," she told one journalist. "She is my lost daughter. I called her Shannon. I eventually got a death certificate for her. That was my way of proving that she existed."[xciv][27]

For abortion activists and their political supporters, however, Miss C had served her purpose. In response to her case, the Government announced that a Green Paper on abortion would be drawn up to "stimulate and to facilitate informed public discussion on the options in relation to the issue of abortion in the light of the range of constitutional, legal, medical, moral, social, and ethical issues involved."[xcv] This Paper would be created by an inter-departmental group, which would form a committee chaired by the then-Minister for Health and Children Brian Cowen. In early 1998, Youth Defence produced a lengthy submission for the Green Paper that

27 Irish pro-lifers would also hold solemn candlelight vigils for Baby C. One held on November 23, 2002 on O'Connell Street in Dublin included a projection screen showing several images of a pre-born child at age 14 weeks, which was Baby C's age when she died. In the years to come, Baby C would often be commemorated along with Baby X and other pre-born children who were killed when mothers in the care of the Irish state were sent to England for abortions.

detailed the medical and legal implications of a range of possible solutions to the X case, and also reiterated their position that "the most democratic and life-preserving solution for both mother and child is a properly-worded pro-life referendum."[xcvi] Their submission included "wording drafted by YD which [had] the approval of retired Justice Rory O'Hanlon," and detailed "how this wording will uphold the pro-life ethos inherent in the majority of Irish people."[xcvii]

To counter the government's efforts, Youth Defence also launched the Right Words Campaign, which utilised bus and billboard advertising to gin up public support for a pro-life referendum that actually gave people the option of voting for a "watertight definition of the rights of the unborn in Irish law," distributing 110,000 booklets and leaflets explaining precisely why this was necessary.[xcviii] As always, Youth Defence was on the offensive, refusing to be satisfied with the status quo and ensuring that they would not be caught off-guard. As they awaited the release of the Green Paper, they kept busy with conferences, daily pickets of the International Planned Parenthood Association on Cathal Brugha Street as well as the Marie Stopes clinic on Blessington Street, and distributed thousands of leaflets. In Northern Ireland, Precious Life also ramped up their activities with a billboard, a bus, and a radio advertising initiative called the Death Threat Campaign. The radio ad, of course, got promptly banned.

The Green Paper was finally published in September of 1999, and it laid out seven options:

1. An absolute constitutional ban on abortion
2. An amendment to the Constitution to remove suicide as a ground for abortion

3. Retention of the status quo as well as legislation reclarifying the prohibition on abortion, which would also restrict the ability to obtain an abortion by claiming suicidal ideation

4. Simple retention of the status quo

5. Pass legislation reflecting the X case ruling

6. The deletion of Article 40.3.3 and reverting to the pre-1983 status quo

7. Permitting abortion beyond the guidelines of the X case[xcix]

A month later, Youth Defence members from all over Ireland descended on Tullamore, County Offaly to protest the home base of Brian Cowen, wielding black flags to commemorate with grief and anger the state-ordered death of Baby C and demand a pro-life referendum. Instead, the so-called Oireachtas Committee on the Constitution began hearings on the issue.

As the year 2000 arrived and a new century dawned, Youth Defence switched offices again, this time setting up their base at 60a Capel Street in Dublin. As they strategised on how to obtain the pro-life referendum they had been demanding for nearly eight years, they struck on a unique way to dominate the political discussion and draw attention to their cause: by hijacking the political convention of Ireland's largest political party, the Fianna Fáil Ard Fheis 2000. Fourteen members of Youth Defence managed to obtain delegate passes to Taoiseach Bertie Ahern's speech on the final night of the convention, and positioned themselves throughout the crowd to ensure that the live television audience that would be tuning in would have their attention drawn to abortion, over and over again.

As Youth Defence described it at the time: "Maurice provides a decoy by walking up to the barriers in front of the stage and asking Bertie when he was going to give the Irish people a pro-life referendum. While security hurled themselves at him, Labhrás and Stephen vault the security barriers and jump onto the stage beside Bertie. Here they unfurl a poster carrying the message *Pro-Life Referendum Now!* before being dragged away. Bertie is clearly shaken by the disturbance, but he is not alone, since everyone else is shaken by Fianna Fáil delegates, who get busy slapping all the interrupters on the head."[c]

That was just the beginning. There were eleven other Youth Defence members positioned throughout the crowd, and each carefully timed their interruptions to ensure that they would dominate the entire speech. One by one, the pro-lifers stood up to shout and demand a referendum, and as the disruptions continued, both security and other delegates fairly flung themselves at the pro-lifers, with the frenzied clapping of attendees arising more out of frustration than of support for the hapless Bertie Ahern, who was beginning to realise that his big speech was going to bomb. After one interruption, he stumbled over his words. TV commentators even occasionally spoke over him to explain to their audiences what the disturbances were all about, and cameras cut away from the stage to show the brusque evictions of the Youth Defence members, with Ahern's speech reduced to background noise. At several points, entire sentences from the Taoiseach were lost in the din.

It worked. The protests hijacked the convention, forced a significant amount of media coverage and, as one commentator on Radio 1's *Sunday Show* admitted, put "abortion back onto the political agenda."[ci]

As the Oireachtas Committee conducted hearings, the pro-life movement kept relentless pressure on the politicians.

Bertie Ahern was confronted by pro-lifers as far away as Australia, when members of Youth Defence Australia showed up to protest his public address at the University of New South Wales on March 12, demanding to know why he wasn't giving Irish pro-lifers their referendum. Throughout that summer's roadshow, the need to lobby local TDs was emphasised. When the Chairman of the Committee told a Sunday newspaper that they had ruled out the option of a referendum during their deliberations, Youth Defence mobilised for action, planning the "most intensive and forceful lobbying of Irish politicians ever to have taken place in Ireland."[cii] The Mother and Child Campaign came into being, a new pro-life initiative oriented towards including the full range of pro-life people in Ireland, as some polling indicated that 70% of the Irish people wanted a referendum.

Hundreds of thousands of lobbying leaflets were distributed, and TD offices were inundated with calls demanding a referendum. As the pressure mounted, many of the politicians went from arrogant and dismissive to suddenly compliant, with "almost panic-stricken reassurances of support for a pro-life referendum."[ciii] Life Days was also launched on Dublin's Grafton Street to celebrate the beauty of human development in the womb, featuring balloons, large photographs of babies in the womb from 6 to 35 weeks lining the thoroughfare, and thousands of shoppers passing by "on a sun-drenched afternoon."[civ] The Chairman backed down, and when the Committee's final report was released, it included the option of a pro-life referendum.

The Committee released its report in November of 2000, and at a hefty 700 pages, the fifth Progress Report on Abortion still did not provide a conclusion as to what should be done about abortion. It did, however, narrow down to three options: a referendum on a bill to reverse the X ruling, the establishment of a Crisis Pregnancy Agency to reduce the number of crisis pregnancies, and legislation to give effect to the X ruling. Everyone was agreed on the proposal of a Crisis Pregnancy Agency, which was duly set up the following year.

In addition to functioning as the core of the Irish pro-life movement's activist wing, Youth Defence continued to develop as a significant political player. In 2001, they launched a billboard campaign aimed at preventing any "backdoor" legalisation of abortion, emphasizing the fact that abortion was never medically necessary. The campaign included 120 bus advertisements and an accompanying pamphlet which was distributed door-to-door, as well as on the ground at shopping malls, churches, and on the street.

The truth, Úna Nic Mhathúna remembered later, was that the pro-life movement and the Irish establishment seeking to legalise abortion were engaged in a nearly perpetual standoff. Attempts to legalise abortion had thus far been unsuccessful, but Youth Defence was working nonstop to foil nearly constant attempts to do so—and it was exhausting. "It was continuous protest," Úna remembered, "and continuously making an absolute nuisance of ourselves." What made Youth Defence unique was that they were unpredictable, which made the political establishment very nervous. It also made them a little bit afraid or unsure of us," Úna said. "They didn't know what we were going to do next. Because, once they have your measure, you're finished as a serious player. Once they know: *If I do this, this is exactly how their organisation is going to react,* you've lost the edge. They study you, they change tack, and if you're left standing there, you're in trouble. So we always needed to be pro-active, to be ahead of the game. So we worked to out-manoeuvre them and do things differently."

As the pro-life movement was strategizing on how to break the stalemate, they came up with an unprecedented idea to knock their political opponents off balance. On June 7, 2001, Irish voters were scheduled to go to the polls to vote on the Twenty-fourth Amendment of the Constitution Bill, which would permit the Irish government to ratify the European Union's Treaty of Nice. The Treaty of Nice proposed to create a new infrastructure as well as new rules for the institutional structure of the European Union to deal with problems related to expansion, the admission of new Member States, potential sanctions against Member States, the creation of subsidiary pan-European courts, financial complications, and other issues. In all of the EU member states, the Treaty could be simply ratified through parliamentary procedure—but in Ireland, the Supreme Court decision *Crotty v. An Taoiseach* dictated that any transfer of Irish sovereignty could only be accomplished by a constitutional amendment. And for the Constitution to be amended, the Irish government would have to call a referendum.

"So we said, right," Úna recalled. "Most of us here don't believe in the increasing encroachment on sovereignty being proposed by the European Union—which was also one of the driving forces pushing Ireland to legalise abortion. So why not get involved in this referendum, and totally blindside them and win it? So we did. And we won. We did totally blindside them—they weren't expecting it at all."

The Irish establishment had never lost a referendum on the European Union, and thus had no inkling that they could lose the first Nice referendum. In 1972, they had achieved a Yes vote of 83%, and in 1987, the Irish public had voted 70% for Yes. Opposing the European super-state seemed like a fool's errand, but the pro-lifers decided to give it a go nonetheless. According to Youth Defence:

"For pro-lifers the suspicion was (and this became a reality when a European constitution was later proposed) that such a state would see abortion as a service much like the majority of European countries. We thought that we might try and do something in opposition to the march of a state modelled on these lines, so over a month before the announcement of the final date set for the referendum, we set about putting the basic elements of the 'No to Nice' Campaign in place."[cv]

From there, the campaign quickly took off. According to Youth Defence's report (which was rendered in their characteristic tongue-in-cheek fashion):

> We began with a series of meetings around the country, both to rally and to test the level of support we could count on in the campaign. In general the meetings were highly successful, building as they did on the network created over the previous summer by the Mother and Child Campaign. So the campaign was cranked into gear and leaflets were shunted onto volunteers… at countrywide meetings with the instructions to knock on doors with gusto. Our egging-on of said volunteers was too effective to ensure a relaxed and blissful life and we had to print piles more leaflets in no time at all. By polling day over 1,000,000 leaflets had been distributed nationwide in a canvass which reached into practically every corner [of] the country.[cvi]

The No to Nice Campaign rocked Europe. Their black and red posters were devastatingly effective; one read *You will Lose! Power, Money, Freedom,* and another punched home a simple and powerful message: *Don't Give Europe Total Control*. "The posters were the talk of the country," Úna said. "The media were reporting them, they were the focus of attention abroad, [and] all the anti-EU groups

Youth Defence Rally, April 1992

At one of the early street sessions, Niamh Úi Bhriain (L) talks with passersby

A funeral for Baby X

Pope John Paul II meets with Niamh Úi Bhriain

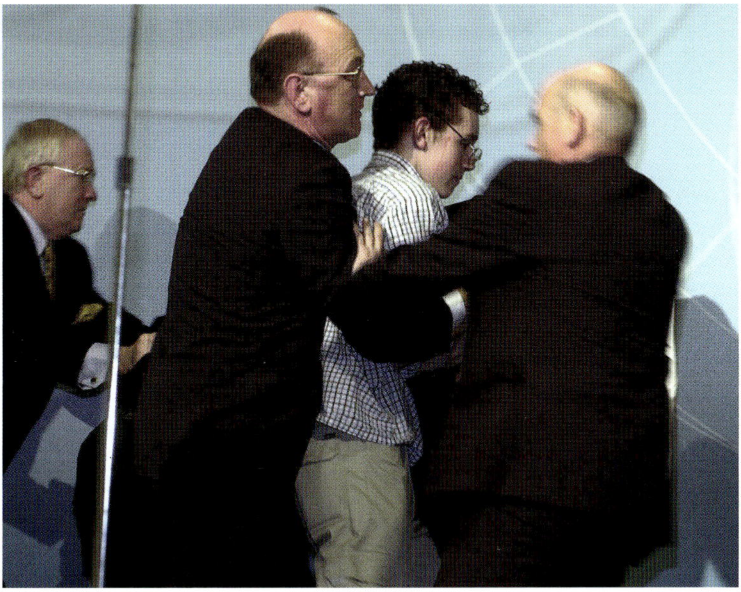

Youth Defence activists hijack Fianna Fáil Ard Fheis, 2000

Headlines of the 2008 Coir victory

Niamh Úi Bhriain (R) at a protest in 2012

Protest of the Protection of Life in Pregnancy Act, 2013

United for Life Rally, 19 January 2013

The crowd gathers at the rally after Savita's death, 19 January 2013

Rally for Life 2013

A Save the 8th billboard

←Abigail Malone, John McGuirk, and Niamh Uí Bhriain at the final Save the 8th press conference

Charmaine and Charlotte Van Maren at the final Save the 8th press conference →

From left to right: Andy Heasman, Amy Cannon, Mary Rose Short, Riaghan O'Callaghan, Martha Green, Patrick Martin, Glenn Mc Dyre, Tim Jackson, Shauna Flynn, and Siobhan Rooney. Bus driver: Anthony McGorian

← Tim Jackson speaks at the All Ireland Rally for Life

The Life Canvass →

Save the 8th Rally, 2018

in Europe were getting in touch saying they loved the campaign." As No to Nice began to gain traction, the Irish establishment started to panic—and that is when Taoiseach Bertie Ahern made a very embarrassing mistake, claiming that the posters alone had cost more than £100,000 and that the campaign was obviously funded with American cash from right-wingers overseas.

Ahern then came out and stated that the No to Nice Campaign was Youth Defence—which was, strictly speaking, untrue, despite the fact that the campaign was manned and driven by Youth Defence leaders and their legions of pro-life volunteers—but more seriously, that the campaign was being funded by US donors. "They went absolutely insane, because they had never experienced this kind of opposition before, and they knew how to deal with Sinn Féin and the Greens, but not this," Úna recounted. "And then they thought they were being clever by throwing this bizarre accusation about foreign funding, but we could show that wasn't true."

At that point, the No to Nice campaign took the unprecedented step of publishing their accounts during an ongoing campaign, calling a press conference and handing over their bank statements to Irish journalists. Ahern, they stated, was being untruthful—they had not received a massive infusion of foreign funds. The Taoiseach's attempt to derail their campaign failed, and on the Friday morning of the vote, it was revealed that early tallies indicated a clear No vote nearly everywhere. The final vote was 54% for No, and 46% for Yes. The Irish establishment was furious. "They were beyond livid," Úna said. "They were on the radio saying this is Youth Defence, this is a terrible injustice to this country [and] our European partners and neighbors…it was just an unforgettable moment." The pro-life movement had successfully gained the upper hand—for the time being.

The Irish establishment, however, had no intention of allowing the results of the referendum to stand. "It is not surprising that the Government didn't like the will of the people," Youth Defence noted in their report on events, "but it was an unprecedented new low for them to reject it altogether. The instantaneous agreement among politicians of all kinds and media commentators was that a new referendum would have to be held until the people gave the right answer."[cvii]

"Bertie Ahern, you have to remember, was the one who negotiated the peace treaty in the North of Ireland," Úna recalled. "He is a very astute politician." Úna and many other pro-lifers with her suspect that Ahern decided to have a divisive abortion referendum before re-running the Nice referendum for this precise purpose—to split, and thus neutralise, the collective power of the pro-life movement. Brilliantly, he cast the Abortion Referendum of March 6, 2002 as a "pro-life referendum." The wording of the referendum was released to much controversy in the movement in October of 2001.

The Twenty-fifth Amendment of the Constitution Bill, titled the Protection of Human Life in Pregnancy Act, would have removed the threat of suicide as legitimate grounds for abortion, included new penalties for anyone committing an abortion, and added two further sub-sections to the Eighth Amendment (the first two dealing with the right to travel and the right to access abortion, were inserted after the 1992 referenda.) The proposed Articles 40.3.4 and 40.3.5 read as follows:

4. In particular the life of the unborn in the womb shall be protected in accordance with the provisions of the Protection of Human Life in Pregnancy Act 2002.

5. The provisions of section 2 of Article 46 and

> sections 1,2, and 4 of Article 47 of this Constitution shall apply to any Bill passed or deemed to have been passed by both Houses of the Oireachtas containing a proposal to amend the Protection of Human Life in Pregnancy Act, 2002, as they apply to a Bill containing a proposal or proposals for the amendment of this Constitution and any such Bill shall be signed by the President forthwith upon his being satisfied that the Bill has been duly approved by the people in accordance with the provisions of section 1 of Article 47 of this Constitution and shall be duly promulgated by the President as a law.

Essentially, the Protection of Human Life in Pregnancy Act would have provided a legislative framework for abortion, which it defined as "the intentional destruction by any means of unborn life after implantation in the womb of a woman"—and it was this definition that split the pro-life movement. For a number of pro-life groups, including Youth Defence, SPUC, the Alliance for All Life, and Human Life International, this meant effectively legalizing the destruction of human life prior to implantation. The pro-lifers who decided to oppose the referendum were concerned that the proposal was too ambiguous with regard to when medical treatment resulting in the death of a pre-born child was necessary, and were also worried that the wording left the door open for research on embryos.

Various changes to the proposal were suggested, but the government effectively told the movement to take it or leave it. After much discussion, several pro-life groups decided to campaign for a No vote. Dana Scallon was a fearless pro-life leader and became one of the key faces of the No campaign. (She was a former recording artist who won the 1970 Eurovision Song Contest as a schoolgirl, and led a very successful music career before running unsuccessfully in the 1997 Irish presidential election, and ended up in the European Parliament as an MEP for Connacht-Ulster from 1999 to 2004.) Another driving factor for the No vote was a profound distrust of Ahern and the other architects of the referendum. They'd been trying to legalise abortion for years, some pro-lifers argued. Why trust them now?

On the other side, many equally passionate pro-life groups emphatically disagreed with this analysis and were campaigning hard for a Yes vote. This referendum, they said, represented an unprecedented opportunity to create a sturdier framework for the protection of human life in the womb and solidify the Eighth Amendment from future attacks. The Pro-Life Campaign, founded by many veterans of PLAC, led the charge with posters telling voters that "The unborn depend on you! Vote YES!" The Catholic Church also endorsed the proposal, and priests read letters from bishops at Mass urging the laity to vote Yes. Literature calling the referendum "An opportunity not to be missed" was distributed, and Cardinal Desmond Connell also called for a Yes vote. The Pro-Life Campaign released a statement detailing the stark contrast between their position and those on the pro-life side campaigning for a No vote:

> We welcome the proposed 25th Amendment (Protection of Human Life in Pregnancy) Bill and are calling for a 'YES' vote. The Amendment restores protection to unborn children. It protects women by ensuring the lawful availability of necessary medical treatment to save their lives. The reality of unexpected pregnancies also challenges us to put resources in place to meet the real needs of women. A clear law on the right to life is an important first step to framing social policies to help reduce our abortion rate.[cviii]

The split in the pro-life movement resulted in a bizarre situation that placed some pro-life activists on the same side as abortion activists, who were also campaigning for a No vote, albeit for very different reasons. Abortion activists wanted Ahern's referendum to fail because it protected human life in the womb, while some pro-life activists wanted it to fail because they did not believe it protected *all* human life in the womb. Also campaigning against the proposal—which was put forward by a coalition of Fianna Fáil and the Progressive Democrats—were Fine Gael, the Labour Party, the Green Party, and Sinn Féin. In the end, the proposal narrowly failed with 629,041 voting (50.4%) voting No and 618,485 (49.6%) voting Yes—a margin of a mere 11,000 votes. A post-election poll indicated that 5% of those who voted No had been persuaded to do so by pro-lifers.

The pro-life movement is divided on the 2002 Abortion Referendum to this day, and there is understandable bitterness concerning the result. To those campaigning for a Yes vote, the 2002 Abortion Referendum represents a tragically lost opportunity, with a different result potentially changing the trajectory of the Irish abortion debate for years to come. It is impossible, of course, to know how things would have unfolded if there was a Yes vote, but many are convinced that it would have provided solid protections for pre-born human life that could have withstood some of the storms that followed. Others argue that the work of pro-life groups continued to successfully stall any legislation from 2002 until 2013, and that the media manipulation of the death of Savita Halappanavar in that year would have been used in precisely the same way to sweep aside legislation and set the grounds for a referendum. However, as a result of the 2002 vote, the pro-life movement emerged from the referendum damaged. Úna remembers a lot of friendships within the movement ending over the duelling campaigns, and "we came out of 2002 a bit demoralised and dejected." Fighting the abortion activists and politicians was one thing. Fighting those who were also profoundly passionate about the protection of pre-born life was ugly and painful.

In an attempt to heal the divide, a Day of Prayer for Pro-Life Unity was held in Knock on June 22, calling on all pro-lifers to come together behind the common cause that they all held dear. A prayer pledge card was distributed that expressed the collective desire to move beyond the division that had wracked the movement throughout the referendum: "Our prayer will be that the entire pro-life community in Ireland may give glory to God through its prayer, through its work, and through one unified voice."

On October 19, 2002, a mere seven months after the Abortion Referendum, the Irish government held another referendum on the Treaty of Nice. This time, they took no chances, pouring millions into ensuring that the Irish public would produce the correct result the second time around. The Yes campaign made use of the media (who were, predictably, only too happy to oblige), and respected European figures such as former Czech president Vaclav Havel were brought out to make the case. Former Taoiseach Garret FitzGerald, then-president of the European Parliament Pat Cox, and a cavalcade of other luminaries joined the campaign, buttressed by the Fianna Fáil, the Labour Party, the Progressive Democrats, Fine Gael, and groups like Ireland for Europe and the Irish Alliance for Europe. The result the second time around was a 60% vote for Yes. When it came to referendums, establishment attitude was simple: If at first you don't succeed, try, try again.

Despite this setback, pro-life work on the ground continued unabated. Pickets continued to be a hallmark of pro-life activism, with Youth Defencers crashing the Alliance for Choice press conference in 2003 and picketing Health Minister Micheal Martin's clinics in Cork after health authorities sent two young girls in their care to England for abortions. Mary Harney had her office protested over her support for research on embryos, and the Irish Family Planning Association clinics, which helped families plan to abort their offspring, were a regular target. In June of 2004, Youth Defence even protested a Bill Clinton book-signing of his memoir *My Life* in Eason's on O'Connell Street due to his pro-abortion policies. Pictures show Youth Defence hoisting signs depicting abortion victims with questions like: "Hey Bill, What About 'My Life'?" Some people waiting for the former president to sign their books even left the lineup and joined the protest when they discovered what the fuss was all about.

It was the increasing sophistication of the Irish pro-life educational campaigns that drew the attention of the international pro-life movement. They held an information campaign on Assisted Human Reproduction, and distributed 100,000 booklets called *Early Human Life and Ethical Issues*. Another 200,000 similar booklets were delivered door-to-door. In 2004, the Mother and Child Campaign released a comprehensive report on the adverse physical and psychological effects of induced abortion called "Women have the right to know," and mailed it to every general practitioner in the country. In 2005, the No Exceptions Campaign was launched to respond to government recommendations found in the Commission on Assisted Human Reproduction, which pro-lifers pointed out would "make Ireland one of the most liberal countries in the world in relation to embryo abuse."[cix] This campaign stretched into 2006, and included a series of meetings as well as radio and TV appearances with Jacki Rabon, a woman paralysed in a car accident but who had recovered feeling in her legs and could walk with leg braces after adult stem cell research.

Their cutting-edge projects and effective education campaigns also landed the Irish pro-lifers on the international pro-life speaking circuit. I first met the Youth Defence contingent at an International Pro-Life Youth Conference in California, where the Irish pro-lifers were the rock star guests from an abortion-free country. In return, the Irish pro-life movement made use of American resources as well, flying in abortion survivor Gianna Jessen and former abortion clinic worker Mark Bomchill in November of 2005 for their Revelation Tour. This featured the two delivering their often chilling testimonies at a string of university campuses, hosted by Youth Defence's student wing, Ultrasound. Each year, new projects and campaigns were rolled out, and the Irish public were confronted with abortion in a new and creative way. In 2009, it was a van with an enormous screen and speakers on the side playing pro-life videos. In 2010, it was a billboard campaign with photos of an embryo, baby, toddler, adult, and elderly person with the slogan *You. Me. Everybody. We're All Just Grown-Up Embryos*. By 2011, Youth Defence alone had done 1,000 street sessions.

In addition to the increasing sophistication of Youth Defence, new wings of the pro-life movement began to develop, as well. The Mother and Child Campaign, for example, was turned into a new research institute and strategic think tank, The Life Institute, headed up by Niamh (who said that at that point, she was no longer young enough to continue on with Youth Defence). She and many of the original founders stepped back to make way for a new generation of leaders, but did not step out of the pro-life movement. Instead, they found new roles in the movement, with organisations like The Life Institute working alongside Youth Defence and other players to broaden the movement and increase its effectiveness.

Throughout all of this, of course, the pro-life movement faced the overt hostility of the media—but in April of 2007, they achieved a particularly satisfying victory. Nearly a decade before, Justine McCarthy, writing in the *Sunday Independent*, had accused Niamh of receiving training from the American pro-life organisation Operation Rescue – an organisation that McCarthy said was involved in blowing up abortion clinics. The claim was a lie on every count: Operation Rescue has a strict non-violence policy, Niamh had not received the fictitious training, and the whole story had been a transparent attempt to smear Niamh and Youth Defence. Niamh sued for libel, and after 56 court appearances (with the *Independent* attempting to oppose a hearing on the matter at every turn), a judge awarded her an undisclosed sum of money and full legal costs. The newspaper also reluctantly agreed to read an apology to Niamh in open court, and print another on page 3 of *The Independent* on April 14. The printed apology admitted that their slander of Niamh had been false, and that furthermore, she is "a person of the highest integrity." These apologies, presumably, were delivered through gritted teeth.

In May 2007, the D case broke. A 17-year-old girl in the care of the Health Service Executive named Amy Dunne became pregnant, and the HSE decided that she needed an abortion—especially after the girl's preborn child was diagnosed with anencephaly, a condition where part of the child's brain fails to develop. Abortion activists, predictably, began to raise a clamour about the various ways in which this case clearly demonstrated the need for abortion in Ireland. But the pro-life movement regarded the unfolding drama with suspicion. As Youth Defence noted at the time:

> The HSE applied to the District Court and the case was referred to the High Court, which soon became crammed with different representatives speaking for each party. [Present] were lawyers representing the HSE, the girl, and the government/people. The government/people had the Attorney General on their side not once but twice. One deputy of the AG's office was watchful of the interest of the right to travel and spoke ably for the cause. The other was there to represent the rights of the unborn and made a good impression of a deaf mute.
>
> The case became very public, with Justice McKenchnie even criticizing the HSE for "trying to turn this into another X Case." It transpired that the girl didn't want to have the abortion. But she was taken aside by her handlers and convinced that she would not be aborting her baby, just delivering it early.[cx]

In response, Youth Defence held several silent vigils for the mother and child, and pointed out that the Health Service Executive was displaying a particularly repulsive version of ableism. After excoriating the HSE for attempting to turn the case into one about abortion, Justice McKenchnie ruled that the right to travel inserted into the Constitution by the 1992 referendum took precedent over the pre-born child's right to life. Many questions were left unanswered—including who at the HSE was attempting to turn the pregnancies of young girls in their care into abortion rights cases. Abortion supporters inside the system were obviously hunting for a case that would reignite the debate and lead to legalisation—but as of yet, despite the fact that they had achieved several dead babies, they hadn't found the case they needed. They would keep hunting.

In the meantime, the Irish establishment were ready to put another referendum to the public. The Twenty-eighth Amendment of the Constitution Bill 2008 would allow the Irish government to ratify the Treaty of Lisbon, an international agreement which would create the constitutional basis of the European Union (and amend a series of previous treaties, including the 1992 Maastricht Treaty). Notably, the Treaty of Lisbon made the European Union's Charter of Fundamental Rights legally binding. This, of course, prompted immediate skepticism from many of the Irish pro-lifers, who were concerned that this gave the European Union a dangerous amount of power over Ireland's laws. While several Euro-skeptic groups already existed, a number of social conservatives and pro-lifers decided to create a new organisation to ensure that their concerns were heard. Cóir was formed for this purpose, and Niamh signed on as one of the spokespeople with Richard Greene, Brian Hickey, and Manus Mac Meanmain. They didn't have much money, but they had the insight, creativity, and drive that had powered so many previous campaigns and they had volunteers—2,600 of them—networks, and a willingness to do the back-breaking campaign work necessary to win.

"They didn't think we'd do it again after losing the second Nice referendum," Úna recalled later. But just as with the first Nice referendum, their anti-EU messaging was perfect: The defining poster depicted three chimpanzees, with one covering his eyes, one plugging his ears, and the other covering his mouth. "The New EU," the poster warned, "Won't see you, won't hear you, won't speak for you." Cóir launched a canvassing roadshow, produced 1.5 million leaflets, 100,000 voter info cards, 7,000 bumper stickers, 11,500 posters, a website, and hit the doorsteps hard. The establishment, apparently, had not learned their lesson from the first Nice referendum, and seemed unconcerned by all of this activity. The Irish people, they figured, had learned their lesson last time, and would thus ignore the No campaigners. But as Youth Defence reported later, they began to get worried when alarming reports began trickling back to them:

> By April, with less than a month to go, panicky reports were working their way back through the party system that the Lisbon idea wasn't being openly celebrated on the streets. They kept finding that a certain issue arose on the canvass—one which they hadn't anticipated. Some "loolaas" were saying they were concerned about the treaty because of its implication for our abortion laws. In one memorable radio showdown Martin clashed with Niamh Úi Bhriain who was now speaking for Cóir. The studio temperature practically came to boiling but while Martin played up the outrage and denial like a seasoned pro, the results showed that the bothersome electorate believed Cóir had won the debate…Some of the feedback that canvassers reported was that people on the doorsteps felt the EU was arrogant; that Irish politicians were only but for themselves; that Ireland's sovereignty was in danger. They believed the Lisbon Treaty was a step too far; that we would lose control of our economy and the right to decide on moral and social issues.[cxi]

The count in Dublin Castle was broadcast all over the world, and the Cóir campaigners and their allies exploded into celebration when the final tally was announced: 46.6% for Yes, 53.4% for No. A photo of two young Cóir members hoisting an exultant Niamh onto their shoulders was beamed around the world, with her joyful face and her hand thrusting a small sign reading

Don't Be Bullied aloft becoming the symbolic image of the night. It was another shocking upset for the elites. "Cóir hit the ground running. The monkeys worked," one Green Party TD remarked glumly.[cxii] Initially, the establishment attempted to assert that their loss had nothing to do with abortion, but they "looked pretty foolish two weeks later when a Red C poll…showed that abortion was a significant issue for a huge majority of No voters and that, in fact, all of the issues highlighted by Cóir were major factors in the No vote." Micheal Martin reluctantly admitted that abortion concerns had fueled the No vote, and Taoiseach Brian Cowen also noted that concerns about the influence of the European Court of Justice on Ireland's abortion and euthanasia laws were key to getting out the vote for the No side.

Undeterred, the Irish government sent voters back to the polls on October 2, 2009, to vote on the Lisbon Treaty once again. This time, with the country spiralling into a severe economic depression after the bank crash of 2008, they assured the public that a Yes vote was the perfect way to stop Ireland from going bust and to staunch job losses. The voters cast their ballots for Yes by a margin of 67.1% to 32.9%, and the Irish government was pleased. According to Cóir, however, the people had been bullied into voting Yes, and anti-EU academic Anthony Coughlan noted that it was the *fear* of the people rather than the *will* of the people that had eventually produced the desired result.

And soon enough, European Union referendums would be the least of the pro-life movement's worries—although their fears concerning European interference would prove founded. In December of 2010, the European Court of Human Rights ruled in the case *A, B, and C v. Ireland* that the State had violated one complainant's rights by not providing concise information as to whether or not she was entitled to get an abortion, and gave the Irish government a year to respond. Following the 2011 election, the newly-elected coalition government set up the Expert Group to advise them in how to respond to and implement the Court's ruling.

Chapter 6
Savita

In years to come, when we look back at the significant women of our history, Savita will be among them.

Kitty Holland

On March 10, 2012, jubilant cheers rocked Dublin's O'Connell Street as one hundred balloons rose slowly into the sky, an explosion of vibrant colour at the climax of Youth Defence's LifeFest celebration. And there were at least 100,000 reasons to celebrate: Each of the balloons represented 1,000 lives saved since 1992 by Ireland's abortion laws. A pro-life flash mob set to cheery music erupted and a huge banner reading "100,000 babies saved! Say YES to life and NO to abortion" was unfurled. Pro-life activists hoisted signs and passed out thank-you cards and heart-shaped lollipops to passersby.

Despite it being the twentieth anniversary of the Supreme Court ruling in the X case, the Irish pro-life movement had much to celebrate. They had kept Ireland abortion-free since 1983, the movement was growing, their political influence and clout was considerable, and the public was largely on their side. In addition to the usual roadshows and street sessions that year, Youth Defence had also rolled out the largest pro-life advertising campaign in Ireland's history in June, with 600 advertising sites nationwide that included metro-panels, billboards, the sides of busses, trains, and transmission screens to send a powerful message that would invigorate the pro-life majority. One billboard featured an ultrasound photo of a baby with a tear dividing the head from the body and the slogan: "Abortion Tears Her Life Apart. There's Always A Better Answer."

The abortion activists, on the other hand, seemed to be spinning their wheels. Political crises that should have sounded the death knell for the Eighth Amendment had come and gone, and yet Ireland's pro-life laws still stood, battered but solid. Tactics that had worked in countless other Western nations had thus far failed in Ireland. In response to the advertising campaign, Youth Defence noted wryly, the abortion campaigners "had a major canary (several of them) and tried to damage the billboards, tried to get their establishment and political friends to ban them, and went on a general rampage of hate. It was fairly intense but everyone was talking about abortion and the damage it does to society."[cxiii]

In September of 2012, the medical community released the Dublin Declaration, which was produced at the International Symposium on Maternal Health at the King's Inn in Dublin. Replete with the signatures (to date) of 244 obstetricians and gynaecologists, 526 medical professionals (primarily doctors), 89 midwives and nurses, 57 neonatologists and pediatricians, the Dublin Declaration laid out clearly why abortion is never necessary to save a woman's life and that an abortion ban does not prevent women from receiving the medical care they need for any condition arising in pregnancy:

> "As experienced practitioners and researchers in obstetrics and gynaecology, we affirm that direct abortion – the purposeful destruction of the unborn child – is not medically necessary to save the life of a woman.
>
> We uphold that there is a fundamental difference between abortion, and necessary medical treatments that are carried out to save the life of

> the mother, even if such treatment results in the loss of life of her unborn child.
>
> We confirm that the prohibition of abortion does not affect, in any way, the availability of optimal care to pregnant women."[cxiv]

It was a succinct summary of the *coup de grâce* that Ireland's pro-life laws presented to the unfounded claim of abortion activists around the world that abortion was necessary, that feticide was healthcare, and that women would die by the thousands if pre-born babies in the womb were protected by law. In fact, Ireland's maternal mortality rate was one of the lowest in the Western world—lower than that of the United Kingdom, where abortion on demand was the law of the land.[cxv] Devastating back-alley abortions of the sort that activists grimly promised would proliferate in nations with pro-life laws stubbornly refused to materialise. In short, the very existence of Ireland and her Eighth Amendment was a constant thorn in the side of the international abortion movement, an always-present reminder that their dire prophecies of a pro-life hellscape were untrue.

Because of this, the entire international pro-life movement pointed to Ireland as a shining example of what was possible: A nation that protected both women and pre-born children. Earlier that year on May 25, 2012, Irish-American pro-life activist Kate Bryan highlighted this in a column for Life Institute titled "Saoirse: The 20-year abortion freedom of Ireland" to celebrate 100,000 Irish babies saved:

> Planned Parenthood's lawyer Julie Kay once described Ireland as the "jewel in the crown of the pro-life movement." This is true. Although Ireland is small, it is a nation that has become one of the pro-life movement's most precious

> jewels. We must stand with Ireland and make sure that this "jewel" is guarded and that life is protected. And then we will add more jewels to this crown and polish them to make them shine brighter than ever before. We will win this battle; Ireland continues to give us hope every day in this battle for life. For many years, Ireland has fought to keep Ireland abortion-free, and I am happy to say that today will be another day without abortion in Ireland.[cxvi]

The abortion activists had also been motivated by the twentieth anniversary of the X case, as two decades without the legislation they desired forced them to confront their failures. In July, the Irish Choice Network was founded to strategise how to bring abortion to Ireland beyond the Expert Group Report that would deliver options to the Government on how to respond to the 2010 ruling from the Grand Chamber of the European Court of Human Rights. Another organisation called Galway Pro-Choice also started up, and other abortion groups began to materialise and mobilise. On September 29, 2012, a few thousand abortion supporters marched in Dublin to mark the International Day for the Decriminalization of Abortion, which had been conjured up by the Women's Global Network for Reproductive Rights the year before.

One month later at 1:09 AM on Sunday, October 29, a thirty-one-year-old dentist named Savita Halappanavar suffered a pulseless cardiac arrest and died at University Hospital Galway four days after giving birth to a dead baby girl named Prasa. On November 4, 2012, several of her friends reached out to Sarah McCarthy, one of the founders of Galway Pro-Choice. They followed up with an email that stated, in short: "We believe that her life could have been saved but for denying her a timely medical termination of pregnancy."[cxvii] According to Savita's friends, including one Dr. Chalikonda Prasad, they were not initially looking for an abortion-related protest, but were merely seeking information. Around twenty of them met with pro-choice activists to discuss this situation in the Meyrick Hotel in Eyre Square on Tuesday, November 6, and the activists hastened to inform Savita's friends that this case was obviously about the denial of an abortion and Ireland's abortion laws. Unsurprisingly, the abortion activists decided to go to the press, and the Dublin-based journalist Kitty Holland got a call on November 7 just before bedtime. It was precisely the sort of story she'd been waiting for.

On Wednesday, November 14, 2012, Holland's story on the front page of the *Irish Times* transformed the abortion debate in Ireland and launched the country on the road to legalisation: "Woman 'denied a termination' dies in hospital," the headline read, and the story ran next to a photograph of Savita's face, the same face that would smile from nearly every telephone pole in Dublin in the leadup to the abortion referendum just over five years later. The story strongly implied that Savita, a young Indian woman living and working in Ireland with her husband, had died because she'd been denied an abortion. That first story was viewed more than two million times on the first day—the most-read story in the seventeen-year history of the *Irish Times* website.

The story exploded from there, with media outlets across Ireland and Northern Ireland picking up both the story and the abortion angle. Then came the international pile-on, with the BBC World Service, CNN, Channel 4 News, and Al-Jazeera reporting with almost gleeful outrage that a woman had died, most likely because she'd been denied an abortion in Ireland. Nearly every news outlet speculated on the political implications of

Savita's death, welcoming the prospect of taking down Ireland's pro-life laws. The word *abortion* made it into nearly every headline, including that of the *New York Times* and the *Washington Post*. The website of the Times of India group ran with the sensational headline "Ireland Murders Pregnant Indian Dentist", while Britain's most famous atheist, Richard Dawkins, tweeted that "Irish Catholic bigotry kills woman."

The media chose to focus special attention on what became known as "the Catholic comment"—the assertion in the *Irish Times* article that Savita had been told in Galway University Hospital that she was being denied a termination of pregnancy because Ireland was "a Catholic country."

Despite the assertion by the Health Minister James Reilly, that there was 'no evidence' that he was aware of that suggested that a '*Catholic* ethos' had negatively influenced Savita's treatment, the speculation continued. The *India Times* asked: "Are Ireland's Catholic Abortion Laws responsible for Savita's death?"[cxviii]

Pro-abortion politicians leapt to speak to the issue, and they spoke with one voice: A young woman was dead because she was denied an abortion, and the only solution was to change the status quo.

Kitty Holland was a long-time advocate of abortion legalisation and the daughter of Mary Holland, a prominent journalist and campaigner for abortion rights. Holland herself had undergone two abortions, the second of which had been performed in Amsterdam and, by her own admission, she regretted terribly. In her 2013 book *Savita: The Tragedy That Shook A Nation* (with a foreword by Mary Robinson), Holland claimed that she had not worked with abortion campaigners to launch the Savita story, and insisted that the pro-choice activists she collaborated with were merely sources rather than allies with a shared goal. She also claimed that her mother's abortion advocacy had nothing to do with her perspective on the events. Considering her version of the facts both at the time of Savita's death and later on, this assertion strains credulity at best.[28]

The outrage at Holland's *Irish Times* story and the tidal wave of domestic and international coverage that followed was immediate and understandable. The Irish public reacted with horror to a simple narrative that was presented to them over and over again: A woman had been denied an abortion even though her baby was already dying, and she had died as a result. It was both personal and powerful: What if it had been *their* wife or *their* daughter or someone *they* loved? If it could happen to Savita, after all, couldn't it happen to anyone? The pro-abortion politicians chimed in: *What are we going to do about it?* It didn't matter that Savita had actually died of undiagnosed sepsis – and that three subsequent inquiries would show that medical negligence meant opportunities were missed to save her life. As the saying goes, a lie gets halfway around the world before the truth has a chance to put its pants on, and even pro-life politicians admitted

28 Kitty Holland is particularly sensitive to this accusation. On November 25, 2017, columnist John Waters told a gathering of the pro-life political party Renua Ireland that no woman in Ireland had ever died as a result of being denied an abortion and that Savita's case was "the closest they can come" but that "We know that's a lie. We know it's a lie that resulted in the journalist who started the lie getting multiple awards from her colleagues." Holland responded by launching defamation proceedings against Waters, stating that, "The idea that what happened to Savita was a concoction on my part, and the attacks on journalists telling the truth and reflecting the family's position, have to be challenged." Of course, Waters was not actually stating that the Savita story was a concoction, just the deliberately-spun angle that she died from being denied an abortion—and Holland ignored the fact that the "family's position" on the matter was heavily informed by abortion activists with a very specific agenda.

that they simply didn't know how to respond to the story, especially in the initial absence of complete facts. Pro-lifers had to wait to discover what had actually happened before they could give a definitive response. Abortion advocates had no such qualms.

Riaghan O'Callaghan, then a music student at Bimm Dublin, remembered how passionate and instantaneous the response was: "The next day I came in, and my professor was like *pro-choice, pro-choice, pro-choice*. At the time I was volunteering in the offices for the Pro-Life Campaign—I was just doing calls—and I would hear the conversations going on in that office. They would be talking about what the records would show, or they would be talking about how the hospitals work, and different things. So when Savita died, I knew instantly that we'd have to wait to find out what happened. But literally the next day at college, it was just *abortion*. It went so quickly. Everything was about abortion. Everything was about choice. So then I started part-time working for [the pro-life cause] because I realised how quickly the misinformation got out."

The case of Baby X had failed to result in abortion legislation. The death of Baby C had also failed to deliver what abortion activists were hoping for. But it was clear from the very beginning that something about Savita's death was different. Finally, abortion activists had the case they needed with an undeniably powerful story attached to it. Savita's baby girl had been wanted—although abortion activists had no desire to linger for too long on Prasa, as that could humanise the babies who would die by abortion. Additionally, Savita wasn't Irish, and as such she could be presented as an unfortunate victim of Ireland's cruel laws. Savita finally gave the abortion movement both a name and a face. Baby X, Baby C, and a handful of subsequent cases had produced dead babies, but those babies were of course nameless and faceless. Savita was different: Here was someone many women could identify with. Her death triggered a passionate response, and many women flooded the airwaves with their own stories of miscarriages or abortions.

The hundreds of thousands of babies saved by the Eighth Amendment were also, in many ways, faceless. Ireland's rock-bottom abortion rate was a mere statistic. Savita was not a statistic, and the false narrative that had been crafted around her passing presented the pro-life movement with an enormous and unprecedented challenge. In terms of public perception, as Joseph Stalin infamously observed, the death of one is a tragedy, while the death of a million is a statistic. The pro-life movement could highlight the thousands of pre-born children that would be killed by abortion if Ireland's pro-life laws were overturned or undermined, and the abortion activists could now respond with a single, powerful counter-argument: *Savita.*

Even Savita's father reportedly said that, "If the Irish law on abortion is changed, I would think my daughter has been sacrificed for a good cause."[cxix] And there it was, said the abortion activists. If Savita's death was to mean something, then the Irish *must* legalise abortion.

The abortion movement moved quickly to take advantage of the outrage and the shifting cultural currents. Rallies and marches were organised. At a massive rally the weekend after the Savita story broke, Socialist Party TD Clare Daly went after Enda Kenny on abortion, screaming that, "This political pygmy has sat in Dail Eireann for over thirty years while 150,000 women have been exported out of here!"[cxx][29] The

29 Kitty Holland puts that number at 100,000.

truth about why Savita died, which had not yet been fully uncovered, didn't matter. The abortion activists relentlessly pounded their simple narrative into the public consciousness. The pro-life movement sensed disaster, pointing out that this was another example of political opportunism and highlighting the fact that the *Irish Times* was using sensationalism to fuel the efforts of abortion activists.

According to Kitty Holland, the primary groups "in Ireland's anti-abortion vanguard are Youth Defence, the Life Institute, the Pro-life Campaign, the Iona Institute, and Family and Life."[cxxi] Life Institute, which shared their offices with Youth Defence, had been founded by older activists who wanted to follow the public engagement model utilised by Youth Defence and who also saw a gap in research and communications requirements for the movement at the time. The Iona Institute had been founded in 2007 by commentator David Quinn as a conservative Catholic lobby group, and focused primarily on family values, the sanctity of marriage, parenting, and on abortion, which it addressed by making the case for a society where abortion is unnecessary (ideas that even Holland admitted made "compelling arguments."[cxxii]) Family and Life, according to Holland, "believes in a total life ethic which requires a commitment to oppose all attempts to undermine the inalienable and imprescriptible nature of human life," and focused on outreach in schools as well as organising pro-life events.

The pro-life movement faced an enormous challenge: Although they knew that the abortion activists were exploiting another tragedy, they had to wait for the full facts to emerge before they could directly rebut the narrative with specificity—but that narrative was rapidly solidifying in a way that was very hard to combat. The same day that the *Irish Times* broke the story, Youth

Defence told the *Journal* that Savita had not died as a result of Ireland's pro-life laws because nothing in those laws prevented women from getting the medical treatment they needed, and stated that abortion activists were using the death to "further their own agenda," noting that the initial evidence pointed to septicaemia as a cause of death rather than anything abortion-related. Niamh Uí Bhriain, now a spokeswoman for Life Institute, also condemned the "rush to exploit" Savita's death, and noted that her "tragic loss" was "not caused by Ireland's ban on abortion." "We need to ensure that mothers and babies are best protected; and abortion is not part of best medical practice. It is medieval medicine," she said.

From the beginning, the pro-life movement could tell that the Savita case was going to hurt them. When she stumbled on an email chat just before the story broke letting her know what was coming, Niamh felt a sense of dread that she couldn't quite articulate: "I remember it left me with a feeling of apprehension that something was coming, and that it was planned and that [the abortion activists] were really excited about it and that it might be something that could be used very badly against the pro-life cause. I didn't have any insight, just a bad feeling." The morning the story broke, thousands of people began spamming the Facebook pages of pro-life groups, calling the Youth Defence office, and sending vicious emails. They were all saying the same thing, Niamh remembered: "You killed Savita."

"The logical side of my brain was saying: Well, that can't be true," Niamh recalled. "We've had the 8th Amendment for all these years, I've had children myself, Irish maternal healthcare is excellent, there is no way a doctor would let a woman die in Ireland. It just wouldn't happen. But it was a crescendo of absolute hysteria from the minute the *Irish Times* story was published. People said things that were later proved to be untrue, but it didn't matter. It was a day when you saw exactly how exploitative the other side was, and how absolutely onside the media were in supporting abortion. But there was a deeper realisation, too. The primary feeling was one of horror, because you realised that they were going to use this story and use this death in the most powerful way that they could, to make people believe that the 8th Amendment had killed a woman." That is precisely what happened. Abortion activists not only in Ireland but around the world were launching an extraordinarily successful campaign of blood libel against the Irish pro-life movement, and it was spreading fast.

The pro-life movement began to push back by attempting to highlight what the abortion activists were doing, launching a website just days after the story broke called Savitatruth, which revealed that "Abortion advocates know the story is going to break at least three days ahead of time and co-ordinate a media strategy exploiting the death to promote their long-standing campaigns to legalise abortion in Ireland."[cxxiii] A November 18 article in the *Sunday Independent* noted that "campaigners had heard of Savita's death three days before the story broke" and detailed how abortion activists planned their response and plotted out how best to capitalise on the "denial of abortion story" to achieve a political result.[cxxiv] A Google discussion detailing the prior knowledge abortion activists had of the Savita case and the *Irish Times* article, and their plans to use the story to their advantage had been uncovered by Life Institute.[cxxv] Included in the discussion were political advisers and researchers working for left-wing politicians such as Mick Wallace and the political party Sinn Féin.

Even when rocked by crisis, Holland writes, the "anti-abortion strategy was and is multi-pronged, slick and brilliantly executed. No opportunity is missed. Most of its spokespeople look great and present their cause as reasonable and rational."[cxxvi] They were about to be put to the greatest test they had ever faced.

Kitty Holland, ironically, claimed in her 2013 account of the events that the fact that pro-lifers stated publicly that Savita's death was not due to a denied abortion before the inquests concluded was distasteful in some way—even though it turned out to be the truth. At the same time, Holland insisted that her original story was accurate even though Savita did not die from being refused an abortion—because she merely reported the fact that it was Savita's husband Praveen's view that she died because she was refused an abortion. The main point of the Savita affair, according to Holland's recounting, is that Praveen wanted an abortion for Savita and she didn't get one.

The key point that pro-lifers were trying to insert into the discussion was that Savita had died of sepsis, caused by a virulent bacteria usually unseen in pregnancy, and that the Eighth Amendment did not prevent doctors from intervening in a pregnancy to save a woman's life. The narrative being presented by the abortion campaigners and their increasingly indistinguishable media partners that a woman died because she was refused an abortion was untrue – but it was fast becoming the only narrative being heard. Abortion activists, of course, wanted to put the sole blame for Savita's death on the Eighth Amendment. Savita's death was a political opportunity too good to pass up.

On the evening of Tuesday, December 4, just under three weeks after the story broke, the pro-life movement organised a response rally of their own in front of Leinster House. The Life Institute, Youth Defence, the Pro-Life Campaign, and Family and Life worked together to make it happen, and over 10,000 people showed up. They came with one message for the ruling Fine Gael and Taoiseach Enda Kenny, emblazoned across placards and posters alike: *Keep your pro-life promise.* Kenny had assured the movement that he would not legalise abortion in Ireland, and in the face of this new storm, thousands of pro-lifers marched through the cold night to put some steel in his spine. Many of them held candles, their faces lit in the darkness by the light of the flickering flames, chants rising up on the puffs of mist emitting from ten thousand throats: *Keep your promise! Keep your promise! Keep your promise!* Thousands of young people were also there to tell the media swarm they would defend babies in the womb, and to make their voices—which were so often ignored—heard loud and clear.

Niamh Uí Bhriain addressed the assembled crowd, a battle cry to the slandered rank and file of the pro-life movement:

> We are not for turning, and we will not yield. We are proud to be a pro-life nation. We are here to tell the politicians in the Dail Eireann that they may have destroyed our economy, but we will never let them kill our children. The lives of our children are worth fighting for and the mothers driven to abortion in fear are worth fighting for, and the pro-life ethos in this country is worth fighting for.[cxxvii]

That December, pro-lifers launched a massive campaign to push back against the spreading lies, delivering booklets to 1.5 million homes asking 4.5 million people to stand up and demand that Enda Kenny keep his pro-life promise. A simultaneous pro-life billboard campaign reinforced this message, with newspaper adverts urging people to contact their local politicians and drive this point home. Youth Defence estimated that 2.2 million people saw the newspaper adverts, and the message "Close the Door on Abortion" was a simple, easy-to-understand response to the equally simple message of the abortion activists.

Enda Kenny did not appear to have any intention of keeping his promise. The day Kitty Holland's story broke in the *Irish Times*, the government announced that the Expert Group, which was working on recommendations for how to respond to the European Court of Human Rights' judgement in *A, B, and C v. Ireland,* had submitted their report to the Health Department the night before. Days later, Sinn Féin tabled a motion in the Dail demanding abortion legislation, and 19 TDs spoke to the motion over the next two days, delivering condolences to Savita's family before hastening on to the politics of abortion. The Labour Party took the opportunity to remind everyone that they had been abortion supporters for quite some time, and accused the Sinn Féin of having been insufficiently enthusiastic on the issue in the past. Fine Gael insisted that a report by the Expert Group should be waited for, and the Sinn Féin motion was defeated, accompanied by the passage of a motion to await the report.

While many of the politicians wanted to buy a bit of time to see where public opinion landed, abortion activists pushed back hard, not wanting the mood to cool with the case. They were concerned that if the government waited too long, the opportunity to use the death of Savita to loosen abortion restrictions would be lost.

Despite this, Enda Kenny was in a difficult position. As the pro-life movement pointed out constantly, he had promised that he would "never" legislate for abortion, and this promise became a theme of pro-life rallies, which continue to swell in size throughout 2013.

The Expert Group's report on abortion legalisation detailed a number of options, and Kenny had to consider how to tackle the issue without losing re-election. The pro-life movement, after all, had proven that it had the ability to make politicians who attempted to legalise abortion pay very dearly for their choice, and as such many had preferred to stay as far away from the issue as possible.

The report of the Expert Group laid out four possibilities for the Irish government to pursue to comply with the Court's ruling:

1. Non-statutory guidelines
2. Statutory regulations
3. Legislation
4. Legislation and regulations

It is impossible to know what Kenny would have decided if the Savita case had not torqued and toxified the discussion, but of the four options presented, the government decided to pursue both legislation and regulations.

In January of 2013, the Oireachtas Joint Committee on Health and Children hosted three days of discussion, inviting various interest groups to weigh in on the government's plans. Several pro-lifers, including Breda O'Brien of the Iona Institute, addressed the hearings to argue against formally legalising abortion in the case of suicidal ideation, which would result, they said, in legislation that essentially allowed for abortion on demand. The pro-life contributions, however, were drowned out by a host of other voices, and O'Brien stated that pro-lifers felt as if they were "battling to be heard."[cxxviii] According to some observers, the hearings showcased clearly how thoroughly the Savita case had transformed the Irish abortion debate: "The Savita story pushed the abortion issue to the top of the media and political agenda in an urgent way that never would have happened on foot simply of the Expert Group report... One of the effects is that what had been the pro-choice argument—seeking legislation for the X case—was now being made by the Government, by the medical profession, by the legal profession. That became the common-sense middle ground."[cxxix]

The pro-life movement fought back. Almost immediately after the successful December 4 vigil, the pro-life movement began planning a second rally for January 19, 2013. In the Life Institute headquarters, a design team was working with Youth Defence creatives to come up with a rally poster that summed up the pro-life position of protecting both mother and baby. The "Love Them Both" slogan, adopted afterwards by pro-life groups across the world, was born.

The Unite for Life vigil was even larger than the first—over 100 buses arrived in Dublin from across the country, and pro-life activists began the set-up early in the morning. People began to drift in, in small knots at first, and then in crowds. There were children carried on shoulders, babies in buggies wrapped snugly in blankets, children clutching hands. As evening fell, the crowd swelled into the thousands.

"An impressive sea of people filled one side of Merrion Square, the majority carrying either pink placards with a picture of a young woman cuddling a baby, saying 'Love them Both,' or yellow ones saying 'Vote Pro-Life,'" Holland noted begrudgingly. "[T]here was a rock-concert-size stage, complete with a mixer desk and a huge screen...so that speakers could be seen from a distance. Between 20,000 and 30,000 people were there in bitterly cold weather and, judging from the TV footage, they were disproportionately young."[cxxx]

There were mothers, fathers, entire families—and all came to defend and give voice to pro-life Ireland, the Ireland where children were welcomed with open arms. The thousands of pro-lifers formed a seemingly interminable column of twinkling torch-bearers, stretching back, back from the stage and into the black. The fragile, shuddering flames of their candles, carefully protected by the cupped hands of young and old, seemed to be the perfect symbol of what was at stake: tiny, helpless babies who could not fend or even speak for themselves. They needed care and protection, and pro-lifers in their thousands were present to signal their willingness. Seen from the air, the vigil was an ocean of ebony pierced by thousands of tiny yellow pinpricks—a flickering army of hope.

A Youth Defence spokesperson took the stage, and the crowd fell silent as he dialed the office of Taoiseach Enda Kenny. He held his cellphone to the microphone, and after a ring, a recorded voice came on the line: "This is Enda Kenny's constituency office...we'll get back to you as quickly as possible." The answering machine beeped, and he spoke into the receiver: "Taoiseach, this is a message from the Irish people." He thrust the cellphone aloft above the crowd, and tens of thousands roared with a single voice: *"Keep your promise!"*

The rally was just the beginning. Life Institute and Youth Defence promptly spearheaded a massive campaign to push back against abortion legislation, replete with all of their hallmark activism: billboards, leaflet drops, demonstrations, newspaper adverts, and daily street information sessions. As the threat of legislation loomed, the pro-life movement called for all hands on deck.

On April 19, 2013, after seven days of evidence from 36 witnesses, Dr. Ciarán McLoughlin delivered his verdict in the case of Savita Halappanavar: medical misadventure. He laid out a number of reasons for her untimely demise:

- Blood tests indicating possible infection were not collected
- Savita's pulse rate was elevated at 114 but the on-call doctor was not aware of this
- Savita's vital signs were not checked for more than nine hours, in breach of hospital guidelines
- Although Savita's pulse rises to 160, with a fever and a foul smelling discharge, the discharge was not relayed to Savita's consultant[cxxxi]

In total, three separate investigations were undertaken into Savita's death—the Health Information and Quality Authority Report, the Health Service Executive Report, and the Coroner's Court inquest. All would report that Savita died of sepsis, an infection of the blood caused by the bacteria Ecoli ESBL. The HSE Report also stated that the bacteria was the most likely cause of Savita's miscarriage. All three inquiries highlighted the fact that Savita's case had been medically mismanaged in the hospital, with the HIQA Report indicating that there were at least thirteen missed opportunities to save Savita's life.

According to the Coroner's Court inquest, a statement made by one midwife to Savita which had been seized upon by the abortion activists that a termination could not be performed because "we don't do that here dear, it's a Catholic thing," turned out to have been a throwaway comment by a woman who emphasised that it was part of a "normal chat," had no bearing on Savita's medical care, and had merely been her clumsy attempt to explain Irish culture to a foreigner. The Coroner's Court inquest also emphasised that religious tenets had no bearing on medical care, despite what was being inferred in the press.

Pro-life groups responded to the Coroner's Court Inquest by reemphasising the fact that Savita had not died because she was refused an abortion. In her book, Kitty Holland responded by asserting her belief that an abortion *could* have saved her, but again the reality—confirmed by lengthy and thorough investigations—is that Savita *could have been saved without an abortion,* and as such, the Eighth Amendment was not the reason for her death. Holland is not alone in her assertion—Dr. Peter Boylan, who would become a prominent campaigner against the Eighth Amendment several years later, also claimed that she might have been saved if she'd had an abortion.[30] A letter rebutting Boylan's view signed by eight consultant obstetricians, a consultant microbiologist, a consultant anesthesiologist and a consultant in emergency medicine, was published on May 1 on the *Irish Times* "Letters to the Editor" page, and this emphatic disagreement with Boylan's abortion advocacy was referred to by Holland as a "co-ordinated attack."[cxxxii] The media, which had given endless coverage to Boylan's assertions and attacks on the Eighth, largely ignored the public refutation of his claims by so many of his peers.

This evidence made no difference to abortion supporters, who were unwilling to relinquish the opportunity Savita's death had provided them. Praveen Halappanavar's response to the inquest was also enormously helpful for their cause. Speaking to the press, he reiterated his opinion that his wife had died

30 In response, Life Institute would publish a fact sheet titled "Who is Peter Boylan?" to expose his blatant biases.

due to being denied an abortion, and then echoed one of their favourite lines: "You lose your rights basically when you are pregnant here, I think."[cxxxiii] He was by far the most powerful advocate the abortion activists had—because even though he was wrong, it was very difficult for the pro-life movement to respond to and rebut the perspective of a grieving and heartbroken widower.

On April 28, just two days before the government released their bill, the *Sunday Independent* published the transcripts of secretly recorded conversations with two Labour TDs, in which they discussed their strategy for utilising X case legislation to push for a liberal abortion regime. "It's a starting point," Aodhán Ó Ríordáin was recorded saying. "Once you get that…then you can move…and of course if I'm on the radio and somebody says to me, 'It's a starting point for abortion on demand' I'm going to say, 'No of course it isn't. It is what it is.'"[cxxxiv] Anne Ferris agreed with him, noting that, "We will legislate certainly for what Europe has told us and then we can go further than that…we get the first bit done and then we go on to the next bit."[cxxxv] Abortion-supporting politicians scrambled to claim that the conversations meant nothing, while pro-lifers said it revealed the intentions of abortion campaigners.

On Tuesday, April 30, the Irish government published their abortion bill, titled the "Protection of Life During Pregnancy Act 2013." The legislation permitted abortion if a woman's life was at risk in an emergency situation from an ongoing condition or illness, and formally declared suicidal ideation to be grounds for abortion.

The pro-life movement, which had been working at a frenetic pace all year, kicked into high gear. Thousands of leaflets were handed out, detailing what would be done to pre-born babies if the legislation were to pass. Clergy spoke out against the bill, and a National Vigil for Life on June 8 drew 40,000 people, a potent display of political force. On July 6, the biggest pro-life event in Irish history was held in Dublin, with 60,000 marching at the All Ireland Rally for Life organised by Life Institute, Youth Defence, and Precious Life. It was a gorgeous, sunny day, and red heart-shaped balloons wafted in the breeze above the heads of the crowd as pro-life leaders riled the troops from the stage, a celebration that was part joy, part warning. Leaflets were handed out at the rally, too, describing different abortion procedures:

> [A] sharp looped knife scrapes the wall of the uterus. Then the baby is cut up before body parts are removed from the womb…The baby is dismembered, limb by limb. The surgeon waits for the baby to bleed to death before proceeding. In some cases he crushes its head to allow it to pass through the cervix.[cxxxvi]

These leaflets were so effective that later that month, the Irish Institute of Obstetricians and Gynaecologists responded to some of them in order to "allay the fears of the public," assuring them that the methods of abortion described "are not currently carried out in this jurisdiction, nor will they be in the future."[cxxxvii][31] Instead, they stated, induction abortions, in which labour is induced early so that the baby could not survive outside the womb and would die as a result, would be primarily utilised instead.

The Pro-Life Campaign also distributed thousands of postcards for voters to send to Fine Gael TDs and Senators, urging them to resist the legislation. Pro-lifers mailed thousands of postcards, with some TDs reporting that they were receiving hundreds of them. In response, Enda Kenny insisted that his abortion bill didn't actually

31 This, unsurprisingly, has turned out to be false.

change the law in Ireland, but merely codified the existing reality brought about by the X case. Furious abortion activists responded with violence, daubing excrement on the premises of Youth Defence's offices and mailing at least three death threats to the office of the Pro-Life Campaign on Baggot Street. The pro-lifers were undeterred, and throughout the three-day debate over the bill, they made up the vast majority of the protestors that gathered outside Leinster House from all over Ireland, kneeling, praying, and carrying signs.

At 12:25 AM on Friday, July 12, 2013, the Protection of Life During Pregnancy Bill passed the Dail by a vote of 127 to 31 with three abstentions and four TDs absent. Altogether, there had been 165 amendments to the legislation. Fine Gael lost five TDs, who defied the party whip and voted against the bill. The debate leading up to the bill's passage had taken an enormous toll on the political system, and abortion activists declared that this was only the beginning. There was now a chink in the armour, and the Eighth Amendment would be next.[32]

Five years later, John McGuirk, who would become the communications director for the Save the 8th Campaign, looked back and saw the seeds of the Eighth Amendment's demise sown in the months leading up to the passage of the Protection of Life During Pregnancy Bill. "We went all out to stop it. All out," he remembered. "We had massive

32 During the debate on the Protection of Life In Pregnancy Bill, Senator Jim Walsh noted that the truth about abortion was almost entirely absent from the discussion and put a description of a D&E abortion by former abortionist Dr. Anthony Levatino on the record of the Seanad (upper house.) The mere description of abortion—which included Levatino's observation that "[m]any times a little face will come out and stare back at you"—prompted one pro-abortion senator to walk out and a headline in the *Irish Times* that read "The air froze in the chamber: Walsh's input was disgusting." Even those who supported abortion couldn't stomach hearing the details of what it was."

rallies, we called in every chip with every politician we had, we had two government ministers resign in favor of our side, we had a huge split in the governing party over it. We made it incredibly painful for the government to pass that legislation. The idea at the time was that we'd make it really bloody for them to move an inch, and they wouldn't dare to move a mile. At the time, I was wholly subscribed to that. Wholly subscribed."

But looking back through the lens of the 2018 referendum, McGuirk's view has changed. "In hindsight, I think it was an...error," he said. "Because one of the things that happened was we lost, for example, two government ministers who were onside. And by the time the 2018 referendum came around, neither of them was in a position to be credible centrist voices on our behalf. A lot of the most prominent politicians who lost their jobs as a result of taking that position in liberal constituencies were no longer around to defend us. So we ended up in a position where, when the actual big fight came around, we had bloodied the government, but we had bloodied ourselves extensively in the process."

In retrospect, McGuirk said later, the 2013 campaign probably hamstringed the movement for the big battle to come. The number of abortions that took place in the year prior to the 2018 referendum under the 2013 legislation was less than ten. Were those lives worth fighting for? "Absolutely it's right to fight for seven lives," McGuirk said, "and I'd do it again in a heartbeat." That said, he believes they would have happened anyway.

Niamh Uí Bhriain sees it differently. "Savita's death changed everything, not because of how she died, which was a travesty of medical mismanagement, but because it was used to push a narrative that said change was not just desirable but absolutely essential," she said. "The 2013 legislation opened the floodgates, not in terms of the number of abortions which took place, but in relation to the public mood and the mindset which saw legal abortion—once considered unthinkable in Ireland—as something which women needed to save their lives. That narrative was false, but it was the myth, as John F. Kennedy said, that is persistent and persuasive and overcomes the truth. Once they had this narrative of the Eighth killing women, they weren't going to stop at legalising abortion on suicide grounds—it was always going to be a full assault on the Eighth."

***

To summarize the path to May 25, 2018, we must briefly go back to December of 2010, when the European Court of Human Rights had ruled in the "ABC case" that the Irish law on abortion lacked clarity, prompting calls for the government to pass abortion legislation to codify the permissible exceptions (such as suicidal ideation). In November of 2011, an expert group with fourteen members was set up to address the outcome of the ECHR's ruling, with many of them being avowed abortion supporters such as Dr. Peter Boylan. The following year, in April of 2012, the *Irish Times*, followed by RTÉ, the state broadcaster, launched a concerted campaign to push for the legalisation of abortion in the cases of life-limiting conditions. Heart-rending and emotional stories were published, but never counter-balanced by the stories of women like those of Tracy Harkin, Sandra Uí Chlónáin, Sandra Nugent, or Tanya Coonan, who as part of the organisation Every Life Counts made a compelling plea for a better alternative than abortion for parents who were told, just as they had been, that their babies would not live for long after birth.

Despite all of this, *TIME* magazine reported on October 5, 2012 that Enda Kenny would not be using the ECHR case to pass abortion legislation. Considering the fact that Kenny governed strictly by the polling data he saw cross his desk, the pro-life movement saw this as a clear indication that Kenny saw no political benefit or public demand for such legislation. That same year, TD Clare Daly put forward two abortion laws as private member's bills, both of which failed to pass but both of which, as she intended, garnered a huge amount of press attention and helped to solidify the narrative of abortion as a necessary response to tragic circumstances. When the Savita case hit in November of 2012, abortion activists had already been laying the groundwork to take advantage of a story like hers.

Between January and May of 2013, the Dáil Committee hearings on abortion also attracted massive amounts of media coverage. Medical witnesses were hand-picked to ensure that much of the testimony highlighted a supposed medical need for abortion, and in February 2015 Clare Daly put forward another abortion bill that once again failed, but kept the narrative front and centre. Her stunt was followed by another abortion bill put forward by TD Mike Wallace, which was defeated in July. In November of 2016, a Citizen's Assembly[33] was established to examine the Eighth Amendment, and despite pro-life submissions and attempts to influence the process, the result was essentially a foregone conclusion.

The Citizen's Assembly, Niamh noted, was "stacked with pro-aborts and abortion-supporting experts." The intent was clear to everyone. The experts trotted out their lines: Savita had been killed by the Eighth Amendment, and abortion needed to be legalised as simply another essential form of women's healthcare. The conclusion was inevitable, and the media reported on it faithfully every step of the way. The All-Party Committee was

33 A Citizens' Assembly is made up of 99 citizens who discuss the issue at hand and make recommendations to the government.

similarly set up, with only a small minority of pro-lifers included. The experts included an abortionist from the British Pregnancy Advisory Services and experts from the Guttmacher Institute, Planned Parenthood's research arm. "The whole thing was a farce, but you had weeks and weeks of it at the beginning of 2018," Niamh recalled, "and the media reporting every day in the headlines. It amounted to endless publicity and public discussion about abortion and it was all pointed one way – a chorus of voices insisting the Eighth had to go." They smelled blood, and pressed their advantage.

"When the Citizen's Assembly was put in place, it was a pretend process with a prearranged outcome," noted Cora Sherlock of the pro-life organisation Love Both. "It was very clear it was intended to result in a referendum."[cxxxviii]

In April of 2017, the Citizen's Assembly had voted to repeal the Eighth Amendment and legalise abortion on demand up until twelve weeks. On June 2, 2017, Leo Varadkar replaced Enda Kenny as Taoiseach, and one of his first acts as Ireland's leader was to announce an abortion referendum. He and his Health Minister Simon Harris had both run for office as pro-lifers (Varadkar had been a doctor), and had consistently assured pro-life groups of their anti-abortion convictions. Their shameless defections were an ominous sign. In October and November, the Oireachtas Committee heard more witnesses, once again hand-picked to support abortion and to hammer home the narrative that abortion was necessary, inevitable, and compassionate, over and over again.

The years that followed would be a nonstop race against forces that had been set in motion—and the abortion activists and politicians were armed with a powerful narrative they intended to use as a club. Both the abortion activists and the pro-lifers knew that everything was different this time, and both sides began making preparations for the fight over the Eighth Amendment. The month after the legislation passed, in August of 2013, a handful of abortion activists met to plan for the future, and in September, twelve organisations joined each other to form the Coalition to Repeal the Eighth Amendment.[cxxxix] For their part, the pro-life movement began gearing up, getting volunteers trained, and marshalling the forces that would be needed for a massive ground campaign.

By the time the referendum campaigns got underway in earnest, as the *Irish Times* put it, "both sides had already started a proxy war."[cxl]

Chapter 7
Save the 8th

For the great Gaels of Ireland
Are the men that God made mad,
For all their wars are merry,
And all their songs are sad.

G.K. Chesterton, *The Ballad of the White Horse*

The leadup to the abortion referendum of May 25, 2018 was so fast-paced that looking back, most of those involved aren't quite sure how they managed to survive it. "Ever since the Savita case," Niamh Uí Bhriain recalled, "We were fighting a running battle." Úna described the period as one where everyone was "constantly wearing riot gear," without a chance to catch a breath. Forces had been set in motion that were speeding inexorably towards a vote that would decide the fate of tens of thousands yet unborn. It often took nonstop effort simply to respond to unfolding events.

Life Institute and Youth Defence were building the team they needed for the referendum that was coming. Most were already part of the movement in some capacity, and included seasoned campaigners, organisers, and creatives such as Katy Robinson, Íde O'Hara, Rebecca Roughneen, Linda Gorman, Scott Schittl, Elaine Sheehan, and Tim Jackson.

"We always had a very strong creative team and a great grassroots network, but we needed to extend and strengthen the existing infrastructure for the referendum," Íde O'Hara, Operations Director for the campaign, remembers. "People took leave from work, they deferred exams, they turned down jobs. Training was ongoing, we were installing dozens of desks and phones in readiness before the date for the vote had ever been called. There was a huge sense of unease and urgency, but people were readying for the fight." Amongst those joining the core team were Christine D'Arcy and Abigail Malone, who would play important roles in media engagement, and Joanna Aiken and Donagh O'Callaghan, who helped manage the volunteer outreach and the myriad of challenges and opportunities the ground campaign involved.

"Every campaign that went before was like a dry-run for this one, for a vote that should never have taken place," said Scott Schittl, who became Field Director for the referendum and was a veteran, like many of the crew, of several national campaigns. His view—that the right to life is intrinsic and inalienable and should not be put to a vote—was shared by many others, including journalist and writer John Waters, who shared his thoughts at many meetings and media events.

In one viral debate on Sky News with a Labour Senator, Niamh Uí Bhriain tackled this fundamental question. Asked by the Sky presenter if Ireland's abortion laws were outdated, she responded: "The right to life can never be outdated. You've got a right to life, so do I. Should we put your right to life to a vote? Should we put mine? The only reason we're even discussing this is that the people whose right to life we're putting to a vote are too vulnerable and out of sight to speak for themselves."

But Niamh and others knew that, however unethical they held the vote to be, it was going to happen. "One of the things that was frustrating was that the media insisted that the referendum was happening because of a public demand for a vote, when that wasn't true," said Rebecca Roughneen. "I remember the RTE exit poll in the 2016 election which showed abortion was only a priority issue for just 2% of voters – and it's likely half of those or more were pro-lifers. If anything, the voter intensity at those margins was actually more pro-life, as evidenced by the rallies for life which were always larger than the pro-abortion rallies. But abortion campaigners now had the political capital they needed: it wasn't just left-wing TDs endlessly pushing bills to make media headlines anymore, now *all* the main political parties were behind repeal."[cxli]

Niamh says the claim made by abortion campaigners that repeal was won by doughty women operating at a grassroots level was "laughable," pointing to the fact that the pro-lifers faced the entire political, media, and civil establishment in the referendum and for years beforehand.

"Since 1992, it has always been the establishment against the unborn. The media, the political elites, the tax-payer funded NGOs, the trade unions, the EU, the United Nations, even billionaires like Chuck Feeney and George Soros, it's been David versus an army of Goliaths," she said. "But without manipulating Savita's tragic death they probably still wouldn't have got Repeal, not in this decade anyway."

Pro-life campaigners knew that they needed to try to bring key issues for middle-ground voters to the forefront in the debate before the referendum was called. Amongst those key issues was unease at abortion rates in other countries, late-term abortions, keeping women safe, and the heartbreaking numbers of babies aborted on disability grounds.

In 2016, the #AbortionDiscriminates campaign launched across Ireland, with mobile billboards featuring a handsome young man with Down syndrome, Joseph Cronin, criss-crossing the country to remind voters that in the UK, 90% of people like him were killed in the womb. Other families, including those of Mary Bridget Kelly, Kevin Trainer, and Hannah Moline also spoke up at media conferences, at rallies, and in powerful personal messages, racking up hundreds of thousands of interactions on social media. Disability rights activists with Down syndrome from Britain—Charlie Fien—and the US—Karen Gaffney—came to speak in Ireland, even going into the Dáil to talk to politicians. The "Abortion Discriminates" message resonated strongly with voters, with opinion polls showing a significant drop in support for abortion on disability grounds in this period—with support registering at 61% in a January 2016 Newstalk poll, then falling to 50% and down to 36% in two successive *Irish Times* polls.[cxlii] The paper described this as a "hardening of opposition" to abortion, but Life Institute said it should more accurately be described as a "softening of hearts, and a growing public awareness that people with a disability have the same right to life as everyone else." In the 2018 campaign these families were joined by the O'Dowds, the Murphys, the Kirbys, the McKees, the Farrellys, and others in Disability Voices for Life, one of the most important voices to emerge in the referendum. For those families, this was deeply personal.

In September 2016, a viral video titled "Repeal Kills" was released by Youth Defence. It was viewed over 180,000 times in the first few days. The following month, Life Institute released "Human," a video message declaring the right to life to be fundamental. It achieved more than one million views within a month of release. The soon-to-be ubiquitous line of "Save Lives, Save the 8th" apparel was launched, with headquarters promptly swamped with requests from the growing legions of volunteers for jumpers and t-shirts.

The groundwork to get a massive campaign ready to rumble was also underway. The Life Canvass, organised by Life Institute with thousands of people eventually going door to door, was first launched in the autumn and winter of 2015. Hours of training were poured into the volunteers, and by the end of the first year, people were coming out in Sligo, Navan, Roscommon, Clare, Cork, Kerry, Galway, and Waterford. It was the largest grassroots endeavour undertaken in the country in decades, Life Institute said.

"Everything was meticulously planned, from the Training Handbook, to the website and materials, and the Leadership initiatives. We wanted to marry decades of experience of public engagement on abortion with what we knew from polling and research. It was as much about answering people's questions as delivering a message. Referendums aren't elections, the questions are more complex, the considerations and conversations more meaningful. A referendum canvass is not a knock and drop: it's an attempt to have an actual conversation, to give space for a real discussion," said Niamh Uí Bhriain. "It was a huge effort, and whatever the outcome, it was undertaken by the real heroes of the campaign, who slogged from door to door to talk to people about saving the Eighth."

"We must have gone to 80 to 100 towns and cities, doing training to give people confidence. Sometimes we'd return two or three times," Scott Schittl recalled. "Then you had your market research, your focus groups, your polling and you were doing all of that not quite knowing exactly what would be in the proposed legislation yet. That was all unfolding, and the Canvass focus was developing with it. It would only be absolutely finalised when the government came forward with its proposal."

The local Canvass leaders were key to making sure the thousands of volunteers were motivated and on message throughout the campaign. "Some of those leaders had been organising volunteers for decades. In Mayo, Eilin Glynn and Pat Cummins had the constituency planned and the canvass started in late 2015, as did the indefatigable Maria Corcoran in Galway. In Cork, Joe Walsh and Ann Hackett led super-efficient teams with Dee Wallace, which grew the canvass to all ten constituencies, while crowds of volunteers had been out every week in Meath since the beginning. The Life Canvass was the back-bone of the campaign, and people really gave it their all; it was real grassroots—something none of the political parties are really capable of mustering anymore," said Katy Robinson. "We'd organise special National Life Canvass Days every couple of months and all the photos coming back were so encouraging, with the teams steadily growing everywhere. I remember looking at them after one mid-2017 drive and thinking, 'Wow the teams in Sligo and Waterford have doubled, and Dún Laoghaire and Donegal are just on fire.' And their feedback was invaluable: We'd be sent detailed reports by people like Philip Norden in Limerick. It fed into the campaign's understanding of what voters needed to hear."

By 2018, Scott, Íde, and their team were talking to local leaders on a daily basis, ensuring the Life Canvass remained a well-oiled machine. "I think people slept with their phones in their hands, or maybe they didn't sleep at all," laughed Íde O'Hara. "Elaine Sheehan and Donagh O'Callaghan developed parish and community group initiatives which doubled the canvass numbers going to the doors. They were incredibly efficient, and they needed to be. The canvass grew so rapidly in the last months, but the structure and the leaders were in place." Student leaders Teresa White and Sandra Parda spent months rallying young volunteers on campus. In an unprecedented show of pro-life unity, 140 local groups eventually joined the Life Canvass, canvassing almost 700,000 homes, close to half of all residences in the country.

"The leaders were astonishing, their commitment was legendary," remembers Schittl. "They motivated thousands of volunteers to knock on hundreds of thousands of doors. To me, their self-sacrifice epitomizes the real spirit of Ireland." One young mum, Aoife de Clár, had a new baby as the canvass intensified, but she was back out knocking doors a week later, her baby in a carrier. She and her sister Ciara, pro-life veterans, were also involved for years, working with homeless women. They were motivated by a deep commitment to the value of every human life, as were countless others like Evelyn Porter, Eithne Black, Emma Quinn, Fionnuala Ní Dhomhnaill, Marion Murphy, Maria Mhic Meanmain, and the hundreds of other young women who canvassed doors and train stations with babies in buggies.

Not that older people weren't equally sacrificial. "They were amazing, out night after night, in cold, wet, and rain, endlessly cheerful and good-humoured," said Íde O'Hara. "I loved working with them, and whatever the result, they patiently and courageously went to hundreds of thousands of homes with the facts and the truth. Their sacrifices might not have produced the outcome we all sought because referendums are essentially a zero-sum game, and all that painstaking information-sharing was swept away in a deluge of media propaganda when it came to the last week, but I have no doubt that the seeds the canvass planted will bear fruit." The feelings were reciprocated. Working with the board members of Life Institute and Youth Defence, Íde, Katy Robinson, and Rebecca Roughneen had managed projects and driven every major event from the office for years. The wealth of talent they and others had acquired fighting against abortion for decades meant that their supporters were fiercely loyal to headquarters.

Then there were the campaign posters, mostly hung on lampposts, which were key to creating talking points in the campaign. The same team that created the messages that swung votes on the Nice and Lisbon campaigns were working on design. The campaign assembled a crew to motivate hundreds of volunteers to spend weeks going up and down ladders in one of the wettest countries in the world, for free, to save the Eighth.

Liam Ó Síocháin, Seán Ó Hara, and Cathal Harte took leave to drive billboard vans carrying tens of thousands of posters the length and breadth of the country. "Postering is tough, and dozens of people were mostly going up and down ladders after work, for hours on end. They never looked for thanks or recognition. You'd have whole families like the Buckleys in Athlone or the Walshes in Waterford doing it. And people like Ron Rossiter and James Hogan, who led teams in postering, canvassing, the whole lot. It meant that we were out first with our key messages, long before the Yes side. Our posters were everywhere, and that meant the message was being seen," Scott Schittl observed. "I remember at one of the Save the 8th rallies a speaker addressed the 'Lads for Choice' group and said that lads pushed women towards abortion—but real men protected women and stood up for life and for the weak and the vulnerable. There were a lot of great men on the campaign, they gave it their all."

The volunteer coordinators working on the Save the 8th plan, Becky Kealy and Siobhán Rooney, found that they had a full-time job dealing with the steady stream of people signing up to volunteer. It was about matching skills with needs and providing training to those new to the campaign. They also started planning a major Save the 8th Roadshow.

For media, the campaign brought on John McGuirk as Communications Director. He would become a high-profile face of the Save the 8th campaign. McGuirk had taken a more circuitous route into the pro-life movement than many of the rank and file activists. He'd always been political, but had considered himself a broad-spectrum conservative who happened to be pro-life, rather than someone animated primarily by the issue. In fact, for a period in his early teens he'd regarded the abortion issue as an irritating distraction that was holding conservatives back in other key areas. As is often the case, that changed when he confronted the issue personally.

"In my late teens, a couple of both personal experiences and people very close to me having experiences with this issue shifted my view completely," he recalled. "I was familiar with one young lady who I knew in college who was pregnant, and I wouldn't say happily so, but had decided to keep the child. Her parents told her that if she kept the child she would be cut off, and I saw what that did to her. It fatally shattered in my mind the illusion of choice."

From that point on McGuirk was a committed pro-lifer, but his career was focused primarily on politics. He worked on the Lisbon Treaty campaign in 2008, on the same side of the question as Niamh, but with a competing campaign. As a result, the two ended up forming a great working relationship. "I've always been close to [Niamh] personally, I think she's a fantastic person," McGuirk told me. "I'm also somebody who tends to have a lot of sympathy for people who are vilified, and Niamh has always been for me a fascinating character because she has been so vilified over the years by the Irish press." That working relationship led to Niamh approaching McGuirk in 2017, when he was working for a telecommunications company, and asking him to assist the pro-life movement in the upcoming referendum. "John is very sharp, he's got a brilliant ability to articulate the most pertinent point at the right time," Niamh explained. "He's also extremely productive and fast, two attributes essential to a campaign where everything moves so quickly."

"I got brought in more through friendship with Niamh than anything else," McGuirk recalled. "I would have been an outspoken advocate of No anyhow, but that's how I formally got involved. Niamh and the people around her in that organisation are probably the most phenomenal organisers I have ever seen. Their ability to activate the grassroots, to organize huge events—the Rally for Life, for example, as a production…is the most professional political event of that nature ever produced in Ireland. I always say that if Niamh was working in the private sector, she could be making, if not millions, then certainly hundreds of thousands annually as an organizer. And she has an incredible team."

McGuirk, on the other hand, didn't see himself as an organizer—his skillset lay in crafting political messaging. "That's why I was brought in, to try and shape, in conjunction with the opinion polling team and Niamh and her creative team, the messages and the matching priorities, and the communications strategy," he said. "When I walked in, I found a team that was incredibly ready and organised for a fight, but we had to deal with how the country had moved on the hard cases."

To help with that assessment, Save the 8th had brought on board Gary Kavanagh as Director of Strategic Research, a man "with the smarts to verify and identify the strategic implications of the tactics and messages the campaign was rolling out." Kavanagh was always pro-life, but got involved "largely because I think society needs to debate issues and that a situation in which every major media organisation, the union for journalists, and every major political party agrees on something is not healthy."

That support for repeal across establishment Ireland was something the government was relying on. Some campaigners thought Health Minister Simon Harris might have overplayed his hand in proposing abortion without restriction to twelve weeks, but the stage had been carefully set.

"The Citizens Assembly in 2017 had recommended that the Eighth be repealed and that abortion without restriction for the first 12 weeks of pregnancy be legalised and that abortion be legalised beyond that point under various circumstances. This seemed totally at odds with the opinion polls from that time, which showed that only about a quarter of people supported that view," Niamh recalled. "In fact, at the end of 2017, just months before the referendum was called, even the *Irish Times* was acknowledging that support for abortion was 'cautious and conditional.' One poll they commissioned in late 2016 found that only 19% of voters supported the British model of abortion-on-demand, which was eventually what was on offer in the referendum. The government and the media—who were the real choreographers of the repeal campaign—needed to tackle that. So the Oireachtas Committee [Parliamentary Committee] held consultations that went on for months and acted like an ongoing daily press conference for abortion. It was very cleverly planned and choreographed. They set the narrative, set the stage, they brought along one pro-abortion witness after another to insist the Eighth had to go or that women would die from taking illegal abortion pills, that there was no other way to provide for the 'hard cases.' It was relentless, it was effective, and it worked."

The Oireachtas Committee, in fact, had been described by two of its own members, Mattie McGrath and Rónán Mullen, as a "charade" which had lost all credibility. At least two medical experts, Professor Patricia Casey and Dr. Martin McCaffrey, declined to participate because the proceedings were so slanted, with Dr. McCaffrey describing the hearings as a "kangaroo court." Niamh agreed. "The whole charade used everything at the disposal of government and media to soften up voters before the referendum. At times it felt like we were fist-fighting a hurricane. Every day, there was a huge media splash about how the Eighth needed to be repealed and a one-line response included from pro-lifers." As expected, the Committee recommended that the Eighth be repealed and abortion legalised on demand to 12 weeks, and without limit in other circumstances.

The barrage had the desired effect. A January 2018 poll, also for the *Irish Times*, showed a complete reversal of the previous position voters had held, with people now supporting the proposal to repeal the Eighth even with the consequence of abortion on demand up to 12 weeks being made available. The government had succeeded in making it a binary choice: Either repeal the Eighth whatever the consequences – or be responsible for endangering women's lives. It didn't matter that it wasn't true, only that it could be spun. The concept that women would die from taking illegal abortion pills was pushed as a particularly strong point in favour of repealing the Eighth. Taoiseach Leo Varadkar spelled it out for voters, claiming that it was only a matter of time before someone died after taking an abortion pill at home unsupervised. "Let's not wait for this to happen. If there is a No vote on Friday, I think it's only a matter of time before someone haemorrhages or bleeds to death after taking one of these pills unregulated," he told RTE's Seán O'Rourke a week before the vote.[cxliii]

Simon Harris, Leo Varadkar, and other senior politicians assured voters that the proposals would be restrictive, flatly denying what was actually in the draft legislation. "The law that the Government is now proposing is anything but unrestricted access to abortion," the Táiniste [VP] Simon Coveney, one of many who had undergone a 'journey' to supporting abortion, told the media.[cxliv]

McGuirk knew pro-lifers could not move to the centre and abandon a single baby to abortion, but that the populace was increasingly sympathetic to the relentless messaging about Savita and the "hard cases." The campaign couldn't pivot to address the concerns of the public on those issues because they couldn't concede that abortion was ever a moral response to a crisis pregnancy, and thus they found themselves pinned down. Politics were restrained by morality, and there was an innate tension between the "undecideds" who would determine the referendum result and the pro-lifers who had never been undecided voters in their lives.

As David Quinn of the Iona Institute put it: "Middle Ireland were homeless. One side wanted total repeal. The other side wanted total rejection. Campaign groups do not attract middle-of-the-road people, they attract people who are totally pro-choice or totally pro-life."[cxlv]

Campaigns are launched to reach the undecided voter, McGuirk noted, but most pro-lifers have never been one. Campaigns are thus not designed to reach the activists and the "true believers," which, according to McGuirk, can at times lead to tension if the base feels the campaign is tilting too far in one direction or another to attract undecided voters. The focus groups and polling carried out for Save the 8th showed that voters were most convinced by messages on key issues like rising abortion rates, disability, and late-term abortion, highlighting the fact that the proposed legislation went far beyond what the Irish public approved of. The Yes side attempted to distract from the actual legislation being proposed by focusing on hard cases and compelling stories, and the No side attempted to reduce the amount of discussion on hard cases by pointing back to the liberality of the proposed abortion regime.

"Once the opposition knows you won't give an inch on hard cases, they want to make the whole debate about those cases," McGuirk said. "Because of that strategic knot [we found ourselves in], the biggest challenge from the beginning was to try and direct the conversation to what was in the proposed legislation, which was a huge challenge because we had a media that was determined to keep the focus on the hard cases."

***

The media's intent to focus the entire discussion on a handful of hard cases became clear right from the very beginning. On March 29, 2018, Save the 8th, a campaign made up of Life Institute, Youth Defence, and 140 local groups (and cooperating and coordinating with many others), launched at the Gresham Hotel in Dublin.

"Before any launch, there is an air of expectancy," Niamh remembered. *"How is it going to look? How is it all going to go down?* Tension and expectations are building. Everything is fast-paced, you're making a lot of decisions, trying not to let the stress take over. The launch day was amazing: a big hotel room, lots of media there, lots of families, lots of young people. There was almost a giddy air in the room." Relief began to shove tension aside. Finally, things could start. Finally, the real battle could begin. Anything was better than more waiting and preparing.

"We had eight young women come up and give their reasons for wanting to retain the Eighth," Niamh recalled. "Eight reasons to save the Eighth: young women, women who had a crisis pregnancy, someone who *was* a crisis pregnancy, people new to the country, immigrants who were saying that *this is what we love about Ireland, you should keep this in Ireland because it makes it special,* nurses. It was one of those days where we just laid out the reasons why the Eighth was so important. The room was full of colour and energy. There were lots of babies and little kids running around, t-shirts and balloons. I think it was a really vibrant, successful launch. You could feel the energy, people were signing up for posters, to do canvassing—they were ready to go. The waiting to find out what the rules of engagement were had been torture, and despite the stakes, there was relief in being able to hit the ground running and feel your muscles burn. There was even optimism."

The podium was backed by an enormous poster of a baby in the womb and the words "Vote NO to abortion on demand."

McGuirk managed the event. After the presentations in which the key messages were rolled out, the floor was open to press questions. "One question was directed to me from an *Irish Times* journalist, [who] didn't even seem to have listened to what was being said, as the first and only question was: *'John, does Save the 8th oppose abortion in the case of rape?'*" McGuirk recalled. The following day, the headline in the *Irish Times* was "Victims of rape and incest should carry babies to full term, say campaigners." Political reporter Sarah Bardon's very first line told readers exactly what they were supposed to take away from the campaign launch: "Women who are the victim of rape and incest should carry the baby to full term, according to the Save the 8th campaign."[cxlvi]

Bardon lingered on that subject for seven paragraphs before finally noting Dr. John Monaghan's testimony that despite delivering between 4,000 and 5,000 babies, the Eighth Amendment had never hampered his ability to protect a woman's life, Dr. Eimear Thornton's statement that abortion results in "a new life snuffed out," and the fact that 320,000 houses had already been canvassed with a goal of another 300,000 over the coming months.[cxlvii] It would be a trend for the entire campaign, McGuirk noted. Journalists would show up at press events about key issues for the No campaign, "and then write their stories about rape anyway." After the referendum, Bardon left the *Irish Times* to take up a role as press adviser to Health Minister Simon Harris, the key government figure campaigning for a Yes vote in the referendum.

Despite the flimsy pretense of objectivity, the media barely disguised its contempt for pro-life groups. "I remember being at a press conference, held by the Iona Institute, and three female journalists walked into the room, armed for battle," McGuirk said. "Lise Hand, Ellen Coyne, and I forget the third. And they literally sat at that press conference and they didn't listen to a word that the Iona Institute said, and peppered them with hostile questions, took over the press conference, walked out of the room, and as they were walking out of the room, they didn't see me standing there at the back. They walked past me and said, 'We got them good.' These are not opinion columnists. These were not young journalists fresh out of college. These were women in their thirties and forties."

Almost immediately after the launch, it became clear that the media intended to box the pro-life movement into a no-win situation. When the Together for Yes campaign rolled out messaging, their desired narrative was faithfully reported.[34][35] When groups fighting for a No vote presented theirs, the reporter's questions were carefully set up so that there "was no way to get a tactical messaging success." The media knew, McGuirk noted, that they could paint the pro-lifers in a bad light regardless of how they answered questions on issues like sexual assault: "Even if we had conceded on the point, which we wouldn't have, the next day's *Irish Times* headline would have been 'Abortion necessary in case of rape, says No campaigners.' So we would have lost either way."

This meant that right out of the gate, Save the 8th had to try and battle the press as a major part of their strategy, which is difficult to do in Ireland. There are just two national TV stations – with RTÉ, the taxpayer-funded platform, being by far the largest and most important in terms of reach. By McGuirk's estimates, the daily national news programme on RTÉ, regardless of what it was airing, would receive between 700,000 and 800,000 viewers: "The Irish media has a massive chunk of the audience locked up, and it's almost impossible to bypass them to get to those people."

But still, Save the 8th had to try. It became increasingly frustrating. "One vitally important press conference was called by pro-life nurses—150 of them representing many more—and RTÉ News came and recorded a lengthy segment which the senior reporter was really happy with. Then the item was just dropped. We were eventually told that the powers-that-be at RTÉ decided not to air it because the Yes side didn't have an equivalent

34 Love Both, the other major campaign working to retain the Eighth Amendment, was derived from the Pro-Life Campaign.

35 The Together for Yes campaign, led by three co-directors, was an amalgamation of three organisations: the Coalition to Repeal the Eighth Amendment, the National Women's Council, and the Abortion Rights Campaign.

they could report on that day. It was unbelievable. That kind of thing kept happening. Maybe we shouldn't have been surprised, but it was still shocking," said Niamh Uí Bhriain. "We went to a meeting at the beginning of the campaign with the Director of News and other senior executives in RTÉ, and it was very obvious from that meeting that it wasn't going to be a fair or equal hearing. We were told they were going to focus on personal stories, when that was exactly what the Yes campaign had sought. As Maria Steen [of Iona Institute] said at the time, the baby can't tell *her* personal story."

But the campaign had many other fronts. Town halls, dubbed monster meetings by the media, were attracting thousands across the country, an initiative spear-headed by Mayo man Adrian O'Boyle along with Paddy Manning and Michael Dwyer. Other meetings were used to pressure politicians and build campaign teams. In Sligo/Leitrim, savvy local leaders from Leitrim for Life and Fionnuala Woods from Sligo had crowds queuing in the corridor to get into their packed-out event. An overflowing meeting in Kerry featured a panel of medical and legal experts. A new political party, Renua, held information events and urged people to get involved. Local newspapers and radio outlets were targeted by media-trained campaign activists. In Donegal, a specially produced video was being released.

Meanwhile, a massive social media operation was underway. Save the 8th had designated a considerable proportion of the campaign's budget for social media spending. "Good content gets additional traction on any platform, but no-one is blind to how algorithms on platforms like Facebook have changed. You mostly have to pay to be seen, especially by undecided voters, in the crowded space of a busy campaign with messages flying out from all sides," said Úna.

Market research and early testing had identified voter attributes and segments and indicated what messages could move the dial for each segment. This was then married on an ongoing basis with feedback from the canvass and from responses on social media, and this helped to tweak messages or flex the messenger. As the campaign intensified however, Save the 8th would hit a roadblock that no-one expected from the Big Tech companies dominating control of social media platforms keeping millions of voters looking at screens every day.

A studio had been set up on the top floor of campaign headquarters, and a crack creative team, including designers, videographers, artists and copywriters were assembled. Rebecca Roughneen said the campaign exceeded all its expectations in terms of quantity and quality of output. Peter Jones and Emmett Glynn were shooting and editing, and the team were producing new content and videos daily.

As Rebecca recalled: "We were working with everyone who had something arresting and important to say. The studio was insanely busy, people coming up and down the stairs all day, or jumping in the car to go shoot a message or film and event. We had families come in from Disability Voices for Life, that was just powerful and a lot of fun, and Patricia who shared her abortion regret story, and Maureen Ward from Travellers Against Abortion who was brilliant. Some pieces went viral straight away, such as a nurse, Caren, sharing how she saw a baby in Australia survive an abortion. Katie Duffy, who was always brilliant at rallies over the years, and Fatima Gunning did some really popular explainer videos. In campaigns we'd always say 'content is king,' and we could see the organic traction was really strong for a lot of the messages. We were testing, too, and we knew what we needed to focus on for the last week or ten days, when people usually make up their minds. A lot of people had such powerful stories to share, and expert voices, pro-life doctors and nurses, were really important. It was all about getting people to see the messages, share the information." Over the course of the campaign some 250 videos were posted and viewed millions of times by voters.

The referendum campaign plan was based on driving key messages to voter segments identified by research, and for each message a series of events and platforms were engaged, including posters, billboards, social media messaging, canvass drives, publicity events, and more. Leaflet and poster designs were tested and revisited. Massive drop-down banners large enough to cover the front of a four-story building were planned. Car stickers and wrap-arounds were ordered, badges were produced, stickers were ordered. The office was literally a whirr of colour and noise and endless effort. "Once you hit the ground running, you eat, sleep, and breathe the campaign," Íde O'Hara remembered. "There's a checklist for the activities every day and planning and execution on a rolling basis. Things begin to blur together. *Is the messaging making an impact? Should we change it? Are we missing anything?*"

It was McGuirk's job to persuade the team to change messaging when he thought it was needed, based on the polling data informing them where the public was at. "You start off with a detailed plan," he recalled. "You have your messaging planned for each week, with those messages subject to shifts as opinion polls come in letting you know how your messaging is being received. Often what you're talking about in the final week is not at all what you were planning to be talking about at the beginning."

McGuirk was a bridge between pro-life activists and the media, attempting to ensure that the narrative most appealing to the "undecideds" was getting out. That job also involved telling pro-lifers to pipe down when necessary, especially in instances where unhelpful altercations erupted between profane abortion activists and pro-life campaigners. In one instance in County Wexford, McGuirk recalled, an older lady out canvassing was told by a young woman that she'd be voting to legalise abortion because if she went on a date, she'd like to be able to hop in the sack without being afraid of getting pregnant instead of just giving oral sex all the time—only, she said it much more crudely than that. The horrified canvasser addressed the situation by flinging holy salt on her and dressing her down before scurrying off. This, McGuirk noted wryly, was the sort of thing sure to end up in the newspaper.

In addition to the Save the 8th media team, senior medical professionals such as Dr. Eamon McGuinness, Dr. John Monaghan, and Dr. Trevor Hayes were arguing the pro-life case, as was professor of psychiatry Patricia Casey and doctors such as Deirdre Gleeson, Brendan Crowley, Niall Maguire, and Andrew O'Regan, among hundreds of others. Representing similar numbers of midwives and nurses were senior healthcare professionals such as Anne Flynn, Paula Berry, Marie Donnolly, and Mary Fitzgibbon who emerged as key voices in the referendum. Pro-life TDs most frequently heard included Peadar Tóibín, Carol Nolan, and Mattie McGrath. Hours of media prepping were ongoing in the office.

When pro-lifers won a debate—which was most of the time—it gave the team a jolt of energy and optimism. Barrister Ben Ó Floinn led Lawyers for Life, which included several prominent retired judges. Legal experts like Geoffrey Sumner, Alan Davern, Cora Sherlock, and Wendy Grace of Pro-Life Campaign were also prominent voices, while Maria Steen, a barrister with the Iona

Institute, was a lethal debater on the pro-life side. As a result, the press began to sideline her as the referendum drew closer. During the final weeks, RTÉ actually reformatted an entire debate rather than have Steen on to represent the pro-life position again. Each debate would be watched with bated breath, and if it went well, everyone would hope that the public had tuned in. Then it was on to the next thing.

***

For the ground game, the Save the 8th campaign was bolstered by the skills of 28-year-old Tim Jackson. As a student in college, Tim went to a Youth Defence conference at the invitation of a friend, "not because I had any strong convictions." At the conference, he saw photographs of aborted babies for the first time. "There was a number of images shown," he recalled, "but there was one where the baby might be around ten weeks, and his body is stretched and torn. He is missing his head, as well. He was just a body." Before seeing the photo, Tim had felt that his friend had perhaps been "a bit over the top" about the pro-life issue. Now, all that had changed: "I needed to see that picture to understand." A seminarian at the time, he began joining a friend outside a referral clinic for sidewalk counseling on the occasional Saturday, where pro-lifers would have just a few seconds to offer people information before they would vanish inside and begin planning their abortions.

It was last-minute ministry, and the urgency was palpable: Tim remembers people turning away just before entering the clinic and crossing the street after seeing their pamphlets, and wondering if a baby had just been saved. After he left college in 2011, he worked at the Life House, which housed both Youth Defence and Life Institute. He worked there for a few years, organising people to take part in street sessions, leafleting drops, postering campaigns, campus demonstrations, and rallies: "Bread and butter stuff. Trying to get people out in the streets and as visible as possible, engaging with the public as much as we could." In addition to all of that, the political attempts to legalise abortion in at least some circumstances were nearly relentless, and pro-lifers worked nonstop to block them.

In September of 2017, as the Oireachtas committee's examination of the Eighth Amendment began and the intentions of Varadkar and Harris became clear, Tim launched a hunger strike after sending a letter to Varadkar and the chairwoman of the committee Senator Catherine Noone, asking that they watch a video illustrating how the abortion procedure is carried out before they proceeded to discuss a referendum on the Eighth. The politicians ignored the letter, and Tim (with long-time pro-life campaigner Kathy Sinnott later joining) vowed to drink only water until the committee changed their minds. After ten days, during which Tim stood outside the Dail, dressed in a suit and holding a white flag in one hand and a sign depicting a pre-born baby clutching a tiny white flag and the slogan "Stop the Killing" in the other, he was forced to cede defeat.

"It was really because I felt helpless at the time," he replied when asked why he did it. "The politicians showed no inclination to watch what they were attempting to legalise. The Orwellian media was really trying to sanitise the whole issue. It was a way, I felt, to help some of them realise the severity of what was being proposed. The specific request was to have them watch a video of an abortion at the committee meeting, and then I would end the hunger strike. They refused. It got to the point where I really couldn't continue much longer."

When Save the 8th asked him to work full-time on the referendum campaign for the final three months and run the Vote No Roadshow, Tim agreed, and promptly quit his job in marketing. He started recruiting immediately, reaching out to people he knew from prayer meetings, youth groups, and pilgrimages. Ireland being such a small place, Tim knew a lot of people, and he had a lot of practice recruiting and fielding a team. People began signing up to get on board—even those who had never done any activism before. Twenty-seven-year-old Shauna Flynn, a schoolteacher who had taken a career break to go traveling in South America and Australia, was not a confrontational person, but she'd been seeing articles and heated arguments about abortion on online forums daily, watching the debate unfold from thousands of miles away.

"As the referendum was impending, I could see many of my friends and acquaintances sharing their reasons for being pro-life for all their Facebook and Instagram followers," Shauna remembered. "In many WhatsApp groups I was a part of, people were organising canvassing and leafleting every evening. I could see my friends becoming more passionately pro-life as the weeks went on. On the flipside I could see many of my Facebook friends, colleagues, and family members sharing their reasons for being pro-choice and encouraging others to have more empathy for women. I read countless articles spun by the Irish media that painted pro-life people as religious bigots that were suppressing women. The lies began to frustrate me, and even though I was so far from home my conscience was telling me I needed to step up and get involved."

When Shauna returned from Australia six weeks before the referendum, she signed up to canvass her local area. Before she could even start, Tim messaged her, asking her if she would join the Vote No Roadshow for a month. "It would involve staying in hostels and relying on the generosity of other pro-life individuals and groups. Initially, I told Tim I would have to think about it. I didn't like the idea of discomfort. I was willing to canvass and help out, but just not that much! I messaged Tim back a day later and told him I'd join the Roadshow. The reason? My faith. I knew deep in my heart that God wanted me to do this and once I decided to do so I felt an overwhelming sense of peace. So with that, I packed my suitcase and joined the team in Donegal for the next four weeks."

The Vote No Roadshow launched on April 23 from Donegal (where many of the volunteers and Tim himself hailed from), embarking on an enormous red bus with the Save the 8th slogan emblazoned across the side in all capital letters: *SAVE LIVES. VOTE NO TO ABORTION,* which was also plastered across the windows in white letters. Following in convoy was a hodgepodge of other vehicles driven by volunteers who came and went over the course of the tour, as well as a flatbed truck sporting a huge billboard featuring the face of a stunned wide-eyed infant and the words, "I had no idea…They want to legalise abortion up to 6 months. Vote NO." Loudspeakers mounted atop the billboard played tunes subliminally suggestive of the pro-life movement's perspective, such as "All You Need Is Love" by *The Beatles*. The goal was to hit over 100 towns and every single county over 23 days, covering Sligo/Leitrim, Roscommon, May, Galway, Kerry, and Cork in the first week alone.

The Save the 8th campaign believed that in order to win, they would have to maximize voter turnout in the towns and rural areas in order to offset what they presumed would be an overwhelmingly pro-choice vote in cities like Dublin. With the media campaigning nonstop to persuade the public that voting Yes was the only sane thing to do, the strategy of the Vote No Roadshow was to encourage the many No voters in the countryside who might have been convinced by the media that the entire country was pro-abortion and to prove to them that they were not alone by being a prominent presence in their towns. At each stop, the roughly two dozen volunteers piled off the bus to wave red *Vote No* flags, wield red *Vote No* banners, and distribute constantly replenished stacks of red literature booklets with titles like "The Abortion Referendum: The More You Know About It, the More You'll Vote NO." The Roadshow team, like the canvassers in Dublin and around the country, wore red hoodies with *VOTE NO* written across the back and *Speak Up For Those Who Can't* across the front. Precious Life, the leading pro-life group in Northern Ireland, sent a crew led by director Bernie Smyth to help, saying that the issue knew no borders.

Even the media couldn't help but notice: It seemed there were pro-lifers in red everywhere you looked. Abortion activists took to calling the omnipresent pro-lifers "the Red Army," and Tim's team crisscrossed the country from Clare to Limerick, from Limerick to Tipperary, from Waterford to Wexford, and then on to Wicklow, Kildare, and Kilkenny. Surprisingly, it seemed as if many people had not yet made up their minds, and conversations erupted wherever the Vote No Roadshow went.

"I had to quickly forget about my dislike of confrontation and arguments," Shauna said. "I had to learn to have open and heated dialogue with people who were pro-choice, despite how uncomfortable I felt at first. I learned so much from the people on the roadshow who could tell me real facts, figures, and statistics. I also spoke to doctors, nurses, and psychologists on the streets that were committed to protecting the lives of the unborn. With all this new information and a lot of practice, I soon became confident in having discussions with the general public and encouraging them to vote no to abortion." Roadshows were trial by fire: People signed up, and promptly found themselves thrust into the middle of Ireland's most contentious and longstanding political debate.

We joined the Vote No Roadshow in Ashbourne, County Meath on May 14; my wife Charmaine, our blue-eyed baby Charlotte, my colleagues Nick and Maaike Rosendal, and myself. Volunteers were fanned out across the town handing out leaflets, while others flapped flags at traffic and erupted in wild cheers whenever they received honks or a thumbs up thrust out a window in response. The billboard truck, playing relentlessly cheery tunes, gave activism a mildly carnivalesque atmosphere, and the Irish pro-lifers greeted us with back thumps and huge smiles ("Fair play t'ya!"). The thing that always strikes me about the pro-life movement around the world is that people are always so happy and kind, despite the personal abuse they often face. I got put to work hoisting one end of a large banner, and the young woman on the other end told me that she was using her university break to volunteer. She was from Northern Ireland, and was frustrated that they couldn't vote in the referendum as she suspected the conservative Protestants in the North could swing the referendum to the pro-life side.

After barely an hour, we were back on the bus and loading up the other vehicles to head to Trim, a little town of 9,000 on the River Boyne (most famous for Trim Castle, the largest Cambro-Norman fortress in the country,) and after a short stay were on the road again, heading to Navan, and then on to Cavan. If there weren't many pedestrians to talk to, Tim ensured that the residents had gotten a good gawk at the sign-wielding pro-lifers swarming past their homes and businesses and, that accomplished, led us on to the next stop. The strategy of the Roadshow made an impact—many people came up to us to thank us for coming specifically to *their* town, while many others took leaflets and appeared to be thoughtfully reading them. A few people marched past looking stiff-lipped and angry, but I was surprised at how little vitriol was directed at us, especially compared to how angrily North Americans often respond. That would change once the teams arrived in Dublin.

In Cavan, the media showed up. Siobhán Rooney, one of the organisers, told me that the foreign press had been following the pro-life efforts nonstop—someone from the *Daily Telegraph* had already stopped by in the morning. A journalist from the *Wall Street Journal* asked to take a group photograph of the caravanners in front of the bus, and she smiled rather thinly as the pro-lifers erupted into enthusiastic chants of *Save the Eighth! Save the Eighth! Save the Eighth!* I wondered, as she surveyed the groups clustered around the bus with a faintly sour expression on her face, what she thought of the packed bus full of young people and the local families who had joined them—one mother even had a beautiful little two-week-old baby trapped to her chest, and nine-month-old Charlotte found the presence of a human smaller than herself extremely fascinating.

At around 7 PM, we boarded the bus to head back to a large retreat centre filled with bedrooms and bunkbeds for the night. En route, an unfortunate few fell asleep—much to the delight of the others, who spent a good portion of the drive taking closeup photos of gaping mouths and flaring nostrils and gleefully sending them to the Vote No Roadshow WhatsApp group. Upon arrival, everyone decamped to toss their bags into the bunkrooms, claim their beds, and get supper ready. By the time everyone had eaten—around 10:30 PM—people had either hit their second wind or were running the very real risk of passing out on their dinner plates. Another abortion debate was airing on RTÉ, and someone got it streaming on a cellphone in the common room. Tim headed outside, announcing that he couldn't bear to watch another of the debates—it wound him up too much.

A cluster of campaigners hunched around the screen to watch one of four major televised referendum debates on *The Clare Byrne Show*. When Dr. John Monaghan, a pro-life OBGYN, informed prominent abortion campaigner Dr. Peter Boylan that if he didn't know that a baby was fully developed at twelve weeks that "maybe you need to go back to school," the room erupted into cheers, fist pumps, and howls of laughter. "He got schooled!" a tattooed ginger named Andy declared. "Smashed!" another agreed from across the room. Within minutes, a GIF had been posted on Facebook of Dr. Monaghan's comment, with the good doctor adorned with an unlikely cigar and shades to the strains of "thug life." The debate seemed a comprehensive win for the No side, with Boylan, who was usually handled with kid gloves by the media, clearly thrown by the robust exchange. The mood was jovial as everyone drifted off to bed.

The pro-life win was short-lived. Abortion campaigners complained bitterly to the RTÉ about the open format of the debate, which according to government spokeswoman Catherine Noone "did not serve the public." RTÉ dutifully changed the format of the rest of the debates.

Despite that, the cheeriness carried into the following day, with the campaigners discussing the debate on the bus as it swung out of the retreat centre parking lot to hit the road. Their optimism was buoyed by the fact that abortion-supporting media personalities were already declaring the debate to have been "unhelpful," by which of course they meant specifically unhelpful to their cause. Especially egregious, in the opinion of several talking heads, was a question a woman in the audience had posed to Boylan, asking what he proposed to do with the bodies of the babies after they'd been aborted. The moderator rushed to inform Boylan that he didn't have to answer such an appalling question, but the final query of the debate had also struck home, perhaps more so because it was left unanswered: *Why, around the entire country, does the word "abortion" not appear on a single Yes campaign sign?* The answer, it appeared, was too obvious to be helpful to the Yes campaigners, and one bearded fellow at our first stop in Delvin told us that the debate had encouraged him: "Swung a lot of people our way, I think." (Incidentally, in the last RTÉ debate, Katie Ascough, of Love Both, spoke from the audience, encouraging people to actually watch what an abortion did to a baby before they voted).

The Vote No crew was a diverse bunch. There was 39-year-old Andy from Blanchardstown, who had broken his back the previous year and was pouring his heart out on the streets for the No campaign. "Even if I could work, I'd quit to do this," he told me with a laugh as we waved our signs at traffic. "This is *real* work." Abortion had impacted his life in two profound ways. His mother had been raped and had an abortion forced on her. "In many ways I lost my mum as she never got over the loss of that baby," he said. He'd also lost a child of his own ten years ago, when the mother of his child "didn't want to keep the baby. As much as I pleaded with her, she went ahead with the abortion. That left me in a bad way and I moved out of Dublin and started to work with pro-life people—that helped me overcome the pain of the loss. So it's always been very personal because I don't want others to go through the pain that I go through."

There was the cheery Séimhín from Carrickmore, a blond, chipper girl who seemed to have endless supplies of energy. There was Lisa, a quiet brunette schoolteacher from Carrickmacross; William, a young pianist from Belfast; Glenn, a relentlessly optimistic fellow from Donegal; Anthony, the endlessly patient bus driver; and Candice, the youngest teenager on the crew (Charlotte promptly fell in love with her.) There was the O'Callaghan sisters, Riaghan and Enya, from Donegal, who looked so different from each other (one with auburn hair, the other black) that I was shocked when I discovered they were from the same family, and Shauna Flynn, who turned out to be their cousin. Along with nearly twenty others from across the country, they had become something like a family in the weeks they had already spent on the road, and it showed. William, who had been sporting an impressive mop of hair he'd taken much ribbing for, received rousing cheers when he climbed back on the bus with a close-cropped haircut after one stop. He turned the cheers to applause when he announced with a grin: "And I got the barber *votin' No!*"

We started the day in the village of Delvin, which like almost every other hamlet in Ireland, features its own castle, a Norman fortress originating from 1172. St. Patrick apparently came this way long ago, preaching Christianity to the pagans. Today, swarms of volunteers headed down the narrow streets, stopping to talk to the few townspeople who were out and about and encouraging them to vote to save the Eighth. Most nodded and told us that was their plan. It was a good start to the day.

From Delvin we headed to Mullingar, where dozens of locals including James Maher were already out canvassing in red "Vote No" vests and wielding huge stacks of information brochures. The entire town had been carpeted from front to back with pro-life signs, and Ray, a local man, told me that after he'd sold the family business he was part owner of—a car dealership—he'd decided to dedicate nine months of his life to turning the local counties of Longford and Westmeath out for the No campaign. They'd been canvassing door to door for months, and were encouraged by the reactions they'd received. The hundreds of signs were Ray's idea. "My aim five weeks ago when the poster campaign started was to dominate the skyline of our major towns," he told me, "and to keep layering on new eye-catching visuals and messaging in phases to give the floating voters a unique reason to Vote No on May 25." It had certainly worked: Looking down the streets in any direction, the word *NO* stood out as far as the eye could see.

There were a few Americans helping out amongst the sea of Irish volunteers, as well—and most of them were familiar faces. I'd met Mary Rose Short in 2014 at the International Pro-Life Youth Conference in California (where I'd also met several members of Youth Defence). I'd met Dave Sao, a hilarious fellow from Philadelphia, on a variety of pro-life missions across the United States. Kate Bryan, an Irish-American who had gone to university in Ireland and worked with Youth Defence, was helping out in Dublin with Public Relations—I'd first met her at a Live Action rally outside an abortion clinic in Washington, D.C. after attending Kermit Gosnell's trial in Philadelphia back in 2013.

It was the North American pro-lifers, Enya said later, that reminded her of just how urgent it all was: "Every moment, every second was so precious." After all, they knew what it was like to live in countries where the corpses of children cooled in dumpsters behind clinics dedicated to the destruction of the smallest lives.

Enya had just finished college when the referendum was announced, and she knew that she needed to get involved—she just didn't know how. Her brother, Donagh, had worked in the pro-life movement for a few years (we would meet him the following week in Dublin, moving about the Life House at an almost frenetic pace, sending out teams with boxes of leaflets to deliver across the city), and her sister Riaghan had volunteered for the Pro-Life Campaign in the past, doing calls. Then Tim messaged her to ask if she'd join the Roadshow, and she knew that this was the opportunity she'd been praying for. She had been nervous about debating abortion on the streets, but the impending referendum meant "You didn't have a choice." You couldn't wait for a couple of weeks or months before getting involved: "Either you do this now, or it's all going to be over and you're going to regret having never spoken up about it," she said. "It was a complete sense of urgency. Get out there now, because it is a warzone. You have to get out now and do your bit."

It was that sense of urgency that bonded the team: a collection of ordinary people from all walks of life, pushed together on a cross-country tour by historical circumstances outside of their control as the passions and bile of pro-lifers and abortion activists poured out onto Irish streets. The Vote No Roadshow was strange because in many ways, the volunteers wished it wasn't happening. They wished the thing that had brought them together didn't exist, and that the threat of abortion didn't loom over Ireland. But yet, they were also somehow *not* sorry that they had been brought together, and they found themselves loving it—the friendship, the camaraderie, that sense of doing something that was profoundly worth doing. It is why old warriors sometimes feel nostalgia for the battlefield: Because the friendships forged in the fires of battle are of such a strength that those who have not lived through such things cannot really understand. "My feeling on the bus, despite what was happening, was often joy," Riaghan recalled. "I remember going to bed at night, and I'd have Shauna and Mary Rose in the same room. We were having fun, and that sounds so odd because we weren't there to have fun. But we were joyful, because every experience affirmed that you were so lucky that you understood the value of life."

And that is how it was. After a long day of campaigning hard, the bus vibrated with laughter and ribbing and people telling stories. As the bus pulled into the countryside to head to where we were staying for the night, I turned to say something to Andy—and nearly everyone was fast asleep.

The camaraderie was a notable contrast to the abortion campaigners, who showed up in handfuls as the Vote No Roadshow moved through Ireland. They would set up a table with some pamphlets, or wave a few "Yes" Signs here and there. But largely, they seemed complacent, if not slightly apathetic. They would not engage with the pro-lifers, and didn't engage the public with too much enthusiasm, either. Perhaps they knew that the media was already doing the job for them, and that they simply needed to stay out the way and not screw it up. Only occasionally did they let their vitriol at the young pro-lifers fly. More often, they simply refused to engage.

In Tipperary, Riaghan recalled, they had a table set up "with loads of pro-choicers, and they were bored stupid. They had nothing to talk about. They could only whine and complain, whereas when we were talking to our people, there was so much concern and love. We *should* be angry. We believe that babies will get murdered—and we're not angry, we're not screaming, we're not shouting, we're not swearing, we're not flipping fingers—we're really happy. They're really angry. They're full of hatred. I was often affirmed over and over again that we were on the right side."

There were good stories, too. "Every day on the Roadshow I became more pro-life," Shauna recalled. "I spoke to one man who found out his child was aborted when he discovered an invoice for an abortion clinic that his wife had hidden in the back of the wardrobe. He suffered with depression. I met parents who had children with life-limiting conditions who described the joy their children gave them, despite the media's claims that they were 'incompatible with life.' I spoke with one woman who had septicaemia during pregnancy and had successfully given birth to a baby girl. She was disgusted by how the media was using Savita Halappanavar's death to push their pro-abortion agenda. All these stories from real people gave me hope that Ireland was more pro-life than the media portrayed."

The next few days were a whirlwind. In Longford, the Roadshow covered the entire town, joined by dozens of grateful locals who hosted an enormous luncheon in the basement of a cathedral to feed the hungry pro-lifers. Many of them had never been active before but were coming out for the final push. In County Monaghan, led by the two Pats (local heroes Pat Greenan and Pat Garvey), we went door to door to deliver Vote No pamphlets in addition to having teams spread out across the city. In Dundalk on Friday the 18th, we passed out hundreds of pieces of literature with the Louth Save the 8th crew, led by Martin McGuill. That evening, we stayed at a gorgeous retreat center just across the border in Northern Ireland, and everyone sat around tables in the dining hall, decompressing after a long week. Tim told us about one of the Roadshow highlights, where Wexford pro-lifers arranged a big convoy of cars to accompany the Save the 8th bus, the O'Donoghue families and many more, in a cavalcade of colour and pro-life flags. The next day, everyone would head down to Dublin for the home stretch.

***

After attending a Presbyterian church in Northern Ireland over the weekend, where an entire day of congregational prayer was announced for the upcoming referendum in the South, we headed back to Dublin to join the campaign team. Everyone was moving at a frantic pace.

One of the bizarre features of the campaign was the slow-moving nature of the formal pro-repeal organisation, Together for Yes, who had launched in March and then seemed to stall. They had already been berated by several mainstream newspapers, including the *Irish Times* and the *Sunday Business Post* for letting the No side get so far ahead of the game. When their posters finally went up, they were clearly based on what had worked in the referendum for same-sex marriage – neutral colours, vague messages. At that point, according to John McGuirk, "their campaign had not fired up their base at all. *Our* campaign fired their base up. I think their posters were anodyne and poor, all about care and compassion. Our focus groups showed they did not relate to them, the tone was not serious enough, too happy and clappy."[cxlviii]

Together for Yes also believed they would marshal the troops for a ground campaign in the same way as had been done for same-sex marriage, but that never materialised. Yes canvasses were thin on the ground and had not always been getting the response they expected, with one sympathetic press report describing Yes canvassers as "shocked and disappointed" at negative reactions in Dublin Bay South, one of the most liberal constituencies in the country.[cxlix]

Niamh Uí Bhriain says these media reports were helpful but not always reassuring. "There were more than 3,000 people out on the pro-life Canvass at the end of the campaign—the Yes side never came anywhere close to that. But they didn't need to, because the media *were* their campaign. I wasn't surprised that pro-abortion canvassers often got the cold shoulder, because most people do not support their position. They see being 'pro-choice' as supporting abortion in all cases and they don't like that. But the media was much smarter than the abortion campaign. They knew that the Eighth meant a total ban on all abortions, and all they needed to do was to convince people of just one hard case for people to vote for repeal. That was the reality."

The polls were also starting to look encouraging. An IPSOS/MRBI poll at the end of 2017 had 62% supporting repeal of the Eighth, the equivalent of a Yes vote in the referendum. That began to slide: by January 18th it was down to 56%, on April 18th it had slipped further to 47% and the following month, on May 18th, support for the referendum had fallen to 44%.

The government and the media took decisive action. The happy-clappy "pro-choice" campaign hadn't worked. Selling abortion as "compassion" or as a "choice" wasn't getting traction. In fact, the numbers seemed to show it was *losing* the Yes side votes. It was time to bring in the fear factor.

Medical professionals who favoured a Yes vote were given maximum coverage in the media, and their assertions that the Eighth prevented best medical care for pregnant women was given widespread and repeated attention in the last week of the campaign. In sharp contrast, pro-life doctors were sidelined by the media. When five of the former Chairs of the Institute of Obstetrics and Gynaecology issued a statement saying that they were "horrified" by the claims made by their colleagues about maternal care in Ireland in support of a Yes vote, they received scant media attention.

Dr. Michael O'Hare, then current chairman of the Irish health department's working group on maternal mortality, was joined by senior OBGYNs Professor John Bonnar, Dr. Eamon McGuinness, Dr. Conor Carr, and Dr. James Clinch in signing the statement which said comments made by Doctors Rhona Mahony and Peter Boylan were a "serious misrepresentation of the Irish maternal health system and must be withdrawn… Ireland is a very safe country in which to be pregnant. The Eighth Amendment does not prevent Irish women receiving care of the highest possible standard. This is why our maternal death rate is so low."

But the media, with the Yes vote sliding, didn't want to hear it. And the No campaign had been dealt a devastating, crippling blow. With time running out and media platforms increasingly closing access to pro-life messages, and especially pro-life medical professionals, Google gave the Yes campaign what they had been looking for: in an unprecedented move, they shut down all advertising related to the referendum.

It was, the *Irish Times* acknowledged, "a significant blow to the [No] campaign. Since last year its strategists had planned a wave of late online advertising targeting undecided and soft Yes voters."

"If you wanted further evidence of whom the Google move favours, look no further than the reaction of Yes campaigners and supporters, who wholeheartedly welcomed and applauded the decision," wrote political correspondent Pat Leahy. "The reasons for the decision, however, remain a mystery. Google declined to supply any rationale, or to answer a series of detailed questions from The Irish Times."[cl]

Pro-life groups saw this as a blatant attempt to rig the election. "We're suddenly being told that we will no longer be allowed to speak to voters on our channels, and that is outrageous," John McGuirk said at a joint press conference.

A joint press statement from the pro-life groups said that "One side in this referendum is terrified of losing and wants to prevent voters from being informed. Online was the only platform available to the No campaign to speak to voters directly. That platform is now being undermined in order to prevent the public from hearing the message of one side." Niamh concurred: "The Yes side in this campaign have rushed out to welcome the ban because, of course, the Yes side doesn't need Google. They already have TheJournal.ie, TheIrishTimes.ie, RTE.ie…the list simply goes on and on." She accused Google of reacting to the concerns of the political and media establishment that support for Yes was sliding.

During the final days of the campaign, John McGuirk scarcely had time to collect his thoughts. "At one point I went six hours on the phone, literally one call after another," he recalled. On one of the final days, he received 142 phone calls. Many of the media outlets wanted to do last-minute "inside the campaign" profiles, hoping to cash in on the last few days of Ireland's most polarizing political battle. As activists poured in and out of the Life House (the Save the 8th headquarters on Gardiner Place) to collect pamphlets for mailbox distribution, fetch signs and banners, or upload new footage to one of the seemingly dozens of social media accounts open on a handful of computers, McGuirk could be seen pacing back and forth in the tiny courtyard behind the building, his phone pressed tightly to his ear.

During the day, the street teams were out with banners, pamphlets, Vote No stickers, and buttons in key traffic areas, such as the main pedestrian thoroughfare beside the General Post Office, where tables set up by the dueling campaigns attracted crowds. The attitude in Dublin was markedly more hostile than in the rural towns and villages, and passersby frequently growled their disapproval at us as we attempted to pass out literature detailing the dangers of the proposed abortion legislation. Many people simply seemed fed up with the relentless campaigning, and occasionally tempers flared. The Yes campaign's numbers on the streets were also being bolstered by students for hire as college exams ended.

"I knew things were bad in Dublin when we [arrived from the Roadshow] and got the welcome," Riaghan said. "One of our friends who was helping out was just gray-looking. They were so excited to see us. Even though we'd been traveling across the country, we were the ones having a good time. We'd met lots of pro-life people. They'd been having more negative experiences."

It was during that final week of campaigning that the O'Callaghan sisters received tragic family news: Their mother, who had been fighting a brain tumor, was told that the tumor had returned. "We knew that it was a matter of a month or so," Enya remembered. "I remember getting the news and crying, being upset. Knowing that *wow, we only have a month*. But also knowing *I have to be here*. My Mom had a life, and she was lucky to have that, and we were losing somebody we loved so much. We had that opportunity, and I knew that she wanted us to be here, giving people the opportunity to have that life, too. It was a *rough* day."

The news put their frontline pro-life activism into a profoundly personal perspective. "I was the hospital-person, the had-to-speak-to-the-doctor person," Riaghan said. "I did it again [the day we got the news], and it was such a contrast. You come from the city [where] everyone's screaming, and it was a break to go to the hospital with my brother Donagh." Riaghan does not remember the arrival of that news as a part of the referendum, even though they received it during that last hectic week. That day has somehow floated free of the others as a standalone moment in her memory, a before-and-after sort of moment that changes everything forever.

But she does remember how that news impacted the life and death conversations she was having about the value of life on the street in Dublin. "I remember one guy, he was trying to be flippant, and I knew he was a bit of a broken person," Riaghan remembered. "He was saying that I was 'on about babies who were terminally ill.' I was saying: Do you think a baby that is terminally ill shouldn't have a right to life? He said: Yeah, they're not worth anything, they're sick, they're going to die anyway. And I [said]: If your mother was sick and going to die, I think every minute would matter to you. He [replied]: No, they're going to die anyway. And I said: No, I know for a fact you would [care]."

Their beautiful mother remained at the forefront of their minds as they sought to reach those they could. "You were out there every day fighting for life, and you knew every moment was precious before she passes away, too," Enya said. "You just had to go back in and keep fighting and keep talking about it, because you knew in your head how precious life is. That was what was keeping me going: Lives are so precious, and if I get an extra—we got an extra two months with mom—and we knew how precious it was." The abortion activists were fighting the referendum in part by asserting that family members with terminal conditions—albeit pre-born ones—could be killed, and for the O'Callaghans, it was very personal.

Back at the Life House, Donagh O'Callaghan and Katy Robinson were working to get tens of thousands of pamphlets into mailboxes. Pro-lifers were delivering them by hand, and so we were picking up boxes of literature at the office along with maps of neighborhoods where they were to be distributed, and heading out to pound the sidewalk. Most mailboxes, we soon discovered, were already stuffed with pamphlets from politicians and campaigns on both sides of the debate. Occasionally, an irritated resident snapped at us, fed up with the abortion discussion. Not many houses here had the red "Vote No" stickers displayed in their windows. Many of them had signs proudly announcing their intention to vote Yes.

At one point we stopped at the office to collect more boxes of pamphlets and Tim was pacing back and forth in front of the door, his face tight with stress. He was ready to head off to a press conference featuring Health Minister Simon Harris and other pro-abortion politicians, with orders from Save the 8th to hijack the proceedings and ensure that the Yes campaign didn't get their message out. Later that afternoon, we watched the footage of the Women's Health in Ireland press conference, and Tim had pulled it off brilliantly. Dressed in a sharp grey suit and wielding an enormous microphone, his voice cut through the media clamour: "Minister, will you resign? Are you in favour of killing innocent human beings? Minister for Health, are you happy that taxpayer's money will be used to fund the killing of innocent human beings?"

As Harris and his colleagues grew stone-faced, an official hastily intervened by loudly suggesting a round of applause for "the Minister," and Harris smiled thinly as his colleagues and members of the media clapped enthusiastically. As it began to peter out, Tim called out: "Can we continue to clap for the killing of Irish children for generations to come?" While journalists scowled fiercely at him, a few clapped defiantly as if to make his point while others demanded to know what he was doing there. Tim got off one last point before the press conference broke up: "Anyone here want to vote on the politicians' right to life?" The headline in *The Journal* later that day (May 22) read "Simon Harris heckled by anti-abortion campaigner at large Yes event." The headline in the *Irish Times*: "Anti-abortion activist confronts Yes politicians at press conference."

While the team in the office worked the media, digital communications, and attempted to coordinate the massive, nation-wide effort, the street teams spread out across Dublin delivering pamphlets, manning tables in high-traffic pedestrian areas, and canvass teams were also heading from door to door. After delivering pro-life literature during the afternoons, we met up with canvass teams at night, meeting in front of churches or in supermarket parking lots to review which neighborhoods still had to be covered, hand out stacks of pamphlets, and team up to begin heading door to door. In groups of two, we headed off to knock on doors, with some of the older volunteers moving at a slower pace but still determined to stay on the streets for the final stretch. Many of them had been out on the Life Canvass for years. One or two, like Mick Hammond in Dún Laoghaire, had voted against the Eighth in 1983 but were now canvassing to save it.

Despite the hostility that the street teams sometimes faced in Dublin, door-knocking was actually quite encouraging. Many people did not seem to understand the pro-life position, but were quite open to talking about it. Most of those who didn't want to talk about it were not particularly rude, but just firmly ended the conversation. At many doors, we found divided households: a mother voting against abortion, her son voting to repeal the right to life. A young mother voting to save the Eighth Amendment, her husband voting to repeal it. Parents voting No, a young daughter voting Yes. Some families were split almost equally, with people no longer speaking to each other. The Irish abortion war truly was a civil war, with the lives and futures of children and grandchildren at stake and emotions running high on all sides. At one point, a few young boys yelled at me from a McDonald's as I headed down a street that a "Yes" vote was the way to go. Wondering if they even knew what abortion was, I walked over to them and described how the abortion procedure tears the body of a pre-born child apart. One by one, they grew pale. One by one, they grew silent. Supporting abortion was just the cool thing to do among the youth—but many of them had no idea what it actually was.

Back at the office, Niamh, Úna, Kate, and the red-eyed campaigners manning the computers asked how canvassing was going, and everyone had good stories. These stories were necessary, as the good news allowed everyone to swallow the panic that crept up their throats as referendum day loomed. It genuinely seemed as if many people were voting pro-life—or at least, that very few people felt passionately pro-abortion. There were a few angry altercations and shouting homeowners, but canvassing was a largely pleasant experience. We did not know at the time that those who had made up their minds to vote Yes had simply decided not to argue about the issue any longer. Instead, they simply agreed with the pro-life campaigners, hustled them along, all the while determining to vote to repeal the Eighth Amendment. After months of being bombarded with pro-abortion and pro-life messaging, people no longer wanted to discuss it.

The final few days went by like a slow-motion blur. Everyone poured their hearts out and strained to expend their last bit of energy as the campaigns headed for the home stretch. In the office, Seán and David McDwyer were running up and down the stairs constantly. "Everybody was out nonstop," Niamh said.

"You'd have to call canvass leaders to tell them to stop, it was too late to be out knocking on doors. People like Mary White and Esme Caulfield, who had fought this fight for decades, were still giving it their all right to the end. It didn't matter how early you got to the office, there would be people there already working. The sense of urgency was very real." There was encouragement, too—in the families of children with disabilities who allowed their love for their children to overcome the viciousness they received for telling their stories, in people who had lived peacefully adjacent to the pro-life movement for years without getting involved but were now signing up for the last surge. The hour was late, but not too late to join the fight.

At the last press conference of the campaign, the international and national media were openly hostile, with antagonistic questions coming from British reporters impatient at Ireland's delay in joining the rest of Europe's liberal abortion regimes. In a speech that went viral, Abigail Malone spoke for a room full of pro-life women when she said she was a "young, proud, ambitious Irish woman" who would be voting No because women deserved better than abortion. "I am sick and tired of being told that without the right to take a human life, I am not equal," she said, pointing out that under Simon Harris's government the country would have abortion clinics before properly-funded rape crisis centres. "This is not a proposal to help women…I am sick of the spin and the yarns and the fake compassion. Do not use women to legalise taking a child's life for any reason at all. We deserve better."

People were still coming together, even those who had never been part of the movement. Niamh recalled the feeling of warmth when someone she'd known years ago would message her after a TV appearance to tell her that they supported her, reaching out from across the years to tap her on the shoulder and let her know that they were behind her. "There was something really lovely about that," she remembered. These flashes of encouragement helped to silence little pinpricks of doubt that surfaced when bad things happened—like the Google ban on pro-life advertising, which came "like a kick in the teeth," or when the media cut stories with badly-needed messaging, or ignored important press conferences with powerful testimonies from medical professionals. These events snapped the blur of the campaign into focus for just a moment, and if the campaigners thought about them for too long, little butterflies of doubt would flutter in their stomachs, brushing their wings gently against the sides. It wasn't panic, exactly. But it was the beginnings of dread.

***

On the evening of May 24, the office was packed with exhausted activists, many of whom had been sleeping at the Life House, bunked down on the floor. People were sitting on tables, cross-legged on the floor, and some were leaning against each other, half-sleeping. It was warm out, and a crowd gathered on the front steps and spilled onto the sidewalk, laughing and chatting, taking photos together, their tense faces alive in the glow of the streetlights. Tim was organising buses to take people back to their towns and villages to vote the next day, and a few members of the admin team were smoking cigarettes to stay awake, the embers burning bright and the smoke *whooshing* out in long sighs. Someone suggested that we go to the pub around the corner for a bit, and a crew in red Vote No sweaters headed down the street.

The last hours before everyone parted were almost surreal. It had been a grueling campaign, and the final week in Dublin had been hard on everyone as the spite and anger they faced had begun to wear down the hopeful enthusiasm created by the weeks on the Vote No Roadshow in friendlier towns and cities. Now, almost everybody was going home, and there was nothing left to do. It had all been left on the field, but the unspoken question hung in the air: *Did we do enough?* As the activists crowded into booths and around tables, the question occasionally surfaced: *Are we going to win?* Even those with doubts pushed them down, and stories of conversations where voters changed their minds, positive reactions at the doors in some of the Dublin neighborhoods, and above all, the *righteousness* of the cause were put forward as evidence that we would. We *had* to.

Despite the hopefulness, everybody was tense. If pro-life Ireland would come through once again and victory awaited on the other side of the night, then everybody wanted to fast-forward to that moment of exquisite relief and jubilation. But if not—if May 25 would bring the devastating news that the Ireland they all loved so much no longer existed, and that the Irish people would be the first to bring in abortion by popular demand—then this night could last forever. Here, in this moment, everything was still as it should be. Babies in the womb were protected, Ireland was one of the only pro-life nations in the Western world, and being Irish still meant something profoundly beautiful. Here, on this island of sanity surrounded by those who had sacrificed weeks, months, and years to pour out their hearts for Ireland's children, was laughter and camaraderie. On the other side lay a new era of unthinkable and unknowable darkness. It was Schrodinger's Ireland: Nobody knew if she was alive, or dead—and nobody knew if they wanted to know.

Chapter 8
The Great Betrayal

There were bands of men and women who were willing to go out and do the most thankless work for people who they'll never meet, and for a cause that won't be of any immediate benefit to oneself. They were willing to make those sacrifices anyway and endure all the animosity and hatred, all to stand up for what's good and what's true and what's beautiful. That to me speaks to a depth of character that isn't often seen today in society. It is often the people who aren't well-known, who aren't in front of the camera, who aren't on a stage, who tend to fill those roles—and not to get any limelight. Those people are the heroes who don't get the recognition they deserve—the bread and butter activists, who just do it because it's right. Unsung heroes.

Tim Jackson

There must be those among whom we can sit down and weep and still be counted as warriors.

Adrienne Rich

Early on the morning of May 25th, as the five of us headed for the Dublin Airport, Tim Jackson's messages were lighting up the Vote No Roadshow WhatsApp group, urging the volunteers to push across the finish line: "There's only 9 hours of work left, please go to working class areas right now, knock on doors, ask them to go out and vote, and have leaflets ready too." Others were heading out to hit up overpasses and wave the enormous red Vote No banners to encourage pro-lifers to get out and vote. As we boarded the plane to fly back to Canada, people began pouring into polling stations across Ireland to cast their history-changing ballots, and the Save the 8th team began one of the most surreal days of their lives with both dread and anticipation.

Mary Rose Short was out with one of the overpass banner teams in Donnybrook, and they headed back into the office around 10 AM before leaving to hoist a banner in front of the General Post Office. It was sunny but windy, and it was difficult to hang on to the banners. Pro-life voters stopped to encourage them and show off their Vote No, Save the 8th, and Love Both pins. Back at the mostly empty office, things were quiet. Mary Rose passed Niamh in the kitchen, and Niamh stopped to thank them for all their hard work, saying that every single bridge and crossing she had passed on the way in from Shankill had been manned by pro-lifers with banners and Vote No messages. Then, Scott Schittl came rushing in to look for someone to help him hold another banner over an overpass to hit the evening rush hour.

"He raced his van through back streets, trying to get ahead of the traffic," Mary Rose remembered. "'I don't like it,' he muttered a few times, before explaining: 'This weather. It's too nice. It makes people confident and unafraid of change.' He had a feeling we were going to lose." After grappling with the banner in the wind for a few hours, they headed back to the office again.

That evening, as the world awaited the results of Ireland's referendum, John McGuirk was with the team he had assembled over the course of the campaign. "We got a lot of beers in, and I was with them," he remembered. "I had been preparing them throughout the day in case the scale of the defeat was devastating because obviously, media communications goes both ways and you hope when you hear things that they're wrong, but I'm a natural pessimist on polling data. I tend to always assume that there's no possible way the public will go the way I want them to.

But I was also speaking to journalists and picking up tidbits. I remember at three o'clock hearing a partial exit poll from a rural box in the west of Ireland that showed us losing 55-45 in a part of the country where we needed to be winning 65-35. So I had some inkling, from about two o'clock in the afternoon, that it was going to go very badly. But the exit poll was not going to be in until eleven o'clock that night."

Niamh Uí Bhriain recalled two things that kept coming into her mind on the day of the vote. The first was a conversation she had with a voter on O'Connell Street in Dublin at the height of the campaign. "He was an older, conservative man, a real Dub, very nice, not antagonistic at all. But he insisted he was voting Yes, and couldn't really explain why. He just kept saying things 'had to change', like a mantra he had heard so often he just believed it to be true. It was indicative of how a public mood can arise and pull people along on a strong emotional level, almost subconsciously. They want to be part of the dominant narrative too, which is, sadly, part of the human condition everywhere."

The second conversation she couldn't shake from her head on that "interminable" day which "seemed to pass in a blur and still stretch to infinity" was one that the core crew that formed Save the 8th had back in 2017. "We were discussing the findings of a new poll, and someone observed that if people voted solely on the hard cases, we'd lose 75:25. Our mission – the whole point of the campaign for years – was to show people the horrific consequences of voting with that narrow understanding, but the danger was always there, and the thought of that sort of landslide was always in the back of our minds. I thought of what Úna said to me at the outset of the campaign too: that we'd work for months to raise funds for billboards and videos, and, as clever and powerful as they might be, it took a huge effort to reach just a section of voters. The other side had it so easy: everything they said and did was faithfully reported by the media, it was endless free publicity for their message. Were we even being heard in the clamour? We were about to find out."

Despite the fact that John was doing his best to warn them of what might be coming, most of the team's younger volunteers couldn't comprehend the fact that after all their hard work, the referendum might be lost. Many of them clung to experiences that indicated otherwise, like an encouraging canvass the night before. So when the exit polls were released, with the *Irish Times* predicting that the Yes side would win by a margin of 68% to 32%, the news was simply devastating.

"I remember Abigail, my deputy," John recalled. "She had poured her heart and soul into it. She showed up with her fiancé, and the poor girl was absolutely shattered and broken-hearted. And I think in moments like that, there's a part of you that puts your own emotions to one side and tries to be a comfort to people. That's how the night was for me. I tried to tell them all for their own sake that they were not to go to any counting centres the next day to be jeered and booed and hassled. I was basically trying to look after them." Abigail went into RTÉ anyway and did an interview where she said she was so proud of everyone on the No side who had fought so hard.

As he tried to comfort his team, John's own feelings were profoundly conflicted—a mixture of both deep sadness and relief. The relief, he remembered, was because if they had lost the referendum by a razor-thin margin, he knew that he—and the rest of the team—would have spent the rest of their lives wondering what they could possibly have done differently. The pro-life campaigners knew that when abortion came to Ireland, babies would die.

To have fought the battle and lost was awful enough. To consider the possibility that it could have been different—that maybe, just *maybe*, all of those babies could have been saved—*that* would have been torture.

"When you lose by [that margin], you know that you bear no responsibility for the result," John recalled. "And that's the thing I spent the evening telling them. When you lose like that, there's not a thing you could have done. You did everything that you could. If you had done twice as much, the result still would have been [the same]. If you had personally gone out there and switched 50,000 voters, we still would have lost."

Niamh, who like many of the team members had not slept at all the night before, had gone home. With nothing left to do, she headed down to the local polling station just before closing time with her husband to check that the boxes had been correctly closed and sealed. They were at the station, she recalled, when "John McGuirk called me and he said, 'Niamh, it's not good. The exit polls are saying 68% Yes.'" Niamh felt a roaring in her ears and John suddenly sounded very far away. She felt as if she'd stepped out of her body, the way you do when you receive terrible news about an illness or a death in the family. The world seemed to tilt on its axis. "We just said a few words to each other, mostly *I don't believe it*. I asked him if he thought it could be wrong, and he said: *Not this wrong*." In a state of shock, Niamh and her husband walked the dog for a little while, and then they went home and she began to call people, "just to see if they were okay and to try prepare them for the next day." On the other end of the line, people were simply broken. "People weren't just fighting for a referendum," Niamh said. "They were fighting for the soul of their country."

After one last, hard day of campaigning, Mary Rose and her sister headed out to wait for the results with some of campaigners. "I don't remember how we got to the pub, but Siobhan Rooney, Patrick Martin, Emma Mykso, Katy and her now-husband Jesus, Rosa, and some of our group were there," Mary Rose remembered. "No one was jubilant. There was some tense excitement, but we were a nervous group. The pub was no longer serving food so some of our group left to get dinner and were still gone when the exit polls were announced. Even then, no one was certain—at least out loud—that we had lost. Several people expressed disbelief that the polls could be accurate. 'The 2016 polls in the U.S. were wrong. Hillary didn't even write a concession speech,' Siobhan reminded us. Then she got a text from Niamh. Given the polls, Niamh said the younger volunteers shouldn't be put through the official count the next day. It was over. Rosa, [whose whole family were stalwarts of the campaign for years,] let loose: 'I don't believe it. I refuse to believe it. I don't believe it. I refuse to believe it.' Katy was in shock, but she and Jesus remained much calmer. Siobhan arranged for Katy and me to get back to the house in Sandymount."

Úna was at home, still working, when she saw the news. "I was online, and I was putting up messages like, 'Thanks for coming out and voting!'," she remembered. "And then I was on Facebook, and the *Irish Times* exit poll came out. When I saw 68%, I actually thought I was going to vomit. My eyes were smarting, I thought I was seeing things, I was just so tired. I was opening and closing my eyes and my eyes were smarting. *It couldn't be. It just couldn't be. It couldn't be 68%.* I just kept refreshing the page and going up and down the page.

The O'Callaghan sisters, who had gone back to Donegal to vote, decided not to stay at home and await the results. Instead, they got in touch with friends and arranged to climb Errigal, the highest mountain in County Donegal. "We didn't want to be home. We didn't want to be sitting ducks, waiting," Riaghan remembered.

"The tension was too much." Enya agreed: "We knew it would be too painful to look at the news. We climbed up, and it was a joyful thing, and it just took our mind off it. Either we were going to walk down and get really good news, or get really bad news." They heard the news at the top of the mountain, and the contrast between the gorgeous scenery of the home they loved so much and the report of what their countrymen had just done made for a strange contrast. "I think it was good that we got the news at the top of the mountain, just looking over Donegal and the beautiful scenery," Enya remembered. "It was a stunning day, which you don't get much of in Ireland. It brought perspective to me. To be at the top of the mountain, and to see the world, how small it was."

There was, at least, one small comfort: Donegal was the only region in the country to vote pro-life, although by a narrow margin: 51.87% for No versus 48.13% for Yes (the headline in *The Guardian* two days later would read "'Life is Precious': Donegal quietly defiant after voting no in referendum").[cli] "I thought, I am so ashamed of my country," Riaghan recalled. "I'm not proud to say I'm Irish anymore. If you think of the American Supreme Court, it was a few people who made a decision on behalf of a country. But for us—we, as a people—chose this. This is what we think of life, and this is what we think of the unborn. I am so ashamed of my people, of my country—but at least Donegal voted pro-life. That was literally all I had: *I hate my country—but at least Donegal is okay to live in for now.*"

Shauna had stayed at home in Donegal with her brother and sister all day after voting to await the result, and when the result was announced, she was genuinely stunned. On the last few days of the campaign on O'Connell Street in Dublin, she had been part of many positive conversations, and as referendum day came, she felt optimistic. "I saw many of my female friends on Facebook out celebrating the results," she remembered sadly. "All I could think [about] was how far Ireland had fallen. It was a dark day in our history, and my heart felt heavy in my chest. Irish people were literally out drinking to celebrate the fact that we can now legally kill our unborn children. I spent the evening with my family and pro-life friends. We prayed, talked, and tried to make sense of the horrible situation. We took a step back, rested, and reflected for a couple of weeks."

Tim had been working in a frenzy right up until the last moment. "It was chaotic, because all of us felt a sense of desperation, that we were really in the final hour," he told me. "It was also a sense, having been in Dublin for the week of the vote, that the referendum was slipping away from us. We were just out trying to get people out of their houses to vote and vote the right way. But even that day, I remember meeting older people in some of the estates in Dublin who had voted Yes. They had been at the ballot boxes early, and really had no qualms about voting Yes. They didn't realise the significance of what they had just done. It was symptomatic of the propaganda people had succumbed to." Like many others on the Vote No Roadshow, Tim had been optimistic until the last week in Dublin: "Walking around the city, every third person had a Yes badge on. The day of the referendum, it felt like time running out in a football match and things are not looking good."

Later that day, Tim left Dublin to go home to Donegal to vote. He was with his then-girlfriend (they've since married) when he heard the results. "I just remember this sinking feeling when the exit polls were released," he recalled. "This sense of loss hit me. There were a lot of tears shed. It was a horrible feeling. We'd lost everything we held dear. Everything. It doesn't get much worse than that, I don't think." On Saturday, May 26, he decided to go to one of the count centres in Donegal, and that, at least, was bittersweet. The country was lost, but Donegal was not. It was a consolation, but a small one—after all, Tim remarked bitterly, abortion would be legal in Donegal, too, despite the fact that the No vote there had won the day.

I heard the results back in Canada, sitting at Pearson International Airport and waiting to board another flight to Ottawa to give a speech. Part of me wished we hadn't left, and that we had stayed with the Irish pro-lifers we had met and worked alongside for the past several weeks. The other part of me was relieved that we hadn't stayed. To be there during that moment of blackness and grief as they grappled with what their fellow countrymen had done would have felt, in some way, like being the only stranger at the funeral of a much-beloved family member, and even to be there and share their sadness would have felt somehow presumptuous. The international pro-life community is in many ways like an extended family, but this loss was deeply personal for the Irish movement in a way that those of us who are not a part of it simply cannot fully fathom.

As I sat there, my phone began buzz with messages coming in the Vote No Roadshow WhatsApp group, one after another. One volunteer said that her heart was breaking as a bunch of girls who had voted Yes were crying with joy next to her. Ireland's people were tearing apart from each other as some were crushed with despair, while others shrieked in gleeful celebration. Dave Sao sent a message that spoke for all of the foreign pro-life volunteers:

> *You are the most amazing people in the world. You are the strongest, bravest, and most dedicated people I've ever met. Because of you, I wish I was Irish. Today is a sad day for so many of us but today can't be the*

end. TODAY must be a new day with more zeal, with more passion, and more conviction. You have fought the good fight, ran the race, you have kept the faith. Thank you for [fighting] for the rights [of] the unborn, for the weakest and for the silenced. Thank you for the fight and I will be with you in prayer and fighting for the pre-born. Don't give up. Fight on. I love you all. You are truly an inspiration.

Riaghan was next:

Love, you guys, and David is right, maybe if it was a no vote then we'd become complacent and take it all for granted, but we saw how much needs to be changed and how little of the truth gets out, [now] we know to what extent we need to work hard for the good! Proud to be part of the red army!! Call me to battle anytime, General Tim!

In response, thanks began to pour in for Tim Jackson, the Red Army's fiercest leader:

Tim is a hero for the unborn. Thank you to our fearless leader.

Tim is a beautiful man.

Tim, absolute hero and legend! Way to go! Thanks for fighting the good fight.

Tim, proud to know you, brother.

And then, finally, Tim:

I just want to thank everyone here for giving every ounce of your heart to the campaign. When the history books are written and when you face God, it will not be forgotten what and who you have stood for. This may be Ireland's darkest day, but 'be of good cheer' for Christ has overcome the world.

As May 26 dawned, abortion activists and campaigners began to gather in the courtyard at Dublin Castle, once the seat of English power, to await the announcement of the results. Leo Varadkar had promised that there would be no celebration if Ireland voted to legalise abortion, but the crowd was having none of it. Buoyed by the exit polls, they waited with barely suppressed excitement. A group of female singers called Voices 4 Repeal serenaded their comrades. When Health Minister Simon Harris arrived, cheers of *Simon! Simon! Simon!* broke out, and women grabbed at him for hugs and selfies and in one case, a kiss on the cheek. The Taoiseach also received wild adulation as he made his way towards the stage, where government ministers waved to the pulsing mob. Still maintaining their cool, the politicians headed to the small room inside Dublin Castle where the final tally would be revealed. The room was packed with politicians of all parties, waiting to find out if they'd gotten a bargain in their deal with the Devil. When the result was read out—66.4% to 33.6% for Yes—cheers erupted, and hugs and handshakes were dealt out left and right.

The cheers spread to the courtyard, where ecstatic chants of *Yes! Yes! Yes!* split the air as clenched fists were thrust aloft and Repeal campaigners with *Yes* tattoos on their cheeks literally wept with joy that abortion would be coming to Ireland. Flags were hoisted, signs waved, and young men and women clutched at each other, many trembling with happiness at the newfound freedom that feticide would bring them. It was a wild and emotion-wracked wake for a nation that had protected pre-born children in the womb, but there were only happy tears here. Compassion, sobbing voters told the equally jubilant journalists, had come to Ireland. They did not explain how forceps, suction aspirators, and other instruments of death could be compassionate. They no longer had to.

On May 27, one of the Vote No Roadshow campaigners sent another message to the WhatsApp group:

> *How is everyone else today. I don't think it hit me [yesterday]. Today feels like a day after a funeral when it hits you that it's actually real and someone has died. The poor babies.*

***

In the days and weeks that followed, the pro-lifers struggled to make sense of it all. The day after the vote, Niamh went into the office, to meet the crew and volunteers. It was a disaster, as many of the Vote No Roadshow volunteers and canvassers had slept on the floor and every inch of the office had been covered in sleeping bags. Now, there were chips, wrappers, discarded signs, and crumpled leaflets everywhere, the debris of a long and hard campaign. The mess, Niamh remembered, made everyone feel worse. "The office kind of matched our mood," she said. "We all felt in disarray, and beaten, and the office really looked beaten. There was an ugly, triumphant atmosphere in the city-centre – people gloating about now having the 'right' to kill babies, though I think a lot of the more vile celebrations actually shocked a lot of reluctant Yes voters, some of whom were posting on social that they didn't vote for what was happening in Dublin Castle. I remember seeing that and thinking 'too late for that now.' Some people said to me that the only comfort in the horrible, heartbreaking sadness was that we didn't have any blood on our hands, and that was true. But the feeling that this was no longer my country was devastating. This was a cruel, selfish, pitiless Ireland now, and every abortion was one that 66% of Irish people voted for – the late-term abortions, the tens of thousands of deaths that would follow, the near-eradication of people with disabilities, that was all on everyone who went into the ballot box and voted Yes. We could hold our heads up high and say 'we didn't vote for that.' It felt like cold comfort though, given that we knew what was lost, and what would follow. There's never any satisfaction in being proved right about abortion. Nothing surrounds it but sadness and despair and death. But as our friend Matt Treacy said later, it's better to be in the right than in the majority."

A priest arrived to pray with people at the office, which gave comfort. Most sat around in silence, smoking and drinking tea or coffee. Many people who had quit smoking quietly resumed the habit. People found it difficult to talk, to verbalize the sorrow they felt for what was lost. Everyone was crying at some stage. But they still wanted to be together. "I remember the Precious Life crew who had come to help from the north and were always full of smiles and hope, brilliant young people, just holding us up that morning," said Rebecca Roughneen.

After a few hours, a group headed out to the Phoenix Park. People trickled in and out, talking and comforting one another. "We just needed to see each other," Úna remembered. The next day, many of the campaigners met again for a barbeque on the north side of Dublin at a park. People didn't understand their country anymore, and didn't understand the neighbours they passed as they drove to join the few they still trusted. The celebrations at Dublin Castle had turned some of the grief into anger, and that was somewhat comforting in some strange way. The pro-lifers looked at the cheering crowds, Niamh said, and were glad that they at least had not become the sort of people who could crow with delight over the impending death of pre-born children.

At the barbeque, one of the canvass leaders, Donal Fallon, started a session and they sang Irish folk songs, even though the tunes were sad and the lyrics tore at their hearts. Úna Mhic Mhathúna sang the song "Seán Ó Duibhir A Ghleanna," which in particular reduced them all to tears.

A ballad of the 1691 Battle of Aughrim in Galway, where the Gaelic chieftans were badly defeated, the final four lines in particular seemed to sum it all up perfectly:

> *And as we part in sorrow, yet Seán Ó Duibhir a chara, Our hope is God save Ireland, pour blessings on her name. May her sons be true when needed, may they never fail as we did, For Seán Ó Duibhir an Ghleanna, we were worsted in the game.*

May they never fail as we did…we were worsted in the game. Those words, Niamh said, put their feelings into words in that peculiar way that perhaps only old, traditional folk songs can, and they felt a bond arching across the years to those other warriors who had fought for their Ireland because they had loved their homes and longed to create a future for her children. We felt, she said, like Shakespeare's band of brothers. Friendships and loyalties were forged on the campaign that would not readily fade.

Although John McGuirk had been prepared for the loss on the day of the referendum, there were still new realities that he had to grapple with, and it didn't really sink in until a week later. "I grew up in a rural area near the border with Northern Ireland, County Monaghan," he told me. "The parish had voted 69% in favor of the Eighth Amendment and was a reliable No vote on cultural issues—voted No to divorce twice. I always thought that those values were widely held across rural Ireland. My own polling box voted 63% No on this occasion, and delivered one of the highest No votes of any box in the country, but it was the only one in all of County Monaghan to turn in a No vote. I'd grown up thinking that where I lived was totally representative of rural Ireland more generally, and it seems that was not the case. So in that sense I was shocked to my core. Before the referendum, I had a totally false impression of the country I was living in."

The campaign had been utterly exhausting, and John was just relieved that he could finally sleep. "Part of you," he said, "is just glad that it's over, and that you survived it." The harsh news coverage he'd been personally subjected to over the campaign was hard on his mother, who was in her sixties, and he was more than ready for a break: "I went into my shell, ignored everyone, switched off, and focused on planning my wedding with my fiancé." Victory had not been enough to make some abortion campaigners happy, however, and after the referendum results came in, they swarmed his social media feeds, mocking him bitterly and doing their best to infect him with their bile. Before checking out, McGuirk responded on Twitter:

> Rarely in my life have I seen people angrier about winning than the repealers. Cheer up folks, it's not that bad. There'll be something along shortly for you all to focus your never-ending anger on, I'm sure.
>
> Today I went to Stonehall Wildlife Park in Limerick (which is brilliant – take your kids) and petted a parrot, and several rabbits and goats. I come home to another 2,000 tweets from the angriest, craziest people in Ireland. Your unhappiness will never be fixed by a vote, folks.
>
> The problem is the 8th amendment was never what was making you angry in the first place. It's not the schools or the hospitals, or the ban on euthanasia either. No social reform is going to make you people happy. You're all looking in the wrong place.
>
> The deep injustice many people feel, and the power to change the country that they now wield, is missing something – there's no vision in it for how to make people feel happy. Once all the "oppression" is gone, they'll have to confront the fact that their misery is their own.

> It was never the journey that was lonely. It was never the country that was cruel. It was never the church that was oppressing you. The movement you are in won't leave you fulfilled and happy. It will just leave you all angry in company.
>
> In terms of the calls to silence me, or others – hah. You guys own the country now. You own the media, the political class, the culture. You can keep pretending that a minority voice is holding you back, or you can realise that it's actually an oppression of your own making.
>
> One thing I kept hearing yesterday was that this was a "symbolic" victory. There are many more symbolic victories to be had – blasphemy, the role of women, the pre-amble. Lots more totems of the past to tear down. None of them will fix the problem.
>
> The problem is that all of those victories are empty of meaning. Even this one. Having an abortion in Louth will not be more fun than having one in London. It remains an abortion. You're not "free". You're just miserable, probably in greater numbers, closer to home.
>
> The Irish liberal left has nothing to offer you whatsoever, beyond days like yesterday. A momentary feeling of togetherness. It can't provide you with a good job, or a loving partner, or security. All it does is provide you with an enemy to hate.[clii]

The Save the 8th campaign's final press release summed it up:

> The 8th amendment did not create a right to life for the unborn child—it merely acknowledged

> that such a right exists, has always existed, and will always exist. What Irish voters did yesterday is a tragedy of historic proportions. However, a wrong does not become a right simply because a majority support it. We are so proud of all of those who stood with us in this campaign—our supporters, our donors, our families, and our loved ones. This campaign took a huge personal toll on all of us who were involved, and we have been so grateful for their support.
>
> The unborn child no longer has a right to life recognised by the Irish state. Shortly, legislation will be introduced that will allow babies to be killed in our country. We will oppose that legislation. If and when abortion clinics are opened in Ireland, because of the inability of the Government to keep their promise about a GP led service, we will oppose that as well. Every time an unborn child has his or her life ended in Ireland, we will oppose that, and make our voices known.
>
> Abortion was wrong yesterday. It remains wrong today. The constitution has changed, but the facts have not.[cliii]

***

One thing was now certain: The country was now profoundly divided in a disturbingly inter-generational fashion.

"My lasting memory of the abortion war in Ireland is not from the referendum campaign," McGuirk recalled later. "It's from the year before, at the March for Life in 2017. I was walking down from O'Connell Street with some friends of mine, and seeing the counter-protests, and realizing that the two Irelands those people represented were fundamentally incompatible—and that one of them was going to be shattered. I remember looking at those faces, and they were mostly in their twenties, and they were *exceedingly* angry—and I mean exceedingly angry. That level of raw antagonism and hatred—that shook me to my core."

The chasm had proven too deep and wide to bridge. Older people who simply could not fathom the idea that young Irish people could be openly advocating the destruction of pre-born children in the streets and young people who hated the older people standing in the way of what they perceived as freedom—it was the Old Ireland and the New Ireland facing off, separated by the vast divide of a generation. Among the 18 to 24-year-olds who voted, 85% of them voted Yes.

"I don't think, unless you're standing there in that moment, that you can get a sense of it," McGuirk reflected. "I remember realizing that this was Armageddon. This was a fight that, if we won, we would be fighting for the rest of our lives, and if we lost, these people would endeavour to punish us for the rest of our lives. That has stuck with me, realizing in that moment that this was not actually about abortion. I always got this sense from the young, militant Yes voters, that this was as much about hurting the older generation and the Catholic Church for their perceived sins as it was about any great cause of female liberation. For many of them, this was a campaign of utter and raw vengeance. I don't even know if they realised that themselves."

"The anger and desire for vengeance in that age group is all the more difficult to understand because it wasn't really based on anything real," Íde O'Hara observed later. "They are the most privileged and pampered generation that have ever lived, working themselves up into a rage against a Church that no longer has any political power, and imagining themselves oppressed because they can't kill helpless babies. It's pathetic to be honest, but in a way it wasn't surprising, because younger people, my generation in particular, are inclined not to be rebellious at all. They're sheep, they want to follow trends and be part of the herd. If the media had told them the 8th should be saved, they'd have rushed out to get No badges."

***

That fall, Riaghan and Enya moved to the United States for several months to attend Thomas More College and see the sights. Meeting new friends and having fresh experiences could help them move on from the loss—but even in America, there were occasional painful reminders of what had happened. In Boston, visiting a modern art museum, the young man behind the counter noted their accents, and they told him they were from Ireland. His face lit up. "He went on and on about how much he loved Ireland because it was the liberal capital of the world now," Riaghan remembered, "because we just had that beautiful referendum, and I really wanted to cry. I'm not easily offended, but I was so close to bursting out crying: *This man loves my country for all the wrong reasons*."

For months, the referendum seemed to follow Tim Jackson around. He bumped into Kitty Holland, the journalist who had crafted the first Savita narrative, at a petrol station. He spotted Enda Kenny, the Taoiseach who had first legalised abortion back in 2013, too. And finally, he got the opportunity he'd been waiting for. "I was in the tiny little town of Bailieborough in the summer," he recalled. "[It was] pouring rain, and who walked out [in front of me] but Leo Varadkar. So I went up and had a few words. He didn't say a word as I told him that he couldn't have all this blood on his hands, and he would have to reverse course. Then he was shooed away. I didn't make a scene. I said it so he could hear it and no one else."

Shauna, who returned to teaching, summed up the feelings of many of the pro-life campaigners perfectly—in my conversations with them after the referendum, I noticed that many of them referenced the work of J.R.R. Tolkien to make sense of what had happened. "There is one quote from Tolkien that helped greatly in comforting me after the results of the referendum," she told me later. *"I am a Christian…so…I do not expect 'history' to be anything but a long defeat, though it contains some samples or glimpses of final victory*. The people I travelled with around Ireland for four weeks and all the wonderful people I met along the way were my glimpses of final victory. We may have lost the referendum, but the passion of the pro-life people has not been diminished. With more stories coming out in the Irish media of the soaring number of women seeking abortions, I am more pro-life than ever. We have to continue to promote a culture of life and keep the conversation going. It may be legal now to kill the unborn in our country. However, the leadup to the referendum started a movement of people committed to giving the unborn a voice. Having something to fight for ignited a fire within us. And that fire cannot be extinguished, regardless of the outcome of the referendum."

Katy Robinson agreed. "The sacrifices everyone made were worth it," she said. "Youth Defence not only shaped Ireland's story, but inspired people across the globe. Keeping Ireland abortion free for so long is such a massive accomplishment that we should still celebrate with joy the huge victory of every life that was saved and every heart that was touched."

Chapter 9: How Ireland lost the Eighth Amendment

Perhaps the greatest irony in this tragic result is that official statistics show that Ireland, without abortion, is one of the safest places in the world to be pregnant. Yet abortion has been legalised here because [the] media managed to convince the people of a lie around the death of a pregnant woman from sepsis.

Life Institute report, "Why the Referendum was Lost"

So how did it happen? Is it true that Ireland changed dramatically on the issue of abortion, and that all of the polls—even those commissioned by the abortion activists—showing high levels of pro-life sentiment were simply mistaken? After all, the general consensus of opinion polls was that only about a third of the Irish people supported abortion on demand. Was the abortion referendum of May 25, 2018 just the completion of a "Quiet Revolution," as Leo Varadkar asserted on May 26? Many people missed the intended meaning of his choice of words, which actually refers to a specific historical event: the decade between 1960 and 1970, when the staunchly Catholic Canadian province of Quebec rejected their previous values almost entirely. Today, Quebec is the province with the highest support for legal abortion and the most aggressively secular population. (Incidentally, it is also the province Varadkar's Canadian friend Prime Minister Justin Trudeau hails from.)

While it is certainly true that Ireland is a much different country now than it was in 1983 or even 2003, there are additional factors to consider. One of those factors is Ireland's leaders. Every single major political party in the Republic of Ireland campaigned for abortion throughout the referendum. Right across the country, lamp posts were festooned with signs featuring the faces of politicians and an enormous *YES* urging voters to cast their ballot for abortion. Three days before the vote, Varadkar released an emotionally-charged video in which he walked somberly towards the camera while delivering boilerplate pro-abortion talking points, falsely claiming that the Eighth Amendment had failed to do what it was put in place to do because some women still flew to the United Kingdom to get abortions.

He also spoke seriously of his own evolution on the issue, and assured voters (again falsely) that "the proposed legislation will be among the most regulated in Europe." He ended by asking voters to imagine that they were a woman who had been raped, or were still "a child," saying, "On May 25, I'm voting yes, because I want us to live in a kinder, more compassionate, warmer Ireland." If *he* had changed his mind, Varadkar was saying, others could surely do the same. Health Minister Simon Harris, too, spent the days leading up to the referendum plugging for abortion like his life depended on it (and considering his scandal-ridden and incompetent tenure in that office, his political life probably did). As Melanie McDonough put it in *The Spectator* on May 26:

> It seems that about a third of the electorate voted No, and the only surprise is that it was that many, given that this not insignificant minority had nil, zero, nada, representation in either politics or media. All the party leaders campaigned for repeal; the only half-recognisable figure

> to campaign for [No] was Peadar Tóibín, a previous unknown from Sinn Féin, who was effortlessly outgunned by the leader of his own party, Mary Lou McDonald, who took the high risk strategy of putting her own picture on Yes posters. So, the Yes campaign had all the heavy hitters, the Taoiseach, the minister for health, the leader of the opposition, and they were faithfully followed by television coverage. As for the media, I can only repeat what I said earlier for this paper: the suffocating consensus in print and broadcast media was such that I can think of only two regular columnists who articulated the arguments against repeal: Breda O'Brien for the *Irish Times* (the paper's token concession to impartiality) and David Quinn for the *Irish Sunday Times*. And that's it.[cliv]

To understand how politicians who had campaigned on pro-life platforms could transform into such enthusiastic abortion activists, we must look no further than the international reaction to the news that Ireland had voted to repeal the Eighth Amendment. UK Prime Minister Theresa May, the then-leader of Great Britain's pathetic Tory party, called the result an "impressive show of democracy" and congratulated "the Irish people on their decision and all of #Together4Yes on their successful campaign." French president Emmanuel Macron tweeted that "this vote will stand as an essential symbol of women's freedom." Canadian Prime Minister Justin Trudeau also tweeted his congratulations, writing: "What a moment for democracy and women's rights. Tonight, I spoke with Taoiseach Leo Varadkar and his team on the Yes Side's referendum legalizing abortion in Ireland."

The leaders of nations with liberal abortion regimes around the world had been waiting with bated breath, hoping against hope that Ireland would join them in the bloody business of abortion. When that moment came, they exploded with praise and celebration. The congratulations came pouring in.

For hip, progressive politicians like Varadkar, Ireland's Eighth Amendment had been an embarrassment. Varadkar styled himself as one of the young, modern leaders like Macron and Trudeau, but the longed-for approval of the progressive elites would always be withheld so long as Ireland protected pre-born human rights, and Varadkar and the rest of his set were desperately embarrassed by their country. He could never be accepted at the cool kid's table with Trudeau and Macron at prestigious international gatherings, despite his intersectional credibility as a minority gay man—not as long as Ireland protected children in the womb. After his trip to Ireland, Trudeau even told the media that he had confronted Varadkar on abortion, stating sombrely that: "On the issue of reproductive rights, I shared our perspective that such rights are integral to women's rights and they are human rights and I asked him to look at it as a fundamental human right and we had a good discussion."[clv]

When Varadkar finally went public with the fact that he would be abandoning his previous pro-life position and campaigning for repeal scarcely two months before the vote on January 27, 2018, he triggered confusion among many Irish commentators by choosing an international media outlet, BBC Channel 4, to make the announcement. Varadkar had assured Irish pro-life groups that he was with them when it was politically expedient to do so, but now he had new friends to impress. When he finally made the decision to show his hand, he made sure his progressive friends in the international community were the first to know.

That said, Ireland's leaders did not dare to move definitively against the Eighth Amendment until they were sure that what political strategists refer to as "middle Ireland" would go with them. After all, as much as they desired to emulate their progressive counterparts, political survival was obviously the primary priority. As recently as 2012, in that TIME magazine interview, Enda Kenny had declared that Ireland's abortion laws would not be changed. Politicians understood that there was always the resolutely pro-life segment of the Irish population, a hardcore faction of abortion supporters pushing for legalisation, and then the broad swathe of the public that lay between those two polar opposites. For decades, relentless waves of pro-life activism had ensured that the Irish people were constantly reminded that abortion was a horrifying act of violence against innocent human beings. Middle Ireland was largely uncomfortable with abortion, and generally satisfied with the status quo. But as Life Institute explained in their report "Why the Referendum Was Lost," released three months after the vote, everything was different in 2018.

As McDonough noted, the entire media was aggressively supportive of abortion on demand. In fact, the Yes campaign was so slow to get out of the gate at first and was providing such a stark contrast to the thousands of pro-lifers canvassing the country that just seven weeks ahead of the vote the media and the political parties were berating them for not campaigning hard enough, with the *Irish Times* noting their "alarm at the apparent lack of urgency in the repeal campaign" as opposed to the "well organised anti-abortion campaign" that was "weeks ahead in its postering and canvassing."[clvi] The media, in short, was doing much of the heavy lifting in shifting the public's perception on the abortion debate, while the Yes campaign was surprisingly lackadaisical and distracted by the "need to sideline extremists in groups like ROSA [a socialist feminist group] and the desire to 'lock Ruth Coppinger [a controversial pro-abortion politician] in a room' for the duration of the campaign," leading to a late launch.[clvii]

But the journalists castigating the Yes campaign needn't have worried. The years-long push by the media to persuade Middle Ireland that the Eighth Amendment was killing women had largely done the job, and the efforts of Yes campaigners—which remained lacklustre right through until May 25—were largely unnecessary. To cite just one example, Life Institute's research indicated that a full 90% of news items on abortion published in the *Irish Times* over a three-year period were biased in favor of abortion, with similar trends existing across the media landscape. And yet, Life Institute concluded that "the media would not have succeeded in shifting the majority of middle-ground voters towards repealing the 8th without the fake-news storm they built around the tragic death of Savita Halappanavar."[clviii]

The first indication of this huge shift in Middle Ireland came the day of the referendum. When exit pollsters questioned voters on why they had voted for repeal, they discovered that voters had not changed their minds on the Eighth Amendment during the campaign. Rather, they had changed their minds a full five years earlier, "precisely the time when they were repeatedly told by the media that Ms Halappanavar died because of the 8th Amendment." The claim that the Eighth Amendment had been killing or brutally hurting women—repeated relentlessly by the media, the politicians, and the abortion activists—had taken root in the minds of the men and women of middle Ireland.

The lie was repeated so often and with such intensity it became an entrenched part of the public narrative. Íde

O'Hara observed that the private polling and focus group research undertaken by Life Institute showed that the belief that Savita Halappanavar had lost her life had been deeply embedded in the cultural narrative by relentless and persistent media reporting. Savita's death had been a tipping point – and had led to a referendum where the hard cases were used to persuade the middle ground.

"A shift had taken place in the mindset of middle Ireland," Life Institute reported. "A search of RTE (the nation's largest news provider) for example, using the terms 'Savita, abortion' yields an astonishing 19,800 results since 2013. In contrast, a search using the terms 'Savita, sepsis' yields only 66 results, while only 114 results are found when searching for the terms 'Savita, medical misadventure'—even though three independent inquiries found that medical misadventure after a delayed diagnosis of sepsis caused her death."[clix] Indeed, the falsehood that Savita had died because she was denied an abortion took root around the world, with pro-life activists facing this argument in debates with abortion supporters right across North America, as well.

The repeal campaigners were fully aware of the fact that Savita's death and the accusation that pro-life laws were harmful to rape victims were their most powerful weapons. As May 25 grew closer and polls appeared to be tightening, they threw their efforts into reminding the Irish public of her untimely demise. Signs featuring Savita's face began to crop up right across the country in the final few weeks—while I was canvassing in Dublin, I headed down one street just as a man was putting up a sign marking a school as a polling station. By the time I came back up the street, there was already a Savita sign zap-strapped to the same pole just beneath it, the accompanying slogan both powerful and inarguable: *Savita Matters. Women Matter.* Throughout the final week, scores of them appeared in Dublin, many erected as close to polling stations as possible. At the Save the 8th headquarters, many of the pro-lifers were enormously frustrated. Savita had not died because of Ireland's pro-life constitution, and all of the evidence clearly stated that. But the truth didn't seem to matter, and the lie had taken root.

Two weeks before the vote, abortion activists even solicited the endorsement of Savita's parents, recording a highly emotional campaign video from India. In the video, Savita's father said he hoped "that the younger daughters of Ireland should not have the fate of Savita. I hope that people in Ireland will remember the fate of our daughter Savita on the day of the referendum and vote Yes so that what happened to us won't happen to any families. And by doing this you will be paying a great debt to the departed soul."[clx]

The video received a huge amount of media attention, garnering millions of views in the days before the vote, and generating more than a thousand news articles.

While pro-life organisations worked incredibly hard to bring the actual facts of the Savita case to public attention as well as rebut the lie that the Eighth Amendment was killing women, it soon became apparent that they were campaigning against the entire Irish media. Despite all evidence to the contrary, the media persuaded the public that the Eighth Amendment had killed Savita Halappanavar, and they compounded this misinformation campaign by pushing misleading statements by abortion campaigners such as Dr. Peter Boylan and refusing to correct the most egregious falsehoods. Boylan, for example, claimed that the Eighth Amendment had also caused the death of a woman named Sheila Hodges, when the truth is that Hodges tragically died of untreated cancer *before* the Eighth Amendment even became law.

Boylan's advocacy resulted in a group of obstetricians asking him to step away from his role as the head of the Institute of Obstetricians and Gynaecologists, as they felt his position on abortion had compromised his role. The media attempted to ignore and bury that story, just as they had buried and ignored other significant statements from pro-life doctors.

In addition to the Savita narrative, voters were constantly told that in a wide range of difficult circumstances, there was "no other way" to help women other than to provide them with an abortion. The spotlight was focused unwaveringly on difficult cases such as sexual assault and instances where the baby had a life-limiting condition, which were inevitably referred to as a "fatal abnormality" by the media.[clxi] The fact that these scenarios make up a tiny fraction of abortions was virtually never mentioned, and the media amplified these claims despite the fact that they were provably false. In almost every interview or debate in the last two weeks leading up to the referendum, the media focused repeatedly on pregnancy from rape, accusing the Eighth Amendment, and the pro-life spokesperson, of "forcing" women to carry a rapist's child. During the last major TV news piece on the referendum on RTÉ, by far the biggest Irish TV channel, the difference between how the Yes and No representatives were interviewed was stark. Yes campaigner Dr. Peter Boylan was permitted to paint the Eighth as oppressive and harmful to women. In contrast, Niamh Uí Bhriain was repeatedly pressed about abortion on the grounds of rape victims, while the presenter also countered pro-life points about the on-demand and late-term abortion clauses in the proposal with the talking points of the Yes campaign. One of the closing TV debates, hosted by veteran broadcaster Pat Kenny, was notable for the overt hostility he displayed toward prominent No campaigner, Maria Steen.

"At the Citizens Assembly and the Oireachtas Committee hearings, abortion supporters argued that the 12-week on demand provision was needed to ensure rape victims could be supported," said Íde O'Hara. "It was a thoroughly dishonest but clever move. They knew polls showed people opposed an on-demand abortion regime, so they dressed that up as a provision for abortion for rape victims. Then the media did their level best to make that the focus of all the debates. The No people were super on the media, but when the producer or presenter is framing the debate to make it all about the hard cases, that's what people hear."

One day while canvassing in Dublin, I was flipping through a newspaper when one of the pro-lifers pointed to it. "Coming from Canada and seeing our media, you must think that every woman who gets pregnant in Ireland was raped and carrying a baby with a fatal fetal abnormality that will threaten her life," he said. He was only slightly exaggerating.

In contrast to this, many courageous families who went on TV programs were often treated with open hostility in interviews: Their selfless stories provided a powerful counter-narrative and inconveniently exposed the selfishness and ugliness at the root of the push for abortion. The Save the 8th Campaign pumped out beautifully-told testimonies of women who had chosen life for their children despite sometimes extraordinarily difficult circumstances, including disability, life-limiting conditions, and conception through sexual assault. They shared stories of women who had faced medical challenges in pregnancy but received any intervention they needed, and gave a voice to women hurt by abortion. The media resolutely ignored these stories, ensuring that many voters went to the polls never realizing that there was another narrative that they were being prevented from seeing. These stories, of course, revealed two things that abortion activists wanted to silence: that women do not need abortion to rise above a crisis, and that the so-called circumstances they were referring to were actually *children*.

One powerful example of this is Vicky Wall, a young woman who worked in a clothing shop and hadn't previously been involved in the pro-life movement. She decided to tell the story of her daughter's death as she discovered the threat that legal abortion would pose to children such as her little girl. She summed up her plea to the Irish people in an op-ed published in *The Journal* two days before the referendum that captures the tenor of those who spoke out on behalf of children with "fatal foetal abnormalities":

> My little girl, Líadán, was diagnosed with Trisomy 18, a life limiting condition also known as Edwards Syndrome, a condition which arises because of an extra chromosome being present. Liadan was born at 32 weeks and passed away that day.
>
> Like too many women in Ireland, I know what it is like to hear a doctor telling you that your unborn child will not survive.
>
> I know that pain. I know that agony. I know that hopelessness and despair. For some women it is accompanied by a feeling of failure. The questions: What did I do wrong? Is it my fault?
>
> There is no grief like the loss of a child. It really doesn't matter how old that child is. There are women in Ireland who have lost adult sons and daughters. There are women who have lost children. There are women like me who knew that loss would come before their child saw even the light of day.

In my case, with Líadán, I knew that above all else, I had to be able to say goodbye in person. To meet her. To let her, if only for a moment, breathe the free air and touch her hand to mine.

She was not a baby with a fatal foetal abnormality, she was my baby, and she was perfect. Her life was short, but her life was full of the kind of love that you cannot express in words.

The bond between a mother and a child is sometimes described as sacred. That word does not do it justice. It is more than sacred – it defines the very nature of us as a species. Our unbreakable commitment to each other. Our solidarity. The way we are not just two separate individuals, but made of the same blood, the same flesh, and the same bone.

When a doctor told me to consider an abortion for Líadán, I recoiled in horror. To someone who does not understand the bond between a mother and her child, it might seem like an imperfect baby is a burden. It might seem like mercy to "end the suffering" or "ease the pain".

We convince ourselves of our own goodness. It's the curse of the human condition. Every horror we perpetrate has some higher goal, some noble purpose.

In the UK, nine out of every ten babies diagnosed with Down Syndrome are not permitted to see a single sunrise. Their lives and their experience are taken from them in the name of mercy. A life that could be so full of joy and happiness is reduced to a potential problem.

> The women who have these abortions are not bad people. I do not condemn them. I do not wish them ill. I do not write this to hurt them. I do not campaign for them to suffer. But the culture that tells them that abortion is a solution, or that abortion is merciful, or that abortion is kind? That has to go…
>
> We are being asked to sanction every future abortion in Ireland on the basis of my pain, and the pain of women like me. Our suffering has been shamelessly used by the YES campaign. Our suffering has been used by the government to bring in abortion on demand in Ireland.
>
> They want the public to feel our sorrow and our misery and our despair, and to turn their sympathy into a licence to kill. Well, I for one, and many others, will not stand by and stay silent while our suffering is used to inflict death on perfectly healthy babies.
>
> That is not medicine. It is not care. It is not compassion. It is indeed change, but not a change that we should ever countenance. That's why I'll be voting NO.[clxii]

One of the key talking points of the Together for Yes Campaign was "compassion," and the media promptly parroted this narrative. But as Niamh pointed out later, people with disabilities and their families played an enormous and special part in the No campaign. "We should be used to that," she noted. "These are families who have always had to fight for every little improvement in services, every small step forward in terms of the rights of people with disabilities. But this was different. This was personal because they were, in essence, asking that their communities be protected from what abortion inevitably brings—the elimination of people with disabilities. The Yes vote felt like a slap in the face for them, a rejection more devastating and more deeply hurtful than they could have imagined. I felt deeply ashamed, that this country—my country—had become so callous and selfish. We once described people with intellectual disabilities as 'daoine le Dia',or 'people with God', but now a majority of Irish people were willing to see the same people killed before birth."

Anne Trainer, the mother of a son with Down Syndrome who had campaigned for a No vote, echoed those sentiments. Months later, she said that the referendum result still felt like "a knife in the heart. I'm so glad we had an opportunity to try to make a difference and show a better way. It is not our fault people didn't listen. But it was such a betrayal of our children, of all people with disabilities. With a heartless and careless swipe of a pen they effectively stole the right to life of our most vulnerable people and tore up the spirit of our country. Their vote approved the eradication of future generations of Irish people like my son, who needed their protection. The Irish of old would have laid down their lives for their brothers, sisters, neighbours, or friends. How could we have lost that?"

The media did more than just ignore essential components of the pro-life argument. As Life Institute noted in their report, they also appointed themselves the pro-life movement's official opposition, and "every factual claim made by the pro-life movement was denied by the media."[clxiii] In some instances, the bias was so obvious that it would have been laughable if the consequences had not been so serious:

> Just one example was when the *Irish Times* wound itself into knots trying to deny the fact that one in five babies are aborted in Britain—a

> figure confirmed by the UK's Office of National Statistics. The Journal.ie went so far as to change their own previous fact-check which had found the statistic to be true, and then issue a 'revised' check supporting their contention that the figure was now untrue…RTE's Prime Time also went to great lengths to try to prove that abortion rates went down when abortion was legalised. The reality—that those rates inevitably climb higher—was airbrushed out by the Irish media. Almost every media outlet denied the reality that the government's proposal allows for later-term abortion, because they were very well aware that polls showed most people were opposed to this.[clxiv]

In contrast to this, the media ensured that the ugliness of the abortion industry and the campaign missteps of the Yes campaign were minimised, covered up, or simply ignored:

> Aisha Chithira travelled from Ireland to a 'safe, legal' abortion clinic in Britain. She bled to death after the abortion, but the Irish media covered up her death just as they under-report or ignore anything that might reflect negatively on the abortion industry. In a similar vein, they also ignored the errors of the Yes campaign, particularly when their spokespeople misspoke or revealed a mindset that would not find favour with middle Ireland. On RTE's Prime Time, Clare Daly denied the humanity of the pre-born child and made horribly offensive remarks about babies who were miscarried. If the No side had made a remark which was this offensive the media would have led a carousel of condemnation to influence voters, but, as usual, they buried Daly's

> misstep. Simon Harris and others repeatedly misspoke about what was actually in the abortion bill without any consequences. Yes campaigners were vicious in social media and thuggish in real life, tearing down half of the No posters and threatening pro-life volunteers. The media ignored all of that and more.[clxv]

There was also the Google factor. The Yes campaign "openly acknowledged that they had repeatedly asked Google to adopt a policy to limit the reach of the No campaign's message, telling the *Irish Times* that they were on to Google about the matter once a week."[clxvi] The media pushed the narrative of "outside influence" hard, with small handfuls of American pro-life activists (some of whom showed up to campaign independently of the Irish movement prior to the vote) getting enormous attention from journalists, while the impact of billionaires like George Soros went almost unmentioned. The media did not have a problem with outside influence on Ireland's abortion referendum, so long as it was influencing Irish voters in what they perceived as the right direction.

The Yes campaign, incidentally, was successful in getting Google to ban all advertising on the referendum, restricting the No campaign's ability to reach voters with messages that the media was also blackballing prior to the vote. Although Google claimed that the ban was fair due to the fact that neither side was permitted advertising, the obvious delight of abortion campaigners was an indication that they were fully aware of the fact that they didn't *need* Google. After all, they had the entire Irish media in lockstep behind their campaign, with the vast resources of print and television pushing their narrative and spiking stories that reflected badly on the abortion activists. While an essential outlet for the pro-life point of view had been cut off, the abortion campaigners benefited from what amounted to millions of euros worth of free advertising. Google's censorship also ensured that medical responses from pro-life doctors to the government's insistence that the Eighth was endangering women's lives went unheard in the vital last days of the campaign. The timing mattered – the media weren't interested in giving any coverage to pro-life medics at a time when they were promoting messages from Leo Varadkar and Savita Halappanavar's parents about repealing the Eighth to ensure women wouldn't die.

"As an example, in the last ten days especially, Save the 8th aimed to get hundreds of thousands of views on a remarkable documentary, *A Silent Killer,* made about Savita's death, which would have countered a lot of the mistruths that were being used to sway voters in those crucial days. But Google shut that avenue down, along with so much of the other vitally important messaging in the last days before the vote – the days that are crucial for undecided voters. Polls just before the Google announcement showed that the No campaign, to that point, had moved many Yes voters into the undecided camp. The Google shutdown was devastating – it was a clear and unwarranted interference in the democratic process for which they have never been called to account," said Niamh Uí Bhriain.

Since the referendum, Google was forced to admit to further interfering in the abortion referendum by manipulating search results and drawing up a secret, internal "black-list" for a significant number of terms used in searches in the abortion referendum.

After the "black-list" was leaked to the American investigative website Project Veritas in July 2019 by a former employee, Google had to confess that voters who searched using certain terms during the referendum had results for their searches manually altered by the company, ensuring that videos and reports chosen by Google appeared first.

Searches affected included "unborn life," "Save the 8th," "abortion is wrong," and "maternal mortality."

Google defended itself by claiming that: "In the midst of the Irish referendum on abortion, our systems brought authoritative content to the top of our search results for abortion-related queries. This happened for both pro-choice and pro-life queries, there was no distinction." However, Úna said this response did not stand up to scrutiny.

"Who decided what the 'authoritative content' was? Was it a government website (which was campaigning for Yes) or a biased, pro-Yes news site like every major media platform in Ireland? Or did they just bring them straight to the official Yes campaign? Who knows? Maybe all three? Google can bluster all they like but the truth is, if they were doing nothing wrong why did they want to hide it? Why was it secret? The reason is obvious: it's the elite interfering to manipulate ordinary voters, and doing it with the full knowledge that even if it is exposed, as this was, the mainstream media won't report it, which they didn't."

The role of Big Tech has increasingly come under the spotlight in other jurisdictions, with Dr. Robert Epstein presenting research to the US Senate Judiciary Committee in 2019 claiming that Google may have swung up to 10 million votes towards Hillary Clinton in the 2016 US presidential election.

As John McGuirk pointed out at the time, Google's decision very likely had little to do with the integrity of elections—instead, this was "about concerns that the No side might win. It is very clear that the Government, much of the establishment media, and corporate Ireland have determined that anything that needs to be done to secure a Yes vote must be done."[clxvii]

In short, Ireland's abortion activists had nearly the entire political, media, and civil establishment on their side "in addition to millions of euros in foreign funding and millions more in domestic funding channeled through domestic NGOs."[clxviii] As Life Institute succinctly put it, the "NO side was out first, reached further, debated better…but the persistent fear that the 8th was killing women, a fear created by years of media lies and misinformation, proved too difficult to overcome." It was a vote *against* the Eighth Amendment rather than a vote *for* abortion. The truth of this analysis is buttressed by the recent revelation that "according to the Edmund Burke Institute, a major poll of some 28,000 voters in 2016 indicated that more than 80% of people, at that time, supported repeal of the 8th."[clxix] In other words, the No campaign actually pushed a substantial percentage of the population *back* into the pro-life camp, as well as solidifying the pro-life vote that already existed.

Post-referendum analyses also found that turnout strongly favoured the Yes campaign. At 64.1%, turnout was fairly high but lower than expected for a debate that had dominated the public consciousness for so many years and with such intensity over the preceding months. Canvassers met dozens of people at the doors in Dublin and elsewhere who were opposed to abortion but hadn't registered to vote. Older people were both far more likely to vote against repeal but possibly less likely to actually get out and vote (one older fellow I spoke with said of *course* he'd be voting no, and then asked me when the vote was. That was on May 24.) Many of them simply did not think things could change so dramatically until they woke up on May 26 in a country they did not recognise. In many other homes, canvassers found that the votes of an entire family were dictated by a single, passionate family member—which may have had more of an impact than originally thought:

> A team of Irish and international observers from UK-based NGO Democracy Volunteers (DV) and Canadian NGO Sustainable Development Assistance International (SDAI) monitored the referendum on the 8th Amendment. They observed a "notable amount" of so-called family voting, which involves two or more people sharing a polling booth. The observers told the Journal that this "can limit voters' right to a secret ballot as it involves two voters, usually partners, sharing a polling booth". Family voting includes sharing the same polling booth when voting, looking at how another individual has voted and even filling in someone's ballot paper on their behalf.[clxx]

This is not to say that the prevailing analysis of a transformed Ireland is entirely untrue. There has, Life Institute stated, "been an undeniable shift amongst some voters, and there are now also greater numbers of people (still a minority of the electorate but more than previously existed) who think abortion should be legal for any reason at all. This culture shift towards a more extreme and callous position was boosted in part by anger at the [Catholic] Church but also by other factors, and was expressed [by] a swing in favour of legalised abortion, particularly amongst younger voters and female voters."[clxxi] Among this segment of the Irish population, the humanity of the pre-born child—beautifully highlighted by impossible-to-miss photographs posted throughout the country prior to the referendum—takes a backseat to the desire for sexual liberation.

The growing hatred of the Catholic Church in Ireland, sparked in part by the horrific sex abuse crisis, the coverup in the 1990s, and a host of other scandals over the past several decades, also contributed to the referendum result. It is a horrible shame, Life Institute noted in their autopsy of the campaign, that pre-born children had to suffer for the desire of some voters to "use a vote to punish the Church and to kick against what is viewed as an oppressive past."[clxxii] The successive scandals struck a shattering blow to the moral credibility of the Irish Catholic Church, and as such even those clergymen who wished to speak out prior to the referendum and urge people to vote to save the Eighth often decided to keep silent for fear of actually achieving the opposite result. Many Catholics voted to repeal the Eighth without ever hearing from their clergy on the issue, and this too contributed to confusion that benefited the repeal campaign. As commentator David Quinn noted after the referendum, one in three weekly Mass-goers voted to repeal the Eighth Amendment.[36]

It must also be noted that much of the clergy itself had also been trending liberal for decades, increasingly associating with left-wing politics and social justice issues rather than family and children as the microcosm necessary for faith to flourish. One of the first indications of this was the hysterical protests aimed at Ronald Reagan during his visit to Ireland in 1984, led in large part by priests and

---

36 That said, the pro-life movement had certainly gotten some support from clergy. "There were always great priests like Fr. Séan Cunningham, Fr. Des Sweeney, Fr. Ronan Cusack, and Fr. Anthony Scully right back to 1992, and then men like Fr. James Cashman, Fr. Clancy, Fr. Brian McKevitt, Fr. Maurice Colgan, Fr. Luuk Jansen, Fr. Colm Mannion, and all the Dominicans who were just tremendous. Lots of priests, including young priests like Fr. Shane Sullivan and Jamie Twohig spoke out repeatedly in the referendum, hundreds of priests did really," said Rebecca Roughneen. "Some of the bishops, like Kevin Doran and Alphonsus Cullinan were very outspoken too."

nuns who also took to the editorial pages to condemn Reagan for a long list of perceived crimes. Because of their exalted position in Irish society, the leftward drift of the clergy, beginning in the 1960s, had a profound effect. "You could have said the Irish were passive to Church authority," Mary Kenny wrote, "and never questioned why an action could be wrong and forbidden one month and suddenly acceptable and right the next."[clxxiii] Adding to that was the abysmal state of Catholic education, which by the early 1980s had barely half of teens affirming God's existence. Fundamental beliefs were not passed on, and so when it came time to put them to the test, they predictably failed. Other clergy were simply worn out, dispirited, and tired of receiving little support from their superiors.

Abortion campaigners heavily exploited the growing bias against the Catholic Church, assisted by a "growing stream of movies...released over the last 20 years purporting to show us what an evil and cruel nation Catholic Ireland was—*Angela's Ashes, The Magdalene Sisters,* and *Philomena* being the most notable."[clxxiv] Many Irish celebrities such as Liam Neeson openly made the connection between a dark Catholic past and the supposed cruelty of Ireland's abortion ban, with Neeson providing the voiceover for an Amnesty International "Repeal the Eighth" video called *Chains*. "A ghost haunts Ireland," he intoned, while the camera panned over the looming outline of a ruined cathedral in the mist and past a cross poking up through the grass, "a cruel ghost of the last century...it blindly brings suffering, even death, to the women whose lives it touches." That spirit, Neeson went on, "lives on in a constitution written for a different time...Ireland doesn't have to be chained to its past."[clxxv]

One example of this was the story of St. Mary's Mother

and Baby Home in Tuam, County Galway, a maternity home for unmarried mothers and their children. Run by a religious order of Catholic nuns known as the Bon Secours Sisters from 1925 to 1961, the Home had been set up to assist unwed pregnant women. In 2012, however, the Health Service Executive began an investigation into children being sent from the Home to adoptive homes in the United States without the consent of their mothers, and research by amateur historian Catherine Corless stipulated that almost 800 children had died at the Tuam Home of malnutrition, disease, and congenital disability, with most of them being buried in an unmarked grave onsite. These discoveries—the details of which are still being debated—received wall-to-wall media coverage as evidence of the profound cruelty of the Irish Catholic Church.

As Piers Shepherd wrote in his essay "Ireland's Anti-Christian Revolution": "Twenty-first-century Ireland measures what is right and wrong, moral and immoral, by discovering what the Catholic Church thinks and assuming the opposite position."[clxxvi] Catholic Ireland, the new consensus holds, was an awful place. One of the things that had made it awful was the Eighth Amendment, which was nothing less than Catholic dogma enshrined in law. Thus, the Eighth Amendment had to go. The baby, as it were, with the bathwater.

***

It took Tim Jackson a week to collect his thoughts before he finally sat down and began to write. When he was finished, he posted a eulogy to Facebook for the country he loved—a lament, with that irrepressible Irish hope rearing its head at the end:

Rest in peace, dear children. Rest in peace, dear land.

A nation has voted to kill its children. The Ireland of St.

Patrick, O'Connell, Pearse and Plunkett was sacked on May 25th as the sovereign people turned persecutor with the stroke of a pencil. The carefully crafted Constitution was also destroyed by inserting a fundamental right to kill, whilst celebrations that followed were as tasteless as they were cruel. Who among the cheering fathomed the darkness of the deed? Who else could celebrate a nation choosing to kill its own children but a propagandised and vacuous generation, bereft of love for country or feeling for the innocent to be slaughtered? Is there a more treasonous deed than this?

In times of persecution, famine and grinding poverty, the Irish were a resilient people, clinging to faith, hope and love with a lion-hearted defiance. Children were blessings, welcomed and sacrificed for, proof that there was a future despite mortal dangers and hardship. Now, babies of burden, they are threatening and therefore disposable, to be sacrificed if chosen on the idol altars of self-fulfilment and pleasure.

The underlying obstacle to abortion in this country was not the 8th Amendment. It was the spirit of the Irish people expressed so beautifully in the Preamble of the Constitution, affirming a willing devotion to the goodness of Christ and a sure sense of justice, purpose and integrity. As the bright flame of Christ was extinguished in soul after soul, it was inevitable that evil would envelope the land. The ship is sinking, the passengers asleep, and everywhere "the ceremony of innocence is drowned." Nihilism reigns. Christ is mocked. And Barabbas is free.

The level of irrationality was astounding: incessant appeals to equality, compassion and care were enough to convince the masses that this murder most foul was not glaringly discriminatory, barbaric and inhumane, but actually progressive. Little thought was given to a proper application of human rights, with a right to kill sought and sanctioned by popular demand.

But this will not be the last word. Whilst the deconstruction of the island of saints and scholars is nearing completion, the architects in their haste have forgotten to ask: who will inherit the land – is it those who kill their young or those who welcome each as gift?

I know the answer, many know the Truth, but the pain of stamping on the faces of Irish saints, martyrs, patriots and children is too much to witness. The land that kept the flame of western civilization alive on Skellig Michael, in Glendalough and Clonmacnoise has become a savage parody of nobler days gone by. Exiled and dejected, it is to the empty tomb that we turn again. He is Risen and with us, and we will not forget.

It is a cruel irony that tens of thousands of the babies who grew safely in their mother's wombs would one day cast their vote to repeal the Eighth Amendment that had protected them from the suction aspirator and forceps of the abortionist. As Michael Dougherty wrote two weeks after the referendum, most of the Irish voters had known what they were voting for: "They knew that in countries with laws comparable to the ones their legislature proposed to enact, the elective-abortion rate had climbed until abortion had become the end for roughly one in five pregnancies. They voted as they did, knowing that Dublin is one of the only European cities where people with Down syndrome are regularly seen in the streets, and knowing that the reason for this was that Ireland had the Eighth Amendment."[clxxvii]

And yet…

Epilogue

Over this campaign, I've met some of the most amazing and beautiful people Ireland has. People that I now call friends. I regret nothing. This isn't the end, just the beginning of a new phase. Thousands of new pro-life activists have come through a baptism of fire and are ready to fight the government and every government to come.

Patrick Martin, Irish Pro-Life activist,
on the day after the referendum

On July 7, 2018, thousands gathered for the annual All Ireland Rally for Life at Stormont in Belfast. For many of them, it was the first time they had seen each other since the referendum—and the first time they had gathered with other pro-lifers. It was sunny, the music was cheery, and people were happy to see each other. If they didn't think too hard, it was almost as if nothing had changed.

But of course, everything *had* changed. When Niamh Úi Bhriain mounted the stage after a rousing speech by Tim Jackson, her task seemed an almost impossible one: How do you deliver a eulogy and a battle cry at the same time? How do you both mourn the loss and hoist the banner?

She began.

Hello Belfast!

It's been a very difficult few months for us in the South, but I'm so delighted to be here today in Belfast, where you are still standing strong for life!

Her voice wavered, then steadied. There were cheers.

Where so many pro-life champions work night and day to protect mothers and protect babies from the unspeakable evil of abortion. And it lifts my heart, too, on the road here to see the good and decent people from the South who traveled to stand with you. Who came from Cork, from Roscommon, from Carlow, from Dublin, and Donegal—because they deserve another round of applause!

Finally, a genuine smile.

Donegal is the county that got this vote right, the county that can still stand proud and hold its head up high. But we came here today to stand with you in this fight, and to make our message very clear: We stand for life, and we will fight on. Because no referendum, no vote in Parliament, no piece of legislation, no unjust law, can ever make it right to kill a helpless child.

There were almost tears now, but she soldiered on.

On May 25th, if I'm to be honest with you, our hearts along with the 8th Amendment were utterly broken. Not for ourselves, but for the babies and for the mothers who will suffer the terrible consequence of what the people have done. Because we have lost, on that terrible day we lost something precious and beautiful. The fall of Ireland's pro-life protection was a wound to the soul.

From the sound of her voice, one could tell that the wound was still fresh. It was for everyone.

And the complicity of our people was a dark stain on our nation. It felt, and I think all of you felt it, on that day, it felt like an unexpected death—because that is what it was. It was the death of decency and kindness and compassion.

There was the applause of agreement, and you could hear her voice catch before she went on.

It was, as Tim Jackson said, the darkest day in Ireland's history, and a terrible cruelty was inflicted on the most innocent of all our people: Our helpless pre-born children. But you, the pro-life people, however, should stand tall, and hold your heads up high! Because your hands are clean! Because your conscience is clear! And because you fought the good fight to protect mothers and babies. And when the day comes, as it surely will, and when our people look back in horror at what they approved, this culture will swing back to overturn this horrific result, and this island, North and South, will be a pro-life nation once again.

Her eyes watered, and the cheers grew louder.

For thirty-five years in the South, you defended the right to life of every human being, and today, together, we continue to do so, because nothing, absolutely nothing, is made better by the killing of a child, and because we are called to defend the most innocent and the most vulnerable—even if we stand alone. But we do not stand alone, as the thousands of you here today can testify! And this movement, even in this year of our terrible loss, has been energized and motivated by the huge influx of newcomers to our cause, and by the young people, North and South, who gave this fight their all and who will continue to do so.

And know this too. In keeping abortion out of Ireland for all these years, you have saved hundreds of thousands of lives, and that is no small achievement. You should feel very proud that because of you and because of your sacrifice and your work and your prayers, Ireland stood strong for many, many years, long after many other countries had fallen. You stood against the greatest injustice in the world, and time will show you were on the right side of history. That should make you proud, and we are proud to stand with you, and to stand with 723,632 people who had the wisdom and the intelligence and the courage to vote No to abortion!

The crowd was hanging onto her words now. She was reading their hearts back to them.

In God's good time, all of those who stood to protect life will be vindicated, and I want to thank you, all of you from the bottom of my heart for your tireless, selfless, heroic efforts. You, each and every one of you, were the unsung heroes not just of the No campaign, not just of the Save the 8th campaign, but of the past thirty years or more. I have never witnessed such absolute dedication from so many thousands of people, and you should know that you are the lifesavers, you are the champions, you are the heroes, and it is my greatest honor to know you and to stand with you in this most noble fight of all as we work to restore our culture and to protect both mother and child.

There were cheers. They were honoured to know her, too. She forged on.

In his poem "The Mother," Patrick Pearse wrote: "Despite the weariness of much sacrifice, yet, I have my joy. My sons were faithful, and they fought." You were faithful, and you fought, and together we will fight on to restore the beauty that Ireland has lost. We are forever grateful to you, and we can never repay you, and you should know that your work was not in vain. Because two years ago, we were a movement, but now we are a risen people, and risen we shall remain!

We will show the world that we are a people that will overcome, even in the darkest hour, because we know that it is always better to light a candle than to curse the darkness. The writer J.R.R. Tolkien in his telling of epic tales of good and evil, made an observation that I think many of us will have felt as we witnessed how abortion campaigners absolutely disregarded the humanity of the living, growing child. Their lack of pity. Their lack of mercy towards an innocent human being. Tolkien said: "So much death. What can man do against such reckless hate?" And we felt that, I think, on May 25th, and in the weeks that followed. So much death. What can we as a people do against such reckless hate?

We can firstly stand strong, and we can then stand proud, and we can know that in our hearts we are a people of life who seek to love both mother and child! It is difficult for us to understand how the killing of a child can be cheered and celebrated in Dublin Castle in the most grotesque scenes possible, overseen by Minister Simon Harris and Taoiseach Leo Varadkar. Leo Varadkar, who made a promise that there would be no celebrations for the legalisation of abortion, a promise that proved itself to be just one more lie. There were many voters who were swayed by the relentless and persistent media lies, which convinced the middle ground of the entirely false claim that the 8th *Amendment was killing women. But I think we need to take stock and to recognise that there are others, campaigners and voters who seem to be driven by that reckless hate, by a cruelty that says if a child gets in the way, then that child must die. Never before, in the history of mankind, has cruelty been so effectively dressed up as compassion—because real compassion doesn't kill a helpless child and real compassion seeks to offer women a better answer than abortion!*

A pause. A deep breath.

But we are also a people of hope. It is important to recognise that there is a significant section of Irish society that do not share that reckless disregard for babies and that reckless support for abortion, that the Irish people are not indifferent to the humanity of every pre-born child. We know that 33% of us had the wisdom and courage to vote against the cruelty of abortion and that exit polls showed that at least half of our voters are unhappy with the abortion on demand provisions being proposed by the Government. Eighty percent of GPs, of doctors, in the South say they will not acquiesce to Leo Varadkar's demands and they will not carry out abortions.

Wild cheering erupted. There were tears, too. Watching it later, my wife and I both wept. I have seen many pro-life speeches over the past decade, but none have moved me quite like that one. Later, Niamh told me that all she could remember was how hard it was not to cry. "Then a lovely big strong man, a farmer, came over to me afterwards and cried his eyes out, said his heart was broken for all the babies," she told me. "I told him he couldn't have fought any harder or better—which was true."

And so, where does the pro-life movement go from here?

To say that the pro-life movement should have hope is certainly true, but to many of those who soldiered on and fought the fight for decades, appeals to hope will sound trite and hollow. Many now survey the nation that they thought they knew so well and wonder where hope can be found. Can laws protecting the lives of the pre-born be re-achieved? Certainly not in the short-term. The magnitude of the betrayal has been for some not only dispiriting, but crushing. "After the referendum people would come up to us, and they were literally suicidal," Úna told me. "They were that dark, depressed. It wasn't like one person had died. It was as if everyone who belonged to them had died."

In the weeks and months leading up to the referendum, the pro-life movement *had* been driven by hope. "We thought we were going to win," said Úna. "We had hope, and hope makes you fight for things." For many, that hope died on May 25, 2018. In its place was a crippling identity crisis: *What does it mean to be Irish now that Ireland has brought in baby-killing by popular demand?*

For many of the pro-lifers, the defeat of the Eighth Amendment represented something much larger than the loss of a pro-life Constitution. Activist after activist told me the same thing: The result of the referendum made them question their very Irishness. The pro-life movement fought for the lives of children first and foremost, but they were also fighting for Ireland because they believed in her history, her heroes, her culture, and her Christian heritage. To many, it was not just the Eighth Amendment that had fallen. It was Ireland herself.

"I was in shock for a period of time," John McGuirk reflected later. "I have decided since then that the scale of liberalism in the country, the scale of the reaction against Catholicism, is so strong as to essentially make political campaigning a fruitless activity for the next twenty years. I have decided to refocus myself towards commentary and journalism and writing and talking on the radio and shifting the culture slowly back, rather than being engaged in political campaigns, because I don't think the political avenues are open in the immediate term."

The shock of the referendum result changed McGuirk's view of his country in a definitive way. "It sickens me to watch the country become the country it has become," he told me. "I have become, in my public commentary, much more scathing about voters. I was usually one of those people who blamed politicians, but I am increasingly convinced that one of the greatest problems we have in our democracy are voters who refuse to think or engage critically. It's not that I've become less patriotic. But I have become far more critical of my country and the people in it, I think."

Some pro-lifers simply could not return to life as it was before the referendum. Vicky Wall spent the night of the referendum having dinner with some friends and the local bishop and avoided looking at the exit polls. But when she saw the results, she was stunned. "The pain was horrific," she remembered. "We knew what was going to come. We knew what this meant. People were going to die." It felt like a death, she said, because that is what it was. Throughout the day of May 25, people kept showing up with cake and tea to comfort her. It felt like a wake for the babies—and for the country.

Vicky had taken six months off for the campaign, and when she went back to her old job at a clothing retailer, everyone was kind to her, even those who had voted to repeal. Despite that, Vicky had a hard time pretending that nothing had changed. She constantly felt like asking her colleagues: *Do you know what you've done?* After another conversation with a colleague about abortion that seemed to go nowhere, Vicky decided that she couldn't live in the world of retail anymore—something she had done for years—and handed in her notice. She went to work for Every Life Counts, assisting parents who received a tragic diagnosis for their child. Her daughter Líadán, she told me, was the one who had led her down this path. Líadán's life might have been short, but it counted. After all, it had transformed the life of her mother and, as a result, the lives of so many others.

It is in stories like Vicky's that the Irish pro-life movement can find the way forward. Perhaps it is not *hope* that is necessary, because hope can fade or die—at least, when it is rooted in faith in fellow man. Hope, in some ways, must be given. And so perhaps what is needed instead is *defiance*—a full-throated rebellion against the evil and destruction of the Culture of Death that threatens the innocents, and an absolute refusal to live a normal life in the face of this betrayal. For examples and inspiration, the Irish pro-life movement does not need to look elsewhere. They need only to look at their own history, and the tens of thousands of lives that have been saved by the relentless efforts of thousands of their fellow citizens.

"It's been my experience in over 25 years of being involved in the pro-life movement that many of those most committed to this cause are the kinds of ordinary, unsung heroes that generally make the world a better place," Niamh told me. "What distinguishes pro-life people in particular, in my experience at least, is that they are often extraordinarily kind. They're the sort of person who will actually give space in their home to a woman in crisis, or fund a pregnancy centre when they are barely scraping by themselves, or comfort the broken-hearted whatever the time or the hour. They're generally also the same people quietly involved in helping homeless people or sick children or in making community games happen or planting trees, not because they are saints but because they care. They practice what Mother Teresa rightly observed is within the ability of all ordinary people: 'do small things with great love.'"

"There's an old Irish saying for it: *Ar scáth a chéile a mhaireann na daoine*, meaning that we thrive in each other's shelter—when we protect each other," she said. "Jesus described it as loving your neighbour as yourself. That mindset is what leads to human flourishing. I see it in the altruism of the ordinary men and women who strive, without recognition or acclaim, to save lives, to make things better, to protect both mother and child. Sometimes in the face of shattering defeats, we can forget that their everyday heroism has already saved so many lives. Now, even since the 8th was lost, the babies that continue to be saved by their kindness and compassion are the pinpricks of hope that light the darkness. Those volunteers are not for turning. They will work to rebuild this broken culture. The alternative is to create a culture so atomised, so callous, and so bereft of human connection that the glue that holds us together comes apart."

These were the people, Niamh reflected, who had juggled large families to make a daily or nightly shift on a canvass team, farmers who gave a section of their field to mount a pro-life sign, men and women who spent untold hours coating the country with posters, students who essentially abandoned their education for months, and lawyers, doctors, and nurses who spoke out despite the professional consequences of doing so. Some stories stand out:

> One man in Cork, Kevin Stromsoe, was diagnosed with pulmonary fibrosis, a severe and sometimes painful condition. He was passionate about the pro-life cause and in spite of his illness, he was determined to spend as much time as possible trying to protect mothers and babies from abortion. And so, despite his illness, he put up posters and dropped leaflets and delivered materials and canvassed doors, and worked and prayed that the 8th would be saved. He passed away shortly after the referendum.
>
> There are many such people. Oliver Doonan spent decades in the good fight, unfailingly cheerful and wise and optimistic. We lost him after the referendum too. And people like Ray Reynolds in Meath and Pádraig Walsh in Waterford, bright and able and full of compassion. They fought so hard, and maybe they know better than we do now what plans God has for us.
>
> What I saw in the referendum was the tremendous resilience, hope, and courage of the pro-life movement. And I feel now that the sense of despondency which was caused by the loss of the 8th is lifting. Hearts that had been broken are healing. There's a new sense of purpose and determination. Groups like Gianna Care are doing incredible work to help mothers who face unexpected pregnancies. New platforms are being built. Our loss has not diminished our resolve.

Abortion, Niamh said, might now be "the new reality in this new, harsh, pitiless, Ireland. But that is not my country. As the actor John Connors said, May 25th was the most shameful day in Irish history—but it is not our shame, because we did not vote for this. Instead, that shame should be felt by Simon Harris, by Leo Varadkar, by the Irish media, and by those who were too cruel or too foolish to know that the only compassionate answer is to love both mother and child. This cruel abortion regime is a stain on what was once a proud, pro-life nation. Time, and the persistence of the few, will change that once more."

There are encouraging signs that Niamh is right about that. In the 2020 elections, all fifteen TDs who voted against legalising abortion in 2018 retained their seats in the Dáil—and by contrast, many of the loudest voices for legalisation, including Catherine Noone, who chaired the Oireachtas Committee on abortion, lost their seats.

Her sister Úna echoed her sentiments. During the days following the referendum, she told me, it was difficult to simply be out and about, surrounded by the very people who had destroyed what was best about Ireland. At first, she said, she felt betrayed. At first, it made her feel profound grief. But then her feelings changed.

"They didn't betray me," she said. "They betrayed tiny, helpless, beautiful children. I got over the sadness, and it turned to anger very quickly. At first I thought: I'm not Irish. But then my perspective changed: No, *they're* not Irish. They are not what the men of 1916 were."

And with this defiance, the last Irish patriots will tirelessly seek to reclaim their nation—even if all of the odds are against them.

References

i Piers Shepherd, "Ireland's Anti-Christian Revolution," *Chronicles*, February 7, 2019, accessed October 30, 2019, https://www.chroniclesmagazine.org/2019/March/44/3/magazine/article/10846080/

ii Jonathon Van Maren, "African woman exposes dark secret behind Western humanitarian aid in new book," LifeSiteNews.com, May 4, 2018, accessed October 30, 2019, https://www.lifesitenews.com/blogs/african-woman-exposes-dark-secret-behind-western-humanitarian-aid-in-new-bo

iii Kitty Holland, *Savita: The Tragedy that Shook a Nation*, (Ireland: Transworld Ireland, 2013),42.

iv Michael Brendan Dougherty, "Ireland Repeals the Eighth," *National Review*, June 7, 2018, accessed October 30, 2019, https://www.nationalreview.com/magazine/2018/06/25/ireland-abortion-vote-catholicism-decline-sadly/

v Emily O'Reilly, *Masterminds of the Right*, (Dublin: Attic Press, 1988),17-18.

vi Rosanna Cooney, "Story of the 8th: How right-wing Catholic groups staged a remarkable political coup," Joe, May 22, 2018, accessed May 5, 2019, https://www.joe.ie/life-style/story-of-the-8th-how-right-wing-catholic-groups-staged-a-remarkable-political-coup-614595

vii Emily O'Reilly, *Masterminds of the Right*, (Dublin: Attic Press, 1988),149.

viii Rosanna Cooney, "Story of the 8th: How right-wing Catholic groups staged a remarkable political coup," Joe, May 22, 2018, accessed May 5, 2019, https://www.joe.ie/life-style/story-of-the-8th-how-right-wing-catholic-groups-staged-a-remarkable-political-coup-614595

ix Rosanna Cooney, "Story of the 8th: How right-wing Catholic groups staged a remarkable political coup," Joe, May 22, 2018, accessed May 5, 2019, https://www.joe.ie/life-style/story-of-the-8th-how-right-wing-catholic-groups-staged-a-remarkable-political-coup-614595

x Emily O'Reilly, *Masterminds of the Right*, (Dublin: Attic Press, 1988),10.

xi Emily O'Reilly, *Masterminds of the Right*, (Dublin: Attic Press, 1988),16.

xii Emily O'Reilly, *Masterminds of the Right*, (Dublin: Attic Press, 1988),16.

xiii Rosanna Cooney, "Story of the 8th: How right-wing Catholic groups staged a remarkable political coup," Joe, May 22,

2018, accessed May 5, 2019, https://www.joe.ie/life-style/story-of-the-8th-how-right-wing-catholic-groups-staged-a-remarkable-political-coup-614595

xiv Emily O'Reilly, *Masterminds of the Right*, (Dublin: Attic Press, 1988),28.

xv Emily O'Reilly, *Masterminds of the Right*, (Dublin: Attic Press, 1988),27.

xvi Emily O'Reilly, *Masterminds of the Right*, (Dublin: Attic Press, 1988),34.

xvii Emily O'Reilly, *Masterminds of the Right*, (Dublin: Attic Press, 1988),34.

xviii Emily O'Reilly, *Masterminds of the Right*, (Dublin: Attic Press, 1988),34.

xix Rosanna Cooney, "Story of the 8th: How right-wing Catholic groups staged a remarkable political coup," Joe, May 22, 2018, accessed May 5, 2019, https://www.joe.ie/life-style/story-of-the-8th-how-right-wing-catholic-groups-staged-a-remarkable-political-coup-614595

xx Emily O'Reilly, *Masterminds of the Right*, (Dublin: Attic Press, 1988),47.

xxi Emily O'Reilly, *Masterminds of the Right*, (Dublin: Attic Press, 1988),49.

xxii Emily O'Reilly, *Masterminds of the Right*, (Dublin: Attic Press, 1988),54.

xxiii Emily O'Reilly, *Masterminds of the Right*, (Dublin: Attic Press, 1988),54.

xxiv Rosanna Cooney, "Story of the 8th: How right-wing Catholic groups staged a remarkable political coup," Joe, May 22, 2018, accessed May 5, 2019, https://www.joe.ie/life-style/story-of-the-8th-how-right-wing-catholic-groups-staged-a-remarkable-political-coup-614595

xxv Rosanna Cooney, "Story of the 8th: How right-wing Catholic groups staged a remarkable political coup," Joe, May 22, 2018, accessed May 5, 2019, https://www.joe.ie/life-style/story-of-the-8th-how-right-wing-catholic-groups-staged-a-remarkable-political-coup-614595

xxvi Rosanna Cooney, "Story of the 8th: How right-wing Catholic groups staged a remarkable political coup," Joe, May 22, 2018, accessed May 5, 2019, https://www.joe.ie/life-style/story-of-the-8th-how-right-wing-catholic-groups-staged-a-remarkable-political-coup-614595

xxvii Emily O'Reilly, *Masterminds of the Right*, (Dublin: Attic Press, 1988),62.

xxviii "Story of the 8th," YouTube video, 9:59, posted by "Joe.ie," February 2, 2018, https://www.youtube.com/watch?v=B6yJH8obJsM&t=20s

xxix Emily O'Reilly, *Masterminds of the Right*, (Dublin: Attic Press, 1988),63.

xxx Emily O'Reilly, *Masterminds of the Right*, (Dublin: Attic Press, 1988),69.

xxxi Emily O'Reilly, *Masterminds of the Right*, (Dublin: Attic Press, 1988),70.

xxxii Emily O'Reilly, *Masterminds of the Right*, (Dublin: Attic Press, 1988),71.

xxxiii Emily O'Reilly, *Masterminds of the Right*, (Dublin: Attic Press, 1988),75.

xxxiv Emily O'Reilly, *Masterminds of the Right*, (Dublin: Attic Press, 1988),76.

xxxv Kitty Holland, *Savita: The Tragedy that Shook a Nation*, (Ireland: Transworld Ireland, 2013),43.

xxxvi "Story of the 8th," YouTube video, 9:59, posted by "Joe.ie," February 2, 2018, https://www.youtube.com/watch?v=B6yJH8obJsM&t=20s

xxxvii Emily O'Reilly, *Masterminds of the Right*, (Dublin: Attic Press, 1988),88.

xxxviii "Story of the 8th," YouTube video, 9:59, posted by "Joe.ie," February 2, 2018, https://www.youtube.com/watch?v=B6yJH8obJsM&t=20s

xxxix Rosanna Cooney, "Story of the 8th: How right-wing Catholic groups staged a remarkable political coup," Joe, May 22, 2018, accessed May 5, 2019, https://www.joe.ie/life-style/story-of-the-8th-how-right-wing-catholic-groups-staged-a-remarkable-political-coup-614595

xl Rosanna Cooney, "Story of the 8th: How right-wing Catholic groups staged a remarkable political coup," Joe, May 22, 2018, accessed May 5, 2019, https://www.joe.ie/life-style/story-of-the-8th-how-right-wing-catholic-groups-staged-a-remarkable-political-coup-614595

xli Rosanna Cooney, "Story of the 8th: How right-wing Catholic groups staged a remarkable political coup," Joe, May 22, 2018, accessed May 5, 2019, https://www.joe.ie/life-style/story-of-the-8th-how-right-wing-catholic-groups-staged-a-remarkable-political-coup-614595

xlii Rosanna Cooney, "Story of the 8th: How right-wing Catholic groups staged a remarkable political coup," Joe, May 22, 2018, accessed May 5, 2019, https://www.joe.ie/life-style/story-of-the-8th-how-right-wing-catholic-groups-staged-a-remarkable-political-coup-614595

xliii Rosanna Cooney, "Story of the 8th: How right-wing Catholic groups staged a remarkable political coup," Joe, May 22, 2018, accessed May 5, 2019, https://www.joe.ie/life-style/story-of-the-8th-how-right-wing-catholic-groups-staged-a-remarkable-political-coup-614595

xliv Emily O'Reilly, *Masterminds of the Right*, (Dublin: Attic Press, 1988),96.

xlv Fintan O'Toole, "Why Ireland became the only country in the democratic world to have a constitutional ban on abortion," *The Irish Times*, August 26, 2014, accessed October 30, 2019, https://www.irishtimes.com/news/politics/why-ireland-became-the-only-country-in-the-democratic-world-to-have-a-constitutional-ban-on-abortion-1.1907610

xlvi Emily O'Reilly, *Masterminds of the Right*, (Dublin: Attic Press, 1988),99-100.

xlvii Emily O'Reilly, *Masterminds of the Right*, (Dublin: Attic Press, 1988),99.

xlviii Emily O'Reilly, *Masterminds of the Right*, (Dublin: Attic Press, 1988),110.

xlix Emily O'Reilly, *Masterminds of the Right*, (Dublin: Attic Press, 1988),110.

l Emily O'Reilly, *Masterminds of the Right*, (Dublin: Attic Press, 1988),110.

li Emily O'Reilly, *Masterminds of the Right*, (Dublin: Attic Press, 1988),125.

lii Kitty Holland, *Savita: The Tragedy that Shook a Nation*, (Ireland: Transworld Ireland, 2013),47.

liii Kitty Holland, *Savita: The Tragedy that Shook a Nation*, (Ireland: Transworld Ireland, 2013),53.

liv Kitty Holland, *Savita: The Tragedy that Shook a Nation*, (Ireland: Transworld Ireland, 2013),54.

lv Kitty Holland, *Savita: The Tragedy that Shook a Nation*, (Ireland: Transworld Ireland, 2013),49.

lvi Kitty Holland, *Savita: The Tragedy that Shook a Nation*, (Ireland: Transworld Ireland, 2013),52.

lvii Monica Miller, *Abandoned: The Untold Story of the Abortion Wars*, (USA: St. Benedict Press, 2012),277.

lviii "Youth Defense Ireland's Pro-Life Activists," YouTube video, 19:59, posted by "Dan Holman," September 22, 2017, https://www.youtube.com/watch?v=bOIjdEejwoQ

lix Youth Defence. "History: 1992." Youth Defence. http://www.youthdefence.ie/history--1992/ (retrieved October 30, 2019)

lx Scott Millar, "Sinister Shadows," *Look Left*, December 2012, accessed October 30, 2019, https://www.lookleftonline.org/2012/12/sinster-shadows/

lxi "Youth Defense Ireland's Pro-Life Activists," YouTube video, 19:59, posted by "Dan Holman," September 22, 2017, https://www.youtube.com/watch?v=bOIjdEejwoQ

lxii Youth Defence. "History: 1993." Youth Defence. http://www.youthdefence.ie/history--1993/ (retrieved October 30, 2019 lxiii Youth Defence. "History: 1993." Youth Defence. http://www.youthdefence.ie/history--1993/ (retrieved October 30, 2019

lxiv Youth Defence. "History: 1993." Youth Defence. http://www.youthdefence.ie/history--1993/ (retrieved October 30, 2019)

lxv Youth Defence. "History: 1994." Youth Defence. http://www.youthdefence.ie/history--1994/ (retrieved October 30, 2019)

lxvi Youth Defence. "History: 1994." Youth Defence. http://www.youthdefence.ie/history--1994/ (retrieved October 30, 2019)

lxvii Youth Defence. "History: 1994." Youth Defence. http://www.youthdefence.ie/history--1994/ (retrieved October 30, 2019)

lxviii Youth Defence. "History: 1994." Youth Defence. http://www.youthdefence.ie/history--1994/ (retrieved October 30, 2019)

lxix Youth Defence. "History: 1994." Youth Defence. http://www.youthdefence.ie/history--1994/ (retrieved October 30, 2019)

lxx Youth Defence. "History: 1995." Youth Defence. http://www.youthdefence.ie/history--1995/ (retrieved October 30, 2019)

lxxi Youth Defence. "History: 1995." Youth Defence. http://www.youthdefence.ie/history--1995/ (retrieved October 30, 2019)

lxxii Pro-Life America. "Noelia Garcia." Pro-Life America. http://www.prolife.com/noelia.htm (accessed October 30, 2019)

lxxiii Pro-Life America. "Noelia Garcia." Pro-Life America. http://www.prolife.com/noelia.htm (accessed October 30, 2019)

lxxiv Suzanne Lowry, "The reinvention of marriage," *The Independent*, October 6, 1998, accessed October 30, 2019, https://www.independent.co.uk/arts-entertainment/the-reinvention-of-marriage-1176411.html

lxxv TruthTV. "Noelia Garcia." TruthTV. http://www.prolifeinfo.ie/mcms_print.php?nav=p-28199 (accessed October 30, 2019)

lxxvi Catherine Cleary, "Paris model addresses anti abortion rally," *The Irish Times*, January 27, 1997, accessed October 30, 2019, https://www.irishtimes.com/news/paris-model-addresses-anti-abortion-rally-1.25891

lxxvii Catherine Cleary, "Paris model addresses anti abortion rally," *The Irish Times*, January 27, 1997, accessed October 30, 2019, https://www.irishtimes.com/news/paris-model-addresses-anti-abortion-rally-1.25891

lxxviii Catherine Cleary, "Paris model addresses anti abortion rally," *The Irish Times*, January 27, 1997, accessed October 30, 2019, https://www.irishtimes.com/news/paris-model-addresses-anti-abortion-rally-1.25891

lxxix Catherine Cleary, "Paris model addresses anti abortion rally," *The Irish Times*, January 27, 1997, accessed October 30, 2019, https://www.irishtimes.com/news/paris-model-addresses-anti-abortion-rally-1.25891

lxxx Youth Defence. "History: 1997." Youth Defence. http://www.youthdefence.ie/history--1997/ (retrieved October 30, 2019) lxxxi Youth Defence. "History: 1997." Youth Defence. http://www.youthdefence.ie/history--1997/ (retrieved October 30, 2019)

lxxxii Kitty Holland, *Savita: The Tragedy that Shook a Nation*, (Ireland: Transworld Ireland, 2013),58-59.

lxxxiii Kitty Holland, *Savita: The Tragedy that Shook a Nation*, (Ireland: Transworld Ireland, 2013),59.

lxxxiv Youth Defence. "History: 1997." Youth Defence. http://www.youthdefence.ie/history--1997/ (retrieved October 30, 2019)

lxxxv Youth Defence. "History: 1997." Youth Defence. http://www.youthdefence.ie/history--1997/ (retrieved October 30, 2019)

lxxxvi Gemma O'Doherty, "C-Case mum: I grieve for my lost baby every day," *The Independent*, May 5, 2013, accessed October 30, 2019, https://www.independent.ie/ca/lifestyle/health/ccase-mum-i-grieve-for-my-lost-baby-every-day-29241584.html

lxxxvii Gemma O'Doherty, "C-Case mum: I grieve for my lost baby every day," *The Independent*, May 5, 2013, accessed October 30, 2019, https://www.independent.ie/ca/lifestyle/health/ccase-mum-i-grieve-for-my-lost-baby-every-day-29241584.html

lxxxviii Youth Defence. "History: 1997." Youth Defence. http://www.youthdefence.ie/history--1997/ (retrieved October 30, 2019)

lxxxix "Miss C: Don't use me to get abortion into Ireland," YouTube video, 1:54, posted by "Save Lives Stop Abortion," May 20, 2018, https://www.youtube.com/watch?v=lfGHlNz10Qs

xc "Miss C: Don't use me to get abortion into Ireland," YouTube video, 1:54, posted by "Save Lives Stop Abortion," May 20, 2018, https://www.youtube.com/watch?v=lfGHlNz10Qs

xci "Miss C: Don't use me to get abortion into Ireland," YouTube video, 1:54, posted by "Save Lives Stop Abortion," May 20, 2018, https://www.youtube.com/watch?v=lfGHlNz10Qs

xcii "13-year-old rape survivor brought to the UK for an abortion after violent rape speaks out," YouTube video, 1:19, posted by "Save Lives Stop Abortion," May 19, 2018, https://www.youtube.com/watch?v=0IkqoLuafUg

xciii Gemma O'Doherty, "C-Case mum: I grieve for my lost baby every day," *The Independent*, May 5, 2013, accessed October 30, 2019, https://www.independent.ie/ca/lifestyle/health/ccase-mum-i-grieve-for-my-lost-baby-every-day-29241584.html

xciv Gemma O'Doherty, "C-Case mum: I grieve for my lost baby every day," *The Independent*, May 5, 2013, accessed October 30, 2019, https://www.independent.ie/ca/lifestyle/health/ccase-mum-i-grieve-for-my-lost-baby-every-day-29241584.html

xcv Kitty Holland, *Savita: The Tragedy that Shook a Nation*, (Ireland: Transworld Ireland, 2013),59.

xcvi Youth Defence. "History: 1998." Youth Defence. http://www.youthdefence.ie/history--1998/ (retrieved October 30, 2019)
xcvii Youth Defence. "History: 1998." Youth Defence. http://www.youthdefence.ie/history--1998/ (retrieved October 30, 2019)
xcviii Youth Defence. "History: 1998." Youth Defence. http://www.youthdefence.ie/history--1998/ (retrieved October 30, 2019)
xcix Kitty Holland, *Savita: The Tragedy that Shook a Nation*, (Ireland: Transworld Ireland, 2013),59-60.
c Youth Defence. "History: 2000." Youth Defence. http://www.youthdefence.ie/history--2000/ (retrieved October 30, 2019)
ci Youth Defence. "History: 2000." Youth Defence. http://www.youthdefence.ie/history--2000/ (retrieved October 30, 2019)
cii Youth Defence. "History: 2000." Youth Defence. http://www.youthdefence.ie/history--2000/ (retrieved October 30, 2019)
ciii Youth Defence. "History: 2000." Youth Defence. http://www.youthdefence.ie/history--2000/ (retrieved October 30, 2019)
civ Youth Defence. "History: 2000." Youth Defence. http://www.youthdefence.ie/history--2000/ (retrieved October 30, 2019)
cv Youth Defence. "History: 2001." Youth Defence. http://www.youthdefence.ie/history--2001/ (retrieved October 30, 2019)
cvi Youth Defence. "History: 2001." Youth Defence. http://www.youthdefence.ie/history--2001/ (retrieved October 30, 2019)
cvii Youth Defence. "History: 2001." Youth Defence. http://www.youthdefence.ie/history--2001/ (retrieved October 30, 2019)
cviii The Pro-Life Campaign. "Welcome." The Pro-Life Campaign. https://web.archive.org/web/20020527102030/http:/www.prolifecampaign.ie/ (retrieved October 30, 2019)
cix Youth Defence. "History: 2005." Youth Defence. http://www.youthdefence.ie/history--2005/ (retrieved October 30, 2019)
cx Youth Defence. "History: 2007." Youth Defence. http://www.youthdefence.ie/history--2007/ (retrieved October 30, 2019)
cxi Youth Defence. "History: 2008." Youth Defence. http://www.youthdefence.ie/history--2008/ (retrieved October 30, 2019)
cxii Youth Defence. "History: 2008." Youth Defence. http://www.youthdefence.ie/history--2008/ (retrieved October 30, 2019)
cxiii Youth Defence. "History: 2012." Youth Defence. http://www.youthdefence.ie/history--2012/ (retrieved October 30, 2019)
cxiv The Dublin Declaration. "The Dublin Declaration on Maternal Healthcare." The Dublin Declaration. https://www.dublindeclaration.com/ (retrieved October 30, 2019)
cxv Ian Gentles, "Ireland's stellar record in reducing maternal and infant mortality," The DeVeber Institute, accessed October 30, 2019, https://www.deveber.org/2017/12/21/irelands-stellar-record-reducing-maternal-infant-mortality/
cxvi Life Institute. "Saoirse: The 20-year abortion freedom of Ireland." Kate Bryan. https://thelifeinstitute.net/blog/2012/

saoirse-the-20-year-abortion-freedom-of-ireland (retrieved October 30, 2019)

cxvii Kitty Holland, *Savita: The Tragedy that Shook a Nation*, (Ireland: Transworld Ireland, 2013),70.

cxviii Gavan Reilly, "Savita scandal: Reilly urges TDs not to prejudge results of inquiries," *The Journal*, November 14, 2012, accessed March 2, 2019, https://www.thejournal.ie/james-reilly-savita-response-investigation-674602-Nov2012/

cxix Kitty Holland, *Savita: The Tragedy that Shook a Nation*, (Ireland: Transworld Ireland, 2013),91-2.

cxx Kitty Holland, *Savita: The Tragedy that Shook a Nation*, (Ireland: Transworld Ireland, 2013),99.

cxxi Kitty Holland, *Savita: The Tragedy that Shook a Nation*, (Ireland: Transworld Ireland, 2013),105.

cxxii Kitty Holland, *Savita: The Tragedy that Shook a Nation*, (Ireland: Transworld Ireland, 2013),102-103.

cxxiii Kitty Holland, *Savita: The Tragedy that Shook a Nation*, (Ireland: Transworld Ireland, 2013),107.

cxxiv Kitty Holland, *Savita: The Tragedy that Shook a Nation*, (Ireland: Transworld Ireland, 2013),108.

cxxv Jerome Reilly, "Pro-choice activists got tip-off on tragic death," *The Independent*, November 18, 2012, accessed March 2, 2019, https://www.independent.ie/irish-news/pro-choice-activists-got-tip-off-on-tragic-death-28902755.html

cxxvi Kitty Holland, *Savita: The Tragedy that Shook a Nation*, (Ireland: Transworld Ireland, 2013),113.

cxxvii Kitty Holland, *Savita: The Tragedy that Shook a Nation*, (Ireland: Transworld Ireland, 2013),122-3.

cxxviii Kitty Holland, *Savita: The Tragedy that Shook a Nation*, (Ireland: Transworld Ireland, 2013),161.

cxxix Kitty Holland, *Savita: The Tragedy that Shook a Nation*, (Ireland: Transworld Ireland, 2013),161.

cxxx Kitty Holland, *Savita: The Tragedy that Shook a Nation*, (Ireland: Transworld Ireland, 2013),123.

cxxxi Life Institute. "The facts about the tragic death of Savita Halappanavar." Life Institute. https://thelifeinstitute.net/info/the-tragic-death-of-savita# (retrieved October 30, 2019)

cxxxii Kitty Holland, *Savita: The Tragedy that Shook a Nation*, (Ireland: Transworld Ireland, 2013),221.

cxxxiii Kitty Holland, *Savita: The Tragedy that Shook a Nation*, (Ireland: Transworld Ireland, 2013),219.

cxxxiv Kitty Holland, *Savita: The Tragedy that Shook a Nation*, (Ireland: Transworld Ireland, 2013),226.

cxxxv Kitty Holland, *Savita: The Tragedy that Shook a Nation*, (Ireland: Transworld Ireland, 2013),226.

cxxxvi Kitty Holland, *Savita: The Tragedy that Shook a Nation*,

(Ireland: Transworld Ireland, 2013),230.

cxxxvii Kitty Holland, *Savita: The Tragedy that Shook a Nation,* (Ireland: Transworld Ireland, 2013),230.

cxxxviii Harry McGee, "How the Yes and No sides won and lost the abortion referendum," *Irish Times,* May 26, 2018, accessed December 3, 2019, https://www.irishtimes.com/news/politics/how-the-yes-and-no-sides-won-and-lost-the-abortion-referendum-1.3509924

cxxxix Harry McGee, "How the Yes and No sides won and lost the abortion referendum," *Irish Times,* May 26, 2018, accessed December 3, 2019, https://www.irishtimes.com/news/politics/how-the-yes-and-no-sides-won-and-lost-the-abortion-referendum-1.3509924

cxl Harry McGee, "How the Yes and No sides won and lost the abortion referendum," *Irish Times,* May 26, 2018, accessed December 3, 2019, https://www.irishtimes.com/news/politics/how-the-yes-and-no-sides-won-and-lost-the-abortion-referendum-1.3509924

cxli RTÉ. (2016). *RTÉ/Behaviour & Attitudes 2016 General Election Exit Poll Report.* Retrieved from https://static.rasset.ie/documents/news/rte-exit-poll-report.pdf

cxlii Newstalk, "Majority want to see abortion in certain circumstances to be legal in Ireland," Newstalk, January 21, 2016, accessed April 15, 2020, https://www.newstalk.com/the-pat-kenny-show/48-of-people-believe-the-8th-amendment-should-be-removed-according-to-poll-619566

cxliii Gráinne Ní Aodha, "Leo Varadkar: It's 'only a matter of time' before a woman dies after taking abortion pills unsupervised," *The Journal,* May 18, 2018, accessed April 15, 2020, https://www.thejournal.ie/leo-varadkar-yes-referendum-4020189-May2018/

cxliv Ralph Riegel, "Coveney reveals what convinced him to back abortion," *The Independent,* April 30, 2018, accessed April 15, 2020, https://www.independent.ie/irish-news/abortion-referendum/coveney-reveals-what-convinced-him-to-back-abortion-36857139.html

cxlv Harry McGee, "How the Yes and No sides won and lost the abortion referendum," *Irish Times,* May 26, 2018, accessed December 3, 2019, https://www.irishtimes.com/news/politics/how-the-yes-and-no-sides-won-and-lost-the-abortion-referendum-1.3509924

cxlvi Sarah Bardon, "Victims of rape and incest should carry babies to full term, say campaigners," *Irish Times,* March 29, 2020, accessed April 25, 2020

cxlvii ibid

cxlviii Harry McGee, "How the Yes and No sides won and lost

the abortion referendum," *Irish Times*, May 26, 2018, accessed December 3, 2019, https://www.irishtimes.com/news/politics/how-the-yes-and-no-sides-won-and-lost-the-abortion-referendum-1.3509924

cxlix Kitty Holland, "Pro-choice canvasser 'shocked' by reaction on doorstep," *Irish Times*, March 11, 2020, accessed April 15, 2020, https://www.irishtimes.com/news/social-affairs/pro-choice-canvasser-shocked-by-reaction-on-doorstep-1.3422778

cl Pat Leahy, "Google abortion-vote ban unprecedented, so why did they do it?" *Irish Times*, May 10, 2018, accessed April 15, 2020, https://www.irishtimes.com/news/politics/google-abortion-vote-ad-ban-unprecedented-so-why-did-they-do-it-1.3489617

cli Sinéad Baker, "Life is precious: Donegal quietly defiant after voting no in referendum," *The Guardian*, May 27, 2018, accessed October 30, 2019, https://www.theguardian.com/world/2018/may/27/life-is-precious-donegal-quietly-defiant-after-voting-no-in-referendum

clii Jonathon Van Maren, "Irish pro-life leader explains why the abortion campaigners are so angry in victory," The Bridgehead, May 28, 2018, accessed April 15, 2020, https://thebridgehead.ca/2018/05/28/irish-pro-life-leader-explains-why-the-abortion-campaigners-are-so-angry-in-victory/

cliii Jonathon Van Maren, "Ireland has fallen—and the battle is just beginning," LifeSiteNews, May 28, 2018, accessed April 15, 2020, https://www.lifesitenews.com/blogs/ireland-has-fallenand-the-battle-is-just-beginning

cliv Melanie McDonagh, "What really happened in Ireland's abortion referendum," *The Spectator*, May 26, 2018, accessed October 30, 2019, https://blogs.spectator.co.uk/2018/05/what-really-happened-in-irelands-abortion-referendum/

clv Chad Pecknold, "Trudeau: abortion should be a 'human right' in Ireland," *The Catholic Herald*, August 21, 2017, accessed October 30, 2019, https://catholicherald.co.uk/news/2017/08/21/trudeau-abortion-should-be-a-human-right-in-ireland/

clvi Life Institute. (2018). Why the Referendum was Lost, pg 8

clvii Life Institute Report, "Why the Referendum was Lost," pg 8

clviii Life Institute Report, "Why the Referendum was Lost," pg 4

clix Life Institute Report, "Why the Referendum was Lost," pg 4

clx "Savita's parents back repeal of Eighth Amendment ahead of referendum," *The Belfast Telegraph*, May 20, 2018, accessed 30, 2019, https://www.belfasttelegraph.co.uk/news/republic-of-ireland/savitas-parents-back-repeal-of-eighth-amendment-ahead-of-referendum-36927114.html

clxi Life Institute Report pg 5
clxii Vicky Wall, "She was not a baby with a fatal foetal abnormality, she was my baby, and she was perfect," *The Journal*, May 23, 2018, accessed December 2, 2019, https://www.thejournal.ie/readme/she-was-not-a-baby-with-a-fatal-foetal-abnormality-she-was-my-baby-and-she-was-perfect-4028600-May2018/
clxiii Life Institute Report, "Why the Referendum was Lost," pg 9
clxiv Life Institute Report, "Why the Referendum was Lost," pg 9
clxv Life Institute Report, "Why the Referendum was Lost," pg 10
clxvi Life Institute Report, "Why the Referendum was Lost," pg 10
clxvii Adrian Weckler, Kyle Ewald, and Nicola Anderson, "Google and YouTube to ban all ads relating to abortion referendum, *The Independent*, May 9, 2018, accessed December 2, 2019, https://www.independent.ie/irish-news/abortion-referendum/google-and-youtube-to-ban-all-ads-relating-to-abortion-referendum-36889599.html
clxviii Life Institute Report, "Why the Referendum was Lost," pg 11
clxix Life Institute Report, "Why the Referendum was Lost," pg 11
clxx Life Institute, "Why the Referendum was Lost," pg 7
clxxi Life Institute, "Why the Referendum was Lost," pg 6
clxxii Life Institute, "Why the Referendum was Lost," pg 6
clxxiii Piers Shepherd, "Ireland's Anti-Christian Revolution," *Chronicles*, February 7, 2019, accessed October 30, 2019, https://www.chroniclesmagazine.org/2019/March/44/3/magazine/article/10846080/
clxxiv Piers Shepherd, "Ireland's Anti-Christian Revolution," *Chronicles*, February 7, 2019, accessed October 30, 2019, https://www.chroniclesmagazine.org/2019/March/44/3/magazine/article/10846080/
clxxv "Chains," YouTube video, 1:35, posted by "Amnesty International Ireland," October 19, 2015, https://www.youtube.com/watch?v=j9W33wCm7Ao
clxxvi Piers Shepherd, "Ireland's Anti-Christian Revolution," *Chronicles*, February 7, 2019, accessed October 30, 2019, https://www.chroniclesmagazine.org/2019/March/44/3/magazine/article/10846080/
clxxvii Michael Brendan Dougherty, "Ireland Repeals the Eighth," *National Review*, June 7, 2018, accessed October 30, 2019, https://www.nationalreview.com/magazine/2018/06/25/ireland-abortion-vote-catholicism-decline-sadly/

The following list is a partial accounting of the thousands of Irish pro-lifers who fought the good fight to save the lives of pre-born children over the past decades. It would be an impossible task to gather all of these names, so those named here are a representation of the legions who fought for the rights of the nameless—and saved hundreds of thousands of people by their efforts.

A Brennan
A de Barra
A Dunphy
A Goodwin
A Hopper
A Lee
A Leonard
A Ryan
Aaron Doherty
Abigail Malone
Adrian O D
Adrian O'Boyle
Adrian Shiels
Afric Ní Fhloinn
Agnes Breen
Agnes Flaherty
Agnes Mc Cauley
Agnes McKeown
Aidan Doherty
Aidan Nolan
Aideen Graham
Aideen Stedman
Aileen McCarthy
Áine Killian
Áine Mc Carthy
Áine Ní Riain
Áine Nolan
Áine O C
Áine Wilkinson
Aisling Armstrong
Aisling Bastible
Alan Chaytor Grubb
Alex Archer
Alexander McKay
Alice Dean
Alice O Driscoll
Alicea Brennan
Ambrose Donnelly
Amy Cannon
Ana Cabeza
Andrew Breen
Andrew O'Regan
Angela & Eamonn Cunningham
Angela Collins
Angela McNally Staunton
Angela O'Connor
Angela O'Neill
Angelo Bottone
Ann & Francie Brolly
Ann Campbell
Ann Creighan
Ann Gallagher
Ann Marie Buckley
Ann Marie Harvey
Ann Marie Murphy
Ann Mc Namara
Ann Murphy
Ann O'B
Ann O'Brien
Ann O'Connor
Anna Brady
Anna Daly
Anne Fitzgibbon
Anne Flynn
Anne Hackett
Anne Herlihy
Anne Johnston
Anne Keeling
Anne McC
Anne Murray
Anne O'Connell
Anne Power
Anne Trainer & Family
Annette & Francis Furlong
Annie Cawley
Annie Ryan
Annie Sherry
Annie Taaffe
Anraoi Buckley
Anthony & Sheila Mc Cauley
Anthony Brennan
Anthony D
Anthony Kavanagh
Anthony Mc Gorian
Anthony O Brien
Anthony O Sullivan
Antoinette Kavanagh
Antoinette Sands
Aoife Collins
Aoife Martin
Attracta Burns
Audrey Wall
Austen Corcoran
Avila D
Avril O Connell
B & A Brady
B & T Mitchell
B Hughes
B Leaper
Barney Burke
Barry & Dana H
Barry Mullen
Becky Kealy
Belinda Hamilton
Ben Dalton O Sullivan
Ben Scallan
Ben Wallace
Bernadette & Derek Smyth
Bernadette Barrett
Bernadette Bonar
Bernadette Smithers
Bernard Wright
Bernie Costelloe
Bernie Grant
Bethany O Mahony
Bill Fitzpatrick
Birute K
Br Jeremy Henehen
Br Kevin Tracey
Breda Mc
Breda Mc Ardle

Breige O Brien
Brenda McG
Brendan Crowley
Brendán Ó Concubhair
Brendan Tarrant
Brian Bonar
Brian Brady
Brian Flanagan
Brian Gallagher
Brian Harney
Brian Lenehan
Brian McGee
Brian O Caithnia
Brian Sexton
Brian Smyth
Brianna Cocuzzo
Bridget Gallagher
Bridie Corbett
Bridie Diver
C Crowley
C Kennedy
C Murphy
C Pembroke
C Quinlan
C Quinn
Caitlin McGlynn
Caitriona Gallagher
Caoimhe Lynch
Caren Hallahan
Carmel Berry
Carmel Moloney
Carmel Shanley
Carmel Swift
Caroline Crehan
Caroline Heraghty
Caroline Mc Carthy
Caroline Mc Donald
Carolyn Uí Mheadhra
Cathal Harte
Cathal Quinn
Catherina O' Sullivan
Catherine Breen
Catherine Collins
Catherine Dilworth
Catherine Flynn
Catherine Hanley
Catherine Kealy
Catherine M
Catherine Manning
Catherine Mc Carthy
Catherine Mc Clelland
Catherine Meaney
Catherine Moriarty
Catherine O B
Catherine O Leary
Catherine O Sullivan
Catherine Ryan & Family
Catherine S
Cathy Molloy
Cecilia Singleton
Charlene Mc Daid
Charles Byrne
Charlie Doherty
Charlie Gallagher
Charlotte Ancona
Chris Fitzpatrick
Chris Hannon
Chris Scanlon
Christina Tobin
Christine D'Arcy
Christine Duignan
Christine Murphy
Christine O Hara Lyons
Christine Reardon
Christy Deely
Christy May
christy quinn
Ciara & Keith Kavanagh & Family
Ciara Breen
Ciara Mc Alister
Ciara Murphy
Ciaran Gallagher
Ciarán O Riordan
Cillian Kelly
Claire O Donoghue
Claire Philbin
Clann Uí Churraoin
Clara Flanagan
Clare Hallahan
Clare Moloney
Clare O Toole
Clare R
Clare Ryan
Clodagh Gallagher
Clodagh Mc Allen
Colm Callanan
Con C
Con L
Con Leddy
Con Lucy
Concepta Quinn
Conor O'Donoghue
Conor, Michael & Audrey O'Dowd
Cormac Corcoran
Crona Bonner
Cronia O Reilly
Daire Fitzgerald
Damian H
Damian Rosinski
Damien Murphy
Damien Richardson
Dan & Geraldine Ryan
Dan Collins
Dan McCarthy
Dan O'R
Daniel Holland
Danny Cooper
Danny Gorman
Darach Mac Mathuna
David Aherne
David Cooney
David French
David Kelly
David Lohan
David McDwyer
David O Donnell
Davina Mc Veigh
De Deirdre Gleeson
Declan O Mahony
Declan Roche
Deirdre Gallagher
Deirdre Moxham
Deirdre Nevin
Deirdre Ui Ghoibin
Delia Bryan
Denis & Helen O'Connor & Family
Denis Donnelly
Denis H
Denis Healy
Denis Meehan
Denis O Riordan
Denis Taylor
Denise O Rourke
Denise Wallace
Derbhile Buckley
Derek Johnston
Derek Smyth
Dermot O'Hara
Dervela O Hanlon
Des Kavanagh

Diarmuid Collins
Diarmuid Gallagher
Diarmuid O Connell
Dick Fleming
Dick H
Doctors for Life
Dominic Deane
Donagh O'Callaghan
Donal & Rita O Driscoll
Dónal & Eleanor Fallon
Donal Griffin
Donal Mac Mathuna
Dónal Ryan
Doreen Malone
Dr Anne McCloskey
Dr Aisling Bastible
Dr Fiona O'Hanlon
Dr Jim Stacey
Dr Kirsten Fuller
Dr Louis Courtney
Dr Maireneasta Nic Gearailt
Dr Maureen O'Carroll
Dr Patricia Thorne
Dr Patrick Kiely
Dr Richard Hurley
Dr Ronan Cleary
Dr Séamus Mac Mathúna
Dualta Roughneen
E Cashman
E Daly
E Dolan
E Foley
E Tynan
Eadaoin Byars
Eamon S
Eddie Meehan
Edel Purcell
Edel Sands
Eileen C
Eileen Coyle
Eileen Donegan
Eileen Gunning
Eileen M
Eileen Moitier
Eileen Mooney
Eileen O'D
Eileen Porter
Eilin Glynn
Eilis Egan
Eilish B
Eithne Cotter
Eithne Lynch
Elaine Healy
Elaine Sheehan
Elaine Wall
Elaine Wolfe
Eleanor Healy
Eleanor McFadden
Eleanor McGee
Eleanor O Keeffe
Elizabeth & Red O'Hanlon
Elizabeth Hogan
Elizabeth Mahon
Elizabeth O Halloran
Elizabeth Twomey
Ellen Cogavin
Ellen O'Shea
Ellen Troy
Elsie Glynn
Emer Tobin-O'Connor
Emma Byrne
Emma O Connell
Ena Spillane
Enda Galligan
Esme Caulfield
Eszter Schittl
Eugene Kealy
Eugene Smith
Eva Kelly
Evelyn Nic Mhathuna
Evelyn Norton
F Lyons
F. O'Dea
Fabio Negrao
Faoiltiarna Nic Charthaigh
Fatima Gunning
Fay Clohessy
Felim
Fergal O Dea
Finian Twomey
Fintan Power
Fiona Carroll
Fiona McHugh
Fionbar Lyons
Fionnuala Ni Dhomhnaill & Family
Fionnuala Woods Darby
Flan Bourke
Fr Anthony Scully
Fr Brian McKevitt
Fr Ciaran Shorten
Fr Colm Mannion
Fr Des Sweeney
Fr Frank Fahey
Fr James Cashman
Fr Jamie Twohig
Fr Joe Clavin
Fr John Joe Duffy
Fr Luuk Jansen
Fr Lynch
Fr M O'Shea
Fr Maurice Colgan
Fr Sean Crowley
Fr Séan Cunningham
Frances Beechinor
Francie Cassidy
Francie McCabe
Francis Mooney
Francis Porter
Frank Cahill
Frank Coyle
Frank Keady
Frank McNeill
Frank Stack
Freda Stout
G Murphy
G Quiglet
Garreth Quigley
Gavin Mc Cafferty
Gemma & Tríona King
Gemma Haire
Gemma Haire
Gene Buckley
Gene Flood
Gene McGinnity
Geoffrey Porter
Geoffrey Sumner
George Osborne
Georgie Cairns
Geraldine Domergue
Geraldine Toal
Gerard Joyce
Gerry Buckley
Gerry Hand
Gerry Ó Flanagáin
Gerry Sheehan
Gill Doherty
Glenn McDyre
Gordon Celender
Grace Cantillon Murphy
Grace McBreen & the McBreen Family

Graham Mooney
Grainne Mc Groarty
Gretta Murphy
H Carroll
Hannelore Harris
Heidi Flanagan
Helen Byrne
Helen Deasy
Helen O'Donovan
Helen Segrave
Helena Byrne
Henry Russell
Hilary Fagan
Hugh Lennon
Hugh O'Rourke
Ian White
Irene Healy
Isabelle Ní Fhloinn
Iseult O Connor
Ita Lenehan
J & S Smith
Jacinta Mc Gorian
Jacinta Skelly
Jack Cullinane
Jack Little
Jackie McLoughlin
James Hogan
James Kelly
James Maher
Jane Flood
Jane Flood
Jane McGurl
Jane Murphy
Jason Hamilton
Javier Silvestre
Jean Moore
Jeannie Coyle
Jennifer Daly
Jennifer McKeown Regan
Jeremiah Costello
Jerry & Catherine
Mulvihill
Jerry Cashman
Jerry Higgins
Jesus Torcat
Jim & Noreen Vesey
Jim & Kitty O'Sullivan
Jim & Phyllis Finnegan
Jim Boyle
Jim Brady
Jim Coen
Jim Comiskey
Jim De Groot
Jim Garvey
Jim Martin
Jim McDonagh
Jim McDonald
Jim O Sullivan
Jimmy & Sally Brauders
& Family
Jimmy McMahon
Jo O Brien
Joan Ahern
Joan & John Herriott
Joan & Seán Kelly
Joan Kavanagh
Joan Kelly
Joan McMahon
Joan Ryan
Joan Walsh
Joanne Cosgrove
Joanne Murphy
Joe & Alice Kearney
Joe & Annette Green
& Family
Joe Duffy
Joe Harte
Joe Kavanagh
Joe Kehoe
Joe Maher
Joe O'Gorman
Joe Walsh
Joel & Cynthia R
& Family
John Woods
John Ahern
John C
John Connors
John D Walsh
John Dill
John Donohoe
John Egan
John Harney
John Heaney
John Jackson
John Joe Culloty
John Joe Murphy
John L
John Lane
John M Cullinane
John Mahon
John Mc Cullen
John Mohan
John Mullins
John Nealon
John O Connor
John O Donovan
John O Riordan
John O'Donnell
John Sorahan
John Stafford
John Stephenson
John Taaffe
John Weldon
John, Lisa, Aine, Roisin,
& Sean Blackwell
Josh O Míocháin
Judith Tait
Julie Connolly
Junia Rezende Jackson
K Downey
K Mrvova
Kaitlyn Cocuzzo
Kala Moline
Karen Brady
Karen Keohane
Karen M C
Karen McTigue
Kate Bryan
Katherina Pettit
Katherine Niedzwiedz
Kathleen Barr
Kathleen Hughes
Kathleen Sheridan
Kathy Bell
Kathy Manning
Kathy O'Hara
Kathy Sinnott
Kathy Synnott
Katie Black & Family
Katie Duffy
Katie Sexton
Katy Robinson
Kay Kearney
Kelly Murlihy
Ken Brennan
Kevin & Geraldine Jones
Kevin Breen
Kevin Collier
Kevin O Connell
Kevin O Flynn
Kevin Smith
Kevin Stromsoe

Kevin Trainer
Killian R
Krzysztof Kiedrowski
L Brennan
L Whyte
Laura O Keeffe
Leah Boyle
Lee Walsh
Lelia O Flaherty
Len Carolan
Leo O Callaghan
Leonard Coughlan
Liadan Herriott
Liam & Moira Hayden
Liam Breathnach
Liam Coughlan
Liam Dooley
Liam Heffernan
Liam Mc Daid
Liam McElroy
Liam Ó Síocháin
Lillian Keane
Lily Whelan
Linda & Dary Farrelly
Linda Boyce
Linda Gorman
Linda Haynes
Lisa Greene
Lisa Russell
Listowel/Duagh Pro-life
Liz Bermingham
Longford Pro Life
Lorcán Mac Mathúna
Loretta O Connor
Lou Metzer
Louise Cronin
Louise Elliott
Louth Pro Life Network
Lúcás O Míocháin
Luka Jagodic
Lucy Kelly
Lucy Mc Donald
M & M Sherlcok
Martin Colfer
M Conlon
M Kinsella
M Maguire
M McManus
M Melichar
M Nolan
M Ó Ceallaigh
M O'Halloran
M O'Regan
M O'Toole
M&T Deegan
Maeve & Evana O Donnell
Maeve Byrne
Maeve McDermot
Maeve O'Hanlon
Magdalen Lawless
Mai McCarthy
Maire Bonar
Maire Ni Bhroin
Mairead Hughes
Mairead Scannell
Mairtin O'Droma
Maithiún Ó Caoimh
Malachy O Brien
Mamie Aherne
Margaret Byrne
Margaret Carey
Margaret Collins
Margaret Friel
Margaret Goulding
Margaret Herman
Margaret Hickey
Margaret Mason
Margaret Mc Geehan
Margaret McGovern
Margaret Roche
Margaret Scanlon
Margaret Smyth
Margaret Ward
Margaret Williams
Margo Hurst
Margot DLP
Marguerite Genocky
Maria & Harry Buckley
Maria C
Maria Casey
Maria Corcoran
Maria Mayes
Maria Maynes
Maria Quinn
Marian Curran
Marian Kane
Marian McGinnity
Marian Regan
Marian S
Mariavi Pueyo
Marie Campbell
Marie Donnelly
Marie Duffy
Marie Lynch
Marie O Donovan
Marie Therese Byrne
Marion Murphy
Marlyn Donegan Hilliand
Martin & Fionnuala Hughes
Martin Colfer
Martin Dunn
Martin Hallisy
Martin Mc Guill
Martin Parker
Martin Sneyd
Martin, Elizabeth & Nicole Moloney
Martina Cummins
Martina Gallagher
Martina Kinsella
Martina Mc Manus
Mary & Arthur McDermott
Mary & Hollie Kenny
Mary & Tony Smith
Mary Anne Collins
Mary Barrett
Mary Bridget Kelly, Clare Kelly & Siobhan Delany
Mary Burke
Mary Burlee
Mary C
Mary Coughlan
Mary Coughlan
Mary Cronin
Mary Crosbey
Mary Cummins
Mary Curran
Mary D
Mary Doherty
Mary Dolan
Mary Dooley Desmond
Mary Duffy
Mary E McKeown
Mary Ellen Hurley
Mary F
Mary F
Mary Fortune
Mary Foy
Mary G Duffy
Mary Gallagher
Mary Gregg

Mary Griffith
Mary Hande
Mary Joe
Mary Kennedy
Mary L
Mary Lawlee
Mary Long
Mary M
Mary Martin
Mary Martin
Mary Mc CArthy
Mary Mc Clelland
Mary Mc Menamin
Mary Mc Namara
Mary McCabe
Mary McCarthy
Mary McEvoy
Mary McGuigan
Mary N
Mary O Neill
Mary O Riordan
Mary O'L
Mary Power
Mary Rose Dennehy
Mary Rose Doherty
Mary Ryan
Mary Smyth
Mary T
Mary T Sweeney
Mary Thornton
Mary Walsh
Mary White
Matt Moran
Matteo Casotti
Matthew McEneaney
Matthew Wall
Maura O'Brien
Maura Sheeran
Maura Simons
Maureen Bashford
Maureen Blackwell
Maureen Devlin
Maureen Devlin
Maureen McIntyre
Maureen O Leary
May Tuite
Meath for Life
Meav Uí Ghallchóir
Melaine Devereux
Michael & Mary Fitzgibbon & Family
Michael B
Michael Burke
Michael C Doonan
Michael Cassidy
Michael Frawley
Michael Griffin
Michael Harkin
Michael Mc Elwee
Michael Mc Ginley
Michael N
Michael O Rourke
Michael O'R
Michael Tanner
Michael Tierney
Michael Tormey
Michéal Ó Coisdealbha
Michelle Quigley
Michelle SD
Mick & Trish Moore
Mick Billane
Mick Bowes
Mick Bowes
Mick Hamilton
Mick Harkin
Mimi Cashman
Miriam Doran
Miriam Goulding
Miriam Pettit
Moira Brennan
Moira O'Regan
Molly McDaid
Mona Stromsoe
Monaghan Pro Life
Monica Gahan
Monica Shinnick
Monika Smulska
MOR
Mr & Mrs David Condell
Muriel Kinsella
Myles Monaghan
Myra O REgan
N & E Feeney
N Mc Areavey
Nellie Fisher
Nellie Long
Niamh Kearney
Nick Folley
Noble Paul
Noel Buckley
Noel Carter
Noel O'Rourke
Noelle Mc Carthy
Noelle Prior
Noelle Tobin
Nora Bennis
Nora Bennis
Nora Harley
Nora Mc Kennedy
Nora Sullivan
Norah Kilcourse
Noreen Hunt
Norma O Leary
Norman Collins
Nuala Keane
O'Donoghue Family
Odon Flanagan
Olive Ni Bhraonain
Oliver Bible
Oliver Doonan & Family
Oliver Maher
Olivia Connolly
Olivia Larkin
Oonagh McCartney
Ora D
Owen Crowley
Owen Kane
P & G McCabe
P Clarke
P Doyle
P Gibbons
P McCaulfield
P Ryder
Paddy & Margaret Despard
Paddy & Anna Grogan
Paddy Connolly
Paddy Early
Paddy Heffernan
Paddy Manning
Paddy Martin
Paddy Scully
Pádraic Walsh
Padraig Forde
Padraig Pyne
Padraig Sands
Pádraig Walsh
Pamela Meehan
Paolo Albanese
Pastor Craig Ledrette
Pastor Lionel Smith
Pat & Katiie Mahoney

Pat & Helena Garvey
Pat Buckley
Pat C
Pat Devlin
Pat Greenan
Pat L
Patricia F
Patricia F
Patricia Friel
Patricia Gardiner
Patricia Mc Gee
Patricia O Connor
Patricia Shannon
Patrick Gallagher
Patrick Slevin
Patsy & Rory Buckley
Paudge Tormey
Paul Aherne
Paul Carroll
Paul Cosgrove
Paul Griffen
Paul K
Paul Keeling
Paul Mc Gregor
Paul Ó Meadhra
Paul O'Loughlin
Paul Twomey
Paula Barry
Paula Donnelly
Paula Geraghty
Paula Mc Hugh
Pauline Coombes
Pauline Hughes
Paulo Albanese
Peadar McMahon
Peadar O'Ceallaigh
Peadar O'Ceallaigh
Peter Carvill
Peter Carvill
Peter Kelly
Peter L
Peter Murphy
Peter Quinn
Peter Ryan
Peter S
Phil & Damien Walsh
Phil Horgan
Phil Minihane
Phil Minihane
Philip Cooke
Philip Mc A
Philip Mc Ardle
Philip N
Philip P
Philomena Lyttleton
Phyllis B
PJ Cormyn
PJ Feeney
Poor Clares
Precious Life
Prof Eamon O'Dwyer
R Hogan
Rachel O RIordan
Raimon Mac An tSaoir
Ray & Aoife de Clar
& Family
Ray McIntyre
Ray O'Regan
Ray Wolfe
Raymond Reynolds
Redempta Farney
Richard & Anne Greene
Richie Mc
Rita & Ann Carolan
Rita & Ann Carolan
Rita Cook
Rita Cooke
Rita Corcoran
Rita Metzer
Robert Swanton
Róisín B
Róisín Mulcahy
Róisín Ní Fhloinn
Roisin Treanor
Ronnie Page
Rory O'Hanlon
Rosari Daly
Rosarie O'Leary
Roscommon for Life
Rose Boyle
Rose Duffy
Rose Gill
Rosemary Lennon Maher
Rosemary Mc Ginley
Rosie Kingston
RRR
Ruth O C
Ruth W
S Austin
S Brady
S de Barra
Sandra M Cullinane
Sandra Mahon
Sandra Parda
Sandra Uí Clónáín
Sandy Collins
Sarah Dilleen
Sarah Doherty
Sarah Ekada
Sarah Gurrie
Sarah Haire
Sarah Standen
Scott Schittl
Séamus Collins
Séamus Connelly
Seamus Connolly
Seamus Mac Mathuna
Seamus Mc Rory
Séamus Ó Riain
Seán Bailey
Séan Barker
Séan Fallon
Seán Gallagher
Sean McHale
Seán Molloy
Sean Mullan
Seán O R
Seán O'Hara
Séimhín Ní Dhonnghaile
Shane A
Shane Kavanagh
Shane O Brien
Shane O'Sullivan
Shay Boylan
Sheila B
Sheila Evans
Sheila Magliozzi
Sheila Wilson
Shiree O Sullivan
Shirley Fisher
Shirley Scannell
Simon & Rose Nestor
Sinead Keane
Sinead Mc Glone
Siobhan Daly
Siobhan O Regan
Siobhan Rooney
Sligo for Life
Sorcha Jagodic
Sorcha Jagodic
Sr Delourde Fahy
Sr Mary Fitzgerald
Sr Miriam Duggan

Stan S
Stella Little
Stephen & Marie Morrissey
Susan & Mick Erbacher
Susan Cremin
Susan Dillon
Susan Riordan
Suzanne Corbett
T Gillespie
T McConville
Tanya Coonan
Teresa Desmond
Teresa Dillon
Teresa Heaney
Teresa Mc Laughlin
Teresa McCabe
Teresa O'Hanlon
Teresa Purdue
Teresa Talbot
Teresa White
Terry Greene
Tessie Lynch
The As Family
The Black Family
The Butler Family
The Carey Family
The Conroy Family
The Cronin Family
The Enright Family
The Gorman Family
The Herriott Family
The Hogan Family
The Keogh Family
The Kirby Family
The Lacken Family
The Lynch Family
The McClintock Family
The McDermott Family
The Mullins Family
The Moloney Family
The O'Callaghan Family
The Quinn Family
The Redmond Family
The Richardson Family
The Ryan Family
The Scanlan Family
Theresa Mc Cormack
Theresa Scanlon
Therese O'B
Therese O'Donovan
Thomas Doherty
Thomas Finegan
Thomas Smith
Tiernan Connolly
Tim Jackson
Tim Mascheler
Tim Murphy
Tina Sexton
Tom Burke
Tom F
Tom Finegan
Tom K
Tomás MacCormaic
Tommy & Mary Halpin
Tommy Burke
Tommy Horan
Tommy Keaveney
Tommy Sheridan
Tommy Sinnott
Tony & Sheena Foy
Tony Barry
Tracy & Tom Harkin & Family
Treasa Ni Mhíocháin
Úna Bn Mhic Mhathúna
Úna Bowe
Úna Hade
Úna Meehan
Ursula Herbert
Valeria S Achille
Valerie Nestor
Ven der Wel Family
Vera Lonergan
Vicky Wall
Vincent Quinlan
Virgillia Killgrew
Will Mc Connell
William O'Shea
Wojciech Cwilag
Y Ferguson
Yvonne Newell
Zornita Kolarova

Fifteen TDs (members of parliament) and five Senators voted No to the Health (Regulation of Termination of Pregnancy) Act 2018 which legalised abortion on demand in Ireland. They did so in the face of prolonged and sustained personalised attacks in the chamber and elsewhere.

Teachta Dála who voted No
Mary Butler
Seán Canney
Michael Collins
Michael Fitzmaurice
Peter Fitzpatrick
Noel Grealish
Danny Healy-Rae
Michael Healy-Rae
Michael Lowry
Marc Mac Sharry
Mattie McGrath
John McGuinness
Carol Nolan
Eamon O'Cuiv
Peadar Tóibín

Seanadóirí who voted No
Terry Leyden
Rónán Mullen
John O'Mahony
Brian O'Domhnaill
Diarmuid Wilson